Yale Russian and East European Studies, 13

The Word and Verbal Art

Selected Essays by Jan Mukařovský

translated and edited by

John Burbank and Peter Steiner

Foreword by René Wellek

New Haven and London   Yale University Press   1977

Designed by John O. C. McCrillis
and set in Baskerville type.
Printed in the United States of America by
The Vail-Ballou Press, Inc., Binghamton, New York.

Published in Great Britain, Europe, Africa, and Asia
(except Japan) by Yale University Press, Ltd., London.
Distributed in Latin America by Kaiman & Polon, Inc.,
New York City; in Australia and New Zealand by Book
& Film Services, Artarmon, N.S.W., Australia; and in
Japan by Harper & Row, Publishers, Tokyo Office.

Library of Congress Cataloging in Publication Data

Mukařovský, Jan.
    The word and verbal art.
    (Yale Russian and East European Studies, 13)
    Includes indexes.
    CONTENTS: On poetic language.—Two studies on
poetic designation: Poetic designation and the aesthetic
function of language. A note on the semantics of the
poetic image. [etc.]
    1. Literature—Collected works. 2. Structuralism
(Literary analysis)—Collected works. I. Title. II. Series.
PN37.M79   809   76-49733
ISBN 0-300-01573-9

Contents

Foreword

In 1936 I published a paper "The Theory of Literary History" in the sixth volume of the *Travaux du Cercle Linguistique de Prague*. There, for the first time in English, Mukařovský's "structuralism" (he had used the term since 1934) and his views on the evolution of literature were expounded with some critical reservations. This long article, which expresses "my profound indebtedness to the work of Jan Mukařovský and Roman Jakobson" and to the "stimulating atmosphere of the Prague Linguistic Circle," of which I was then a junior member, attracted, I believe, no attention at that time: it appeared in a publication of limited circulation, printed in Prague, and read almost exclusively by linguists. In 1939, after the invasion by Hitler, I emigrated to the United States and there restated and developed my views, often referring to the work of the Prague Linguistic Circle. In 1946 in a lecture at Yale University, "The Revolt against Positivism in Recent European Literary Scholarship," which appeared in the same year in a collective volume *Twentieth Century English* (ed. William S. Knickerbocker, New York, 1946, reprinted in *Concepts of Criticism*, New Haven, 1963), I gave an account of the Prague School, singling out Mukařovský for special attention and praise. "The most productive member of the school is Jan Mukařovský, who not only produced brilliant studies of individual works of poetry, of the history of Czech metrics, and poetic diction, but also has speculated interestingly on fitting the formalistic theory into a whole philosophy of symbolic forms, and on combining it with a social approach which would see the relationship between social and literary evolution as a dialectical tension. I trust that my view is not falsified by years of membership in the Prague Circle, if I express my conviction that here in the close cooperation with modern linguistics and with modern philosophy are the germs of a future fruitful development of literary studies" (p. 85).

Then, in *Theory of Literature*, a book written in collaboration with Austin Warren from 1944 to 1946 but delayed for reasons beyond our control until January 1949, Mukařovský is referred to several times and expressly commended for his "brilliant dialectical scheme of 'aesthetic function, norm and value as social

facts,' " the title of Mukařovský's pamphlet dating from 1936. The
paper "Intonation as a Factor of Poetic Rhythm," translated here,
is quoted, and the elaborate bibliography lists several items by
Mukařovský in French, in periodicals and proceedings of congresses.
Still, I have the impression that in the mass of reviews of *Theory
of Literature*, both in the United States and in Great Britain, and
later in the reviews of its translations into many other languages
(twenty to this date), little attention has been paid to these
references, or at most they were ascribed to my "Continental eru-
dition." I am giving this account not in order to claim any merit
for the introduction of Mukařovský to the English-speaking world
but, on the contrary, to show that while I was the first to quote
and praise him, my advocacy remained without immediate effect.

Victor Erlich's book *Russian Formalism* (The Hague, 1955),
with a short preface by me, contains a chapter on the Czech movement with special reference to Mukařovský. Erlich treated the
Czech movement understandably as a repercussion of the Russian
Formalist school but also pointed out that Mukařovský went
beyond Russian Formalism by replacing the term with "structuralism" and by considering "poetics an integral part of semiotics
rather than a branch of linguistics" (p. 132). In the same year
Paul L. Garvin published (in mimeographed form) *A Prague School
Reader on Esthetics, Literary Structure and Style* (Washington,
1955), which contains four articles translated from Mukařovský.
As my review in *Language* (31 [1955]:584–87) pointed out, the
choice of articles is sometimes injudicious. "Standard and Poetic
Language" served a local polemical purpose against a Czech purist
journal with a defense of poetic deviations from current standard
language. "The Esthetics of Language" is a diffuse and repetitive
paper moving from minute questions about the "beauty" of Czech
words to such problems as the oscillation, in the history of poetry,
between acceptance and violation of the norms in standard speech
(for example, the extremes of Boileau and Mallarmé). The third
and fourth papers are excellent examples of Mukařovský's studies
of prosody and style but are narrowly focused on texts in Czech.
In my review I tried to define Mukařovský's special position. He
has "gone beyond the original close collaboration between linguistics and literary theory into a general theory of esthetics, in which
key concepts such as function, structure, norm and value point
to an overall goal in a theory of semiology, of meaning in a social

and historical context." Garvin's selection hardly afforded a glimpse of the scope of Mukařovský's achievement.

The great new interest in Mukařovský's work developed only in the late sixties and early seventies in ways which would have to be investigated in detail. Some of the stimuli are obvious. In the United States (and less so in England) there was a growing realization of the necessity of a collaboration between linguistics and literary studies. The conference "Style in Language" (Indiana University, 1958) was a landmark, even though Mukařovský's name does not appear in the printed proceedings (Cambridge, Mass., 1960; two items, however, are listed in the bibliography). Two of Mukařovský's essays, in Garvin's translation, were reprinted in anthologies (see Seymour Chatman and Samuel Levin, eds., *Essays on the Language of Literature*, Boston, 1969, and Howard S. Babb, *Essays in Stylistic Analysis*, New York, 1972), and one comes across passages that show that Garvin's translation of the Czech "aktualisace" as "foregrounding" has caught on (see, for example, Roger Fowler, *The Languages of Literature*, London, 1971, p. 41, and Geoffrey N. Leech, *A Linguistic Guide to English Poetry*, London, 1969, chapter 4).

Undoubtedly the enormous vogue of French structuralism drew attention to its antecedents and anticipations. The impact of the return of Roman Jakobson from decades of preoccupation with linguistic and Slavistic problems to an analysis of literary texts brought his long association with the Prague Linguistic Circle and Mukařovský back into memory. Slavicists in the United States translated some of the key texts. Mark E. Suino brought out the important pamphlet *Aesthetic Function, Norm and Value as Social Facts* (Ann Arbor, 1970) and Ladislav Matějka and Irwin R. Titunik most recently, in *Semiotics of Art: Prague School Contributions* (Cambridge, Mass., 1976), included Mukařovský's seminal lecture "Art as Semiotic Fact," originally delivered at the VIIIth International Congress of Philosophy held in Prague (1934, printed in French in 1936), the paper "Poetic Denomination and the Aesthetic Function of Language" (1938), and the essay "Essence of the Visual Arts," written in 1944 but first published in 1966.

In the meantime my pamphlet *The Literary Theory and Aesthetics of the Prague School* (Ann Arbor, 1969, reprinted in my collection of essays, *Discriminations*, New Haven, 1970) gave a fuller account of Mukařovský's doctrines and development than was before available in English. Teun A. Van Dijk's *Poetics: Inter-*

national Review for the Theory of Literature (No. 4, 1972), published in English and French at The Hague, assembled a whole new
of contributions from Mukařovský's Czech pupils to honor his
eightieth birthday, a tribute unimaginable even a decade ago. Other
new accounts in English are L. Doležel and J. Kraus, "Prague
School Stylistics," in *Current Trends in Stylistics,* ed. D. B. Kachru
and H. F. Stahlke (Edmonton, Alberta, 1972), and Thomas G.
Winner, "The Aesthetics and Poetics of the Prague Linguistic
Circle," in *Poetics,* No. 8 (1973), an especially well-informed and
acute analysis. Peter and Wendy Steiner wrote a postscript on "The
Relational Axes of Poetic Language" for the translation *Of Poetic
Language,* published separately in Holland in 1976, printed here
as the first item in this anthology.

When Mukařovský died in February 1975 at the age of 83, he
could have surveyed with satisfaction the growth of his reputation
abroad, in Germany in particular. In Germany the decisive break-
through was accomplished even earlier than in the United States. A
small selection, *Kapitel aus der Poetik* (1967), in the cheap and
widely distributed series Edition Suhrkamp, was followed by another booklet in the same series, *Kapitel aus der Ästhetik* (1970),
and finally by a large volume, *Studien zur strukturalistischen
Ästhetik und Poetik* (Munich, 1974), which contains a knowl-
edgeable postscript by the two translators, Herbert Grönebaum
and Gisela Riff. A lively discussion of Mukařovský's position accompanied these translations and is well summarized in Hans
Günther's *Struktur als Prozess. Studien zur Ästhetik und Literatur-
theorie des tschechischen Strukturalismus* (Munich, 1970). Some
of the writings of Mukařovský's pupils are beginning to appear in
German translations. Květoslav Chvatík's *Strukturalismus und
Avantgarde* (Munich, 1970) is studded with references to his
teacher's work, and so is Felix Vodička's *Struktur der Ent-
wicklung* (Munich, 1976), for which Jurij Striedter, a newcomer
from Konstanz to Harvard, has written a long and searching
introduction.

In German, an intense and well-informed discussion of Prague
structuralism is going on. Not to mention articles in periodicals, I
would single out Miroslav Červenka's "Die Grundkategorien des
Prager literaturwissenschaftlichen Strukturalismus" in Victor
Žmegač and Zdenko Škreb's collection, *Zur Kritik literaturwissen-
schaftlicher Methodologie* (Frankfurt, 1973), and Elmar Holen-

stein's "Der Prager Strukturalismus—ein Zweig der phänomenolo-
gischen Bewegung" in his new book *Linguistik Semiotik Her-
meneutik* (Frankfurt, 1976), which propounds an unusual thesis
persuasively.

In France, where Mukařovský's French papers in the thirties
caused hardly a ripple, his work also is beginning to be known.
The magazine *Change* published a whole issue on the Circle
(1969), and Tzvetan Todorov, a Bulgarian settled in France who
has done much to bring the Russian Formalists to the notice of
the French, reprinted two of Mukařovský's French essays in an
early number of the main structuralist review, *Poétique* (No. 3,
1970), with an informative note.

In Italy, two substantial selections from Mukařovský's writings
appeared recently: a translation of *Aesthetic Function, Norm and
Value as Social Facts* with an appendix containing other papers
(1971), and another large selection called *Il significato dell'estetica*
(1973). There is also a Spanish translation entitled *Arte y
semiología* (1972).

This little sketch of Mukařovský's reputation abroad must lead
to the crucial question posed by any prospective student of his
work: Why should we care about Mukařovský in particular? No
doubt some of the interest in his work is justified on historical
grounds. If we want to understand the origins of structuralism,
Prague is an indispensable link in the chain leading from Moscow
to Paris. A book in German by a Dutch author, Jan M. Broekman's
Strukturalismus—Moskau, Prag, Paris (Freiburg, 1971; English
translation, Dordrecht, 1974), formulates this sequence expressly.
Ewa Thompson, in her *Russian Formalism and Anglo-American
New Criticism: A Comparative Study* (The Hague, 1971), glanced
rather casually at Mukařovský's work to support her strained
parallelisms. But surely historical considerations are not enough.
One can rather claim that Mukařovský's thought is still relevant
today, that he has elaborated a system of literary theory and
aesthetics which has lucidity, coherence, and sanity not easily
matched elsewhere.

We must, however, distinguish between the different stages of
Mukařovský's long scholarly career. He began with concrete inves-
tigations of Czech verse (1926) which, methodologically, were still
in the wake of his teacher, Otokar Zich, an aesthetician primarily
interested in the psychological motivation of stylistic differences.

Then, in 1928, Mukařovský's minute analysis of the romantic poem *Máj* by Karel Hynek Mácha (1810-36) showed that he had mastered and developed the techniques of the Russian Formalists. He gives a close look at sound patterns and their integration with other aspects of the poem: the way words are used, motifs are clustered, plot and point of view are organized. The study is a model of close analysis which overcomes the contrast of form and content in a total view reaching from sound to meaning. Then Mukařovský turned to the problem of evolution in literature, which he also inherited from the Russians, and brilliantly demonstrated its value for a history of modern Czech versification, which lends itself to a dialectical scheme of "actualization" and "automatization," convention and revolt. About this time, in 1934, Mukařovský gave up his close adherence to the Russian Formalists. He criticized Victor Šklovskij's *Theory of Prose* (1925), then newly translated into Czech, for its narrow focus, calling his own view "structuralism," which he felt had achieved a synthesis of content and form and made allowance for the role of society (and hence of sociology) in the study of literature. Very properly this review is included in this volume.

In the same year Mukařovský broadened his scheme by embracing an all-inclusive theory of signs in which literature appears as only one subdivision. He developed more and more a consistent system of aesthetics which, assuming a semiological approach, allows for the relations of the work of art to the speaker and the addressee and accounts for such old problems as the world view implied in a work, the relation of a work of art to external reality and hence to society. During the war years in particular, Mukařovský discussed "The Individual and Literary Development," "The Poet," and the relation "Between Literature and Visual Arts," in papers translated in this volume.

Many years elapsed before, in 1966, he consented to the publication of his unpublished papers in a volume entitled *Studies in Aesthetics* (1966). Also a later collection, *On the Track of Poetics and Aesthetics* (1971), contains only papers written before 1948.

The selection of his papers in this volume ranges from an early, rather technical analysis, "Intonation as the Basic Factor of Poetic Rhythm" (1932), to a paper written late in the war (1943-45), "The Individual and Literary Development." It offers a conspectus of his literary theory which shows his clear grasp of abstract issues combined with a remarkable power of close observation and discrimination. The forthcoming volume on the general problems of aesthetics and the other arts should give an idea of the full range of Mukařovský's achievement.

RENÉ WELLEK

Publisher's Note

In the above Foreword, Professor Wellek had hoped to provide a fuller account of Jan Mukařovský's career between 1948 and 1971 (cf. Wellek, "The Literary Theory and Aesthetics of the Prague School," in *Discriminations: Further Concepts of Criticism*, published by the Yale University Press in 1970). However, under the conditions of the contract with the Czech copyright holder we were compelled to delete this information, despite all efforts to reach an agreement.

Preface

The Word and Verbal Art is the first half of a project begun nearly five years ago to make available to the English reader a substantial selection of Jan Mukařovský's critical writings. Originally we envisioned all twenty-seven essays as forming a single volume, but the length of the manuscript made this plan untenable. As a result, the text has been divided into two volumes, the present one devoted to literature, and a second one, *Structure, Sign, and Function* (forthcoming), on general aesthetics and arts other than literature.

The title of the present volume is a translation of *Slovo a slovesnost*, the name of the journal of the Prague Linguistic Circle, Mukařovský was one of the early members of this group and participated actively on the editorial board of its journal. Two of the articles in this volume appeared there for the first time, most significantly the comprehensive study "On Poetic Language." Moreover, this title captures the essence of Mukařovský's approach to literature as an art of language.

Translating Mukařovský's work necessarily entails certain problems. First, since Czech is a highly inflected language, long sentences are not only frequent in writing but typical. The length and complexity of the sentence, moreover, causes the paragraph to play a relatively insignificant role, so that extremely long, loosely constructed paragraphs are quite common in scholarly Czech prose. Therefore, part of translating consisted in dividing excessively long sentences into shorter ones and in some instances in reparagraphing the text.

Secondly, Mukařovský indulged in certain stylistic idiosyncrasies as a reflection of his theoretical outlook. For example, he conceived of structures as processes—dynamic wholes whose elements are charged with energy and interlocked in an ongoing struggle for domination. This point of view accounts for the unusual animation of his descriptions of poetic structures, often created by the use of animate verbs with inanimate subjects. We have been forced at times to tone down this stylistic trait, as it leads to rather ludicrous English formulations.

Thirdly, we encountered the eternal stumbling block of terminology. Whenever possible, we used equivalent English terms, footnoting them if they seemed in any way problematic. In a few cases, however, it was necessary to coin a new English term (for example, *deautomatization*), but we hope that these sports of translation are self-explanatory. For the considerable number of terms for which there was no exact English equivalent, we have had to choose among several synonyms. For example, the term *pojmenování* has at least four roughly equivalent English counterparts: "naming," "denomination," "nomenclature," and "designation." We opted for the latter, fully aware that some other translator might easily have chosen any of the remaining three. These were not arbitrary choices, however, but involved as careful a weighing of a word's advantages as possible in a deliberative procedure whose origin Herodotus ascribes to the ancient Persians (I.133).

Finally, since several of Mukařovský's essays were originally lectures or rough drafts, they lack full documentation. Whenever possible, we have rectified this difficulty, although in a few instances we have been unable to obtain the books or periodicals referred to or even to establish the source altogether. In addition to bibliographical footnotes we have provided some essays with editorial notes where further clarification seemed advisable. Originally we intended to append a brief glossary of the Czech writers whose names appear in Mukařovský's essays, for the convenience of those not familiar with Czech literature. However, Arne Novák's comprehensive volume, *Czech Literature* (Ann Arbor, 1976), has now appeared, which in every respect does more justice to these writers than our short glossary could possibly have done.

We wish to acknowledge with much gratitude the assistance of many people in this project. Professors Peter Demetz, Victor Erlich, Jaroslav Pelikan, René Wellek, and Thomas Winner introduced us to the Yale University Press and personally intervened on behalf of our project. The staff of Yale Press were consistently encouraging and efficient, in particular Whitney Blake, under whose guidance we began our translation, and Ellen Graham, who helped bring it to a conclusion. We owe special gratitude to Lynn Walterick, our copy-editor, who went through the manuscript several times, painstakingly picking up stylistic lapses and terminological inconsistencies. Our appreciation also goes to Wendy Steiner, who read many of our drafts and advised us on questions of English usage, to Michelle Burbank, who assisted us in translations of French quotations, to Professor Vadim Liapunov, whom we consulted on critical terminology and problems in translating from German, to Dr. Bedřich Steiner, who spent many hours in the reading room of the Charles University Library in Prague finding answers to our bibliographical inquiries, and to Dr. Jaroslav Kolár for his help with the notes for "The Poet."

September, 1976   JOHN BURBANK
                                                     PETER STEINER

1

On Poetic Language

I. Poetic Language as a Functional Language and as a Material

In the last few years the study of poetry in general and poetic language in particular has undergone a profound change. This has been made possible because modern linguistics has become aware of the differentiation of language according to the goals toward which discourse is directed and according to the functions for which both particular linguistic devices and entire sets of them are designated and adapted. Thus poetic language appears as a part of a linguistic system, as an enduring structure having its own regular development, as an important factor in the development of human expression through language in general.

This study concerns poetic language as one of the functional languages. Because until recently there have been many different concepts of poetic language, it would not perhaps be inappropriate to state briefly by way of introduction everything which poetic language *is not* from the contemporary standpoint, that is, where its essence does not lie.

Above all, poetic language is not always *ornamental* expression. Of course, it has this characteristic in certain developmental periods, namely, those which feel the bifurcation between expressed content and linguistic expression, when expression is evaluated as the garment of content. However, there are also periods when both these components merge indistinguishably and when this close linkage becomes the characteristic feature of poetic expression.

Nor is *beauty* the constant token of the poetic word. The history of literature is full of examples in which the poet has sought his linguistic material in lexical spheres indifferent to the standards of beauty or even negative with respect to them. Thus Neruda—according to Šalda's famous statement—had "the frightful audacity to take words from the street, unwashed and uncombed,

This essay is translated from "O jazyce básnickém," *Slovo a slovesnost* 6 (1940).

and to make of them messengers of eternity.''[1] Nor is poetic language identical with language designated for the expression of feelings, *emotive* language. The basic difference is in the orientation of these two languages. Emotive language tends, in its essence, to express the emotion which is most immediate and which is therefore limited in its validity to the unique psychic state of the speaking individual. The goal of poetic expression, on the other hand, is the creation of suprapersonal and lasting values. Of course, literature can use the devices of emotive language for its own purposes, and it uses them abundantly, especially in periods when poetic expression emphasizes its relation to its creator's unique individuality. Nevertheless, emotive expression is only *one* of the many devices which poetry adopts for its goals from the rich stock of language. In the same way it borrows from other linguistic strata. There are even periods when the departure from the emotiveness of expression becomes a programmatic requirement in literature: Joseph Machar and František Gellner in our poetry.

Furthermore, poetic language is not fully characterized by *concreteness* ("plasticity"). There are periods when—again programmatically—it tends toward abstraction, non-concreteness. Thus, for example, periods of classicism tend to avoid any pronounced concreteness of designation. After all, even the very meaning of the word *concreteness* is ambiguous; in every case it means something different: sometimes the evocation of a distinct image, sometimes the accompaniment of a word by a cluster of indefinite associated images. In the course of its development, then, poetic language oscillates between concreteness and non-concreteness rather than always inclining toward the first of these poles. In connection with this, we should mention that neither is a *figurative* nature unconditionally characteristic of poetic language. On the one hand, figurative designation, even "vivid"[2] figurative

---

1. "Alej snu a meditace ku hrobu Jana Nerudy" [An avenue of dream and meditation to Jan Neruda's grave], *Boje o zítřek,* 3rd ed. (Prague, 1918), p. 67.

2. In colloquial speech, for example, we sometimes encounter figurative designations (metaphors, similes, etc.) improvised for the purpose of an immediate characterization of the situation. K. M. Čapek-Chod has illustrated this property of colloquial language very well in the short story "Deset deka": "Postaví se tuhle Lucka nad nůší, kterou napěchovala prádlem, a místo aby se s nůší konečně 'hnoula' k hokynáři na mandl, stojí a stojí 'jako ten elektrickej transportátor—nebo jak se to řekne—na chodníku, kady nejvíc lidí chodí'. Jak vidět, milovala Réza ve svých metaforách variace." ("Once Lucka was standing over a pannier which she had stuffed with laundry, and instead of finally

designation, is common in language in general, not only in poetic language; on the other hand, there are in the history of literature examples of a departure from figurative designation or at least from its domination.

Finally, not even *individuality,* the emphasized uniqueness of linguistic expression, characterizes poetic language in general. Regardless of the fact that a distinctly individual style is possible outside of literature (in scientific discourse, for example), we should keep in mind that there are entire developmental periods in which poetic language avoids individuality of expression. For instance, periods of classicism usually establish which words, indeed, even which images, can be used in poetry in order to limit individual invention. There are even entire realms of literature, the stylistic canons of which are composed of fixed, concrete conventions, formulae obligatory for every individual creator of poetry (in this respect, consider examples from the Greek or Slavic heroic epic: "long-shadowed lances," "white breast," "azure sea"). In *Studies in Linguistic Psychology,* Jousse comments on this: "The narratives of the guslars, similar in this respect to the narratives of Homer, the prophets and the rabbis, to the Epistles of Baruch, St. Peter and St. Paul . . . are a juxtaposition of relatively few clichés. The development of each of these clichés happens automatically according to fixed rules. Only their order can vary. A good guslar is one who plays with his clichés as we play with cards, who arranges them in different ways according to the effect which he wishes to produce from them."[3] Thus individuality in such poetic configurations is obviously relegated to a secondary position, and what is left to it is merely an influence on the arrangement of a priori given formulae.

Such is the enumeration of the properties which have usually been and in part still are declared as characteristic of poetic language in general but which in reality mark only individual developmental periods or particular special aspects of literature. From this enumeration we can assume that no single property characterizes poetic language permanently and generally. Poetic language is permanently characterized only by its function; however, function

'moving off' to the mangle at the grocer's, she kept standing and standing 'like that electric conveyeror—or whatever it's called—on the sidewalk where most of the people were walking.' As can be seen, Reza was fond of variations in her metaphors.")

3. M. Jousse, *Etudes de psychologie linguistique* (Paris, 1925), p. 113.

is not a property but a *mode of utilizing* the properties of a given phenomenon. Poetic language belongs among the numerous other functional languages, each of which is an adaptation of a linguistic system to a certain goal of expression. Aesthetic effect is the goal of poetic expression. However, the aesthetic function, which thus dominates in poetic language (being only a concomitant phenomenon in other functional languages), concentrates attention on the linguistic sign itself—hence it is exactly the opposite of a practical orientation toward a goal which in language is communication.

The aesthetic "orientation toward the expression itself," which is, of course, valid not only for linguistic expression and not only for verbal art but for all arts and for any realm of the aesthetic, is a phenomenon *essentially* different from a logical orientation toward expression whose task is to make expression more precise, as has been especially emphasized by the so-called Logical Positivist movement ("Viennese Circle") and in particular by Rudolf Carnap. First of all, the very notion of language is quite different for logic from what it is for aesthetics, although the Logical Positivists (in agreement with other trends in contemporary logic) rely more than older logic on real language in proceeding from a total context to a sentence and only from a sentence to concepts.[4] For the aesthetics of poetic language and language in general, "language" means a particular national language with all its concrete properties which have originated and continue to originate in its historical development. For the Logical Positivists, however, "language" means a particular logical contexture characterized by the fact that within it semantic units linked by logical interrelations determine its meaning. One disregards "the meaning of the signs (e.g., the words) and . . . the meaning of the expressions (e.g., the sentences)" and takes into account only "[the] type and concatenation of the signs, of which the expressions are constructed."[5] Therefore, according to the Logical Positivists' views, syntax creates the only basis and law of semantic context in the "language" of logic. But in "natural" language, as we shall see, the semantic context is governed simultaneously but not always entirely concurrently by two kinds of relations: on the one hand, by

4. M. Schlick, "L'Ecole de Vienne et la philosophie traditionelle," *Travaux du IXe Congrès international de philosophie* 4 (Paris, 1937).

5. R. Carnap, *Logische Syntax der Sprache* (Vienna, 1934), p. 1.

syntactic relations; on the other, by purely semantic ones (the semantic structuring of the text). Even an individual scholar can create for himself a language of the kind which the Logical Positivists have in mind.[6] Each of the sciences has such an independent language, and all the sciences together tend to create a "unified" scientific language (consider the Logical Positivists' well-known efforts at creating a "unified science").

Hence the Logical Positivist notion of language is completely different from the notion of language as a means of communication in everyday life. What is valid for one does not necessarily have to be valid for the other. Therefore, the orientation toward expression, as aesthetics considers it, is absolutely incompatible with the one that the Logical Positivists have in mind. It would not make sense to consider the specific difference between these two orientations. The Logical Positivists themselves, however, pose the question of the specific difference and consider poetry a matter of emotional expression. Although in this respect they agree with Bally, the fallaciousness of this view is obvious from the standpoint of contemporary study.

But not even the concept "orientation toward expression" has the same meaning for the Logical Positivists as it has for contemporary aesthetics. In aesthetics it means a concentration of attention on the expression in all of its variety, especially functional variety. In this process the perceiver in no way loses sight of the extraaesthetic functions of the linguistic sign, especially the three basic ones which Bühler designated as the presentational, the expressive, and the appellative[7] in his *Sprachtheorie*. Linguistic expression in its aesthetic orientation oscillates freely among them; at any time it can attach itself to and also detach itself from one of them; it can combine them in various ways. This is precisely the epistemological consequence of its liberation from a unilateral bond with any one of them achieved by "being enveloped" in itself. Logical "orientation toward expression" means, on the contrary, the subordination of linguistic expression to a logical consideration. Hence *only one* of the functions of the linguistic

6. See R. Carnap, *Philosophical and Logical Syntax* (London, 1935), p. 77.

7. *Editors' note.* These three basic functions of the linguistic sign are now commonly called the referential, the emotive, and the conative, respectively; cf. R. Jakobson, "Linguistics and Poetics," *Style in Language,* ed. Thomas A. Sebeok (Cambridge, Mass., 1960), pp. 353-57.

sign is clearly emphasized, and this functional isolation is manifested distinctly by its effort to purify the utterance of all extralogical considerations. From the viewpoint of logic a real language is never perfect enough.[8] Both the extreme limit and the ideal of the language of logic is "absolute" signs in which the meaning given by the relation to empirical reality completely yields to the "sense" drawn from the logical context (the "language" of mathematical formulae). But if it is a matter of the relation to reality ("synthetic" sentences according to the specialized terminology of logic), then this relation is controlled as far as truthfulness is concerned (the "validity" and "contravalidity" of a synthetic judgment, according to Logical Positivist terminology). In contrast, the question of truthfulness does not make any sense in poetry where the aesthetic function prevails. Here the utterance "means" not that reality which comprises its immediate theme but the set of all realities, the universe as a whole, or—more precisely—the entire existential experience of the author or, better, of the perceiver. The incompatibility of the aesthetic "orientation toward expression" with the logical one is thus proven not only with respect to the notion of language but also with respect to the very notion of "orientation."

Having made this digression, let us return to poetic language. The fact that poetic discourse has expression itself as its aim does not deprive poetic language of practical import. Precisely because of its aesthetic "self-orientation" poetic language is more suited than other functional languages for constantly reviving man's attitude toward language and the relation of language to reality, for constantly revealing in new ways the internal organization of the linguistic sign, and for showing new possibilities of its use. The domination of the aesthetic function in poetic language is not, of course, exclusive. There is a constant struggle and a constant tension between self-orientation and communication so that poetic language, though it stands in opposition to the other functional languages in its self-orientation, is not cut off from them by an insurmountable boundary. After all, it has very few of its own linguistic devices, so-called poeticisms which are most often lexical but sometimes also morphological or syntactic. For the most part poetic language draws from the stock furnished by other levels of

8. Carnap, *Logische Syntax der Sprache*, p. 3.

language, often taking from it very specific means of expression which in normal usage are limited to a single linguistic level. This both distinguishes poetic language from other linguistic levels—for, as a rule, they use only their own means, except, of course, for common linguistic property—and closely connects it to them because poetic language is the mediator of their interrelations and interpenetration.

Nevertheless, among the functional languages there is one to which poetic language is especially related: the standard literary language.[9] Literature and, of course, poetic language have no difficulty existing in national languages that lack a standard literary form or in linguistic structures that have nothing to do with the standard literary language (folk poetry). In what is called "artificial" literature, however, the link between poetic language and the standard literary language is so close that the examples cited in dictionaries and grammars codifying the standard literary language, for instance, are often from poetic works. What kind of connection is this?

Scholars sometimes explain this connection by discussing poetic language as one of the variants of the standard literary language, a variant governed by the general regularity of this higher structure. Purists in particular conceive the interrelation between poetic language and the standard literary language in this way; they purge the standard literary language of all alien elements, not only foreign but also domestic, elements inconsistent with the norm of the standard literary language. But if they also attempt to discipline poetic language in this way, a considerable number of its artistic devices will appear to them as arbitrary violations of linguistic "purity," precisely because a limitation to a single

9. *Editors' note.* In an encyclopedia article, Bohuslav Havránek, the leading expert of the Prague Linguistic Circle on questions of the standard literary language, has characterized it as follows: "The standard literary language [*spisovný jazyk*] is the vehicle and the mediator of culture and civilization; it is an indicator of independent national existence. It differs from the popular language of a given nation primarily in its function: its tasks are much broader than those of the popular language, and they are, above all, more precisely and deeply differentiated. For this reason the standard literary language exhibits a much richer functional and stylistic stratification. Furthermore, the norm of the standard literary language is more conscious and more obligatory than the norm of the popular language, and the requisite of its stability is more emphatic. Finally, public and written (printed) utterances predominate among the utterances in the standard literary language" ("Spisovný jazyk," *Ottův slovník naučný nové doby* 6[Prague, 1940]: 180).

sphere of linguistic devices is alien to literature. Hence the struggles between poets and purists for the right of freedom of creation and the right to limit creation. Not long ago we experienced such a campaign in our own country.[10] The difference between poetic language and the standard literary language is therefore clearly evident. But this is not to the detriment of their close connection, which lies in the fact that even in periods when poetry violates the norm of the standard literary language most radically, the standard literary language constitutes the background against which the linguistic aspect of the poetic work is perceived. It is precisely the *deviations* from standard literary usage which are evaluated in poetry as artistic devices. This does not apply to any other level of language (functional, social, etc.), not even to that level from which poetry draws most at a given moment. For instance, insofar as poems written completely in argot or dialect are felt as belonging to "artificial" poetry, they have the standard literary language as their background, even though they radically violate its norm.

As for poetic language, its intimate relation to the standard literary language manifests itself in the influence which poetry exerts on the development of the standard literary norm. This influence is not, of course, such that everything created by poetry with respect to language immediately and automatically becomes part of the standard literary norm. It is precisely the most striking linguistic creations of poetry, that is, neologisms, that take root in the standard literary language most rarely. Poetic language influences the organization of discourse more effectively, for example, by providing standard literary usage with new phrasing, new types of semantic sentence structures, and so on. The influence of poetic language on the standard literary language also varies in different periods. For instance, in our country it was strongest in the period of the National Revival when a consciously intentional reconstruction of the standard literary norm was undertaken; the very fact that this reconstruction began with Jungmann's *poetic* translations is characteristic in itself. Nevertheless, both the stan-

10. *Editors' note.* Mukařovský is referring to the polemics between some Czech writers (O. Fischer, Iv. Olbracht, Vl. Vančura et al) and J. Haller, editor-in-chief of the journal *Naše řeč*. The members of the Prague Linguistic Circle took part in these polemics, which began in 1930, and sided with the writers. Their views may be found in the anthology *Spisovná čeština a jazyková kultura* [Standard literary Czech and the culture of language], ed. B. Havránek and M. Weingart (Prague, 1932).

dard literary language and poetic language maintain the independence of their development and the sovereignty of their norms. What may be a revolutionary change for the standard literary language is a simple artistic device in poetry; on the other hand, frequently a certain stylistic form, which appears very individual and peculiar from the viewpoint of poetry, is quite regular from the standpoint of the contemporary standard literary norm. Bohuslav Havránek has demonstrated the fundamental validity of this on the basis of Mácha's language.[11]

We have ascertained the position of poetic language within the entire linguistic system. Now, however, we must examine it from the opposite side, that is, we must devote our attention to the place of language within the literary work. What is language in literature? It is a *material* like metal and stone in sculpture, like pigment and the material of the pictorial plane in painting. Language, too, enters the work of art from outside as a sensorily perceptible phenomenon in order to become a vehicle of the non-material structure of the work; in the work of art it also undergoes elaboration, reorganization for that purpose. Nevertheless, there is a considerable difference between other artistic materials and language. Stone, metal, and pigment enter art as mere natural phenomena which gain a semiotic nature only in art; they begin to "mean" something. Language in its very essence is already a sign. Even the natural phenomenon which is its basis—the sound of the human voice—comes from the speech organs already formed for this purpose. Only the material of music, tone, which is not merely a natural sound but a component of a tonal system (we understand it only as part of a tonal system), approximates language as an artistic material in its semiotic character. Musical tone is also to a certain extent independent of its sound realization: trained musicians can read a score silently just as a reader can a book.

Unlike language, however, tone is limited in its existence almost entirely to music; nature does not, with negligible exceptions, have tones (the tone of downsliding sand dunes is usually cited as an almost unique case of natural tone). Outside of music, tones appear only on the very periphery of human activity and in close connection with it; such are, for example, horn signals. Tone is

---

11. "Jazyk Máchův" [Mácha's language], *Torso a tajemství Máchova díla* [The torso and the mystery of Mácha's works], ed. J. Mukařovský (Prague, 1938), pp. 279-331.

not, therefore, rooted in everyday life and does not become the vehicle of a particular meaning. The "meaning" of a musical melody remains a mere intention without a specific quality, an intention capable of absorbing an almost unlimited number of concrete meanings. Language, on the contrary, exists and operates outside literature as the most important system of signs, as a sign κατ᾽ ἐξοχήν: it is the cement of human coexistence and regulates man's attitude toward both reality and society.

Hence, unlike the materials of sculpture and painting, language has a semiotic character and for that reason a relative independence from sensory perception. Poetry does not, therefore, appeal directly to any human sense (if, of course, we disregard its sound realization, which is from the artistic viewpoint the subject of a special art, recitation) but indirectly to all of them. Unlike the material of music, language also exists and operates outside art to which it is indebted for its semantic definiteness and its close contact with the contexts of everyday human life. If we thus extol the advantages of language as an artistic material, we nevertheless must not forget its disadvantages. The main one is that the literary work based upon language, a historically changeable phenomenon, is more easily liable to changes after its completion than are the works of other arts. Its artistic structure can be palpably disturbed and even broken down by the further development of the language. What the poet intended to be aesthetically effective can lose this effect, while, on the contrary, components which the poet's artistic intention did not touch can acquire aesthetic effectiveness.

The first case occurs if an aesthetically intentional transformation of a particular linguistic component becomes common usage; the second occurs if the common usage of the poet's period appears unusual, extraordinary on the basis of changed linguistic sensibility. Another disadvantage of language as poetic material is that it limits the literary work to the members of a given linguistic community. A literary work does not exist for people who do not know its language, and it is only imperfectly and not completely accessible even to those who know its language but not as their mother tongue. That is to say, they do not command the entire wealth of associations connecting the words and forms of the given language together and to reality. The more the linguistic aspect asserts itself in a literary work, the more strongly it is bound to a given national language. Hence the difficulty in the translation—or even the untranslatability—of certain poetic works, especially lyric works.

Therefore, poetic language—like, after all, every functional language—is rooted in the system of a *particular* national language. This fact for all its seeming obviousness has important consequences which have not until recently been apparent even to theoreticians of poetry and literary historians. These consequences result from the fact that a particular poetic device acquires characteristics in one language which are entirely distinct from those it has in other languages because of their different natures. We could cite copious examples from studies of recent years, but we shall content ourselves with only one taken from Roman Jakobson's *Foundations of Czech Verse.*[12] V. A. Jung translated Pushkin's trochaic tetrameter "Burja mgloju nebo kroet" word for word in Czech "Bouře mlhou nebe kryje" ("The storm covers the sky with fog"); nevertheless, the Czech version is profoundly different from the Russian, on the one hand, in quantity (which is the component of stress in Russian but which is free in Czech) and, on the other hand, in that the precise coincidence of the foot boundary with the word boundary which occurs here is very common in Czech, with its stress on the first syllable, but is relatively rare in Russian, with its free stress, and is therefore onomatopoetically effective in the given line.

The same dependence of poetic expression on the nature of a given linguistic system occurs in other cases as well. Therefore, pan-European literary movements like Symbolism and Futurism, in applying the same programmatic requirements in different languages, can attain results which are considerably different from each other in individual national literatures. Czech Symbolism is, in essence, a different phenomenon with a different significance in the local literary development from, for example, French Symbolism in France or Russian Symbolism in Russia, although the theoretical ideas of the Symbolists themselves are quite similar throughout Europe. And from this we can understand why European literary development demonstrates much greater heterogeneity even in the nineteenth and twentieth centuries, periods of such great international contacts, than does either the development of painting or architecture at the same time.

---

12. *Základy českého verše* (Prague, 1926), pp. 52 f.

II. The Developmental Changeability of Poetic Language, Its Generic Differentiation, Its Perfectibility

Closely connected, on the one hand, with the fate of the local language and, on the other, with the development of local and world poetry, poetic language cannot remain without change in the midst of this dual movement. After all, even its prevailing aesthetic character leads it to changeability, for the aesthetic effectiveness of any device vanishes after a certain time because of automatization, that is, vulgarization and generalization. But in what does the development of poetic language consist? In the fact that poetry's use of the linguistic devices furnished by its entire national language constantly changes and that the entire stock of these devices is also subject to change. Change is very often quite rapid. Not even the works of one generation are likely to be linguistically uniform over its entire course; indeed, we frequently observe changes in language from work to work in the same author. How Vladislav Vančura's poetic language, for example, has changed in a relatively short period! Although biblical language has remained the basis of the sentence structure in Vančura's entire creation up to now, there is an essential difference between the sentences of, for example, *Pekař Jan Marhoul* (1924) or *Poslední soud* (1929), full of Dadaistic semantic reversals, and the monumental sentences of his last book, *Obrazy z dějin národa českého* (1939–40).

Renewal in poetic language appears, both with respect to the previous developmental period and in comparison with the norm of the standard literary language, as a certain violence against language, and therefore one speaks about the *deformational* character of poetic language. It is, however, necessary to use this term, albeit a rather telling one, carefully. Only in some schools and in some periods is it a matter of *apparent* violence tending toward real destruction or at least toward a loosening of the previous forms of poetic expression or the forms of standard literary communication. At other times deviations from poetic tradition or from standard literary usage are less discernible, being instead only a special application of a given means of expression. In some periods (and also in some literary genres) a considerable convergence of poetic language and the standard literary language may take place so that the impression of the deviation of poetic expression almost

vanishes, and poetic genres stand undifferentiated in close prox-
imity to the communicative genres of literature. This happens
especially when both parties meet head on in the middle of the
road, that is, when the language of communicative literature takes
on a strong aesthetic coloration. We see such a state of affairs
particularly during periods of classicism, and this is the desire of
all classicistically minded theoreticians. None of these states—
neither the greatest mutual separation of the standard literary
language and poetic language, nor their maximal convergence, nor,
finally, the golden mean—is, however, a permanent ideal, for
poetic language is constant change.

But what is the essence of the developmental changes in poetic
language? It consists in the constant rebuilding of the set of
linguistic components with respect to the aesthetic effect of an
entire utterance. Each time a different component comes to the
fore, and thereby the arrangement of all the others changes, for all
the components of a literary work are interconnected by multiple
relations pervading its structure. As soon as a certain component
takes the lead, it pulls along those which stand closest to it and
pushes others into the background. Let us say, for example, that
intonation becomes the dominant component. It acquires the leading position by merging into an unbroken line capable of carrying
a great span of meaning. Everything that may interfere with this
continuity immediately withdraws into the background: the sharp
articulation of individual phonemes, emphasis on stress and with it
the phonological independence of the word, the distinct articulation of the sentence by means of syntactic stresses and pauses. All
of these things lose their distinct contours and merge into a single,
gentle undulation (for example, Vrchlický's or Nezval's verse). At
the same time the influence of this shift involves the semantic
sphere: the poet avoids words which are sharply delimited
semantically and chooses expressions rich in imagistic and emotional associations. The sentence structure will also yield to the
continuity of the intonational line. Subordinate clauses will not
accumulate, and the opposition of superordination and subordination which requires sudden transitions in tonal height will be suppressed. Main clauses will accordingly follow one another without
distinct syntactic and semantic boundaries, very often merging
into syntactically indistinct patterns. Sometimes it is even possible
to ascertain the influence of intonation in the very mode of

developing the theme, in the composition. Intonation sometimes becomes the vehicle of thematic articulation in shorter lyric poems. And thus we see how the entire complex structure of the utterance is set into motion under the influence of a single component and how the poet's expression thereby differs from the common mode of expression.

If, then, a change in the dominant component takes place along with a change in poetic movement, a new reconstruction occurs, alienating anew poetic language from the previous state and common linguistic usage. The simple scheme which we have outlined has, of course, both the advantages and the disadvantages of any scheme. To be sure, it elucidates graphically the way in which changes occur in poetic language, but it does not do justice to their actual complexity and heterogeneity. If we wanted to become acquainted with them, we would have no other choice but to examine in detail at least a certain section of an actual concrete development. This would, however, exceed the limits of a basic study.

What we must still mention is that when we say "poetic language" we are already making a schematizing abstraction. As a matter of fact, there is a multitude of poetic languages not only among nations but also within a given national literature. Every literary genre represents a linguistic structure, self-sufficient to a certain degree; sometimes the linguistic differentiation of individual genres is underlined by the use of different dialects, as in ancient Greek poetry. In particular, three basic literary structures are distinguished from one another linguistically: the narrative, the lyric, and the dramatic. Drama is the poetry of dialogue, whereas the narrative and the lyric are monologic structures. This very difference causes the variety of linguistic devices and the ways in which they are used.

The lyric, then, is usually defined specifically as the poetry of language, and it is also the main vehicle of the development of poetic language. Here especially rhythm is the catalyst which sets the linguistic components of the poem into constant motion. All the linguistic (and, of course, the extralinguistic) components are related to rhythmic schemes. For example, euphony[13] can be

---

13. *Editors' note.* Mukařovský uses the term *euphony* to mean the aesthetically intentional organization of the speech sound material in a poetic work. He discusses this phenomenon in the third section of this study.

directly superimposed upon them (see Mácha's *Máj*), intonation may support or oppose the division of the poem into lines or the internal division of the line created by rhythmical breaks, and words are chosen according to the number of syllables because of the requirements of the metrical scheme (hence the Czech trochee prefers parisyllabic words, especially disyllabic ones). The syntactic and semantic structure of the sentence can either yield to or diverge from the rhythmic articulation.

All of this means a great deal from the linguistic viewpoint. What a victory it was, for example, for Czech verse and its further development that the Lumírians, and especially Vrchlický, loosened the usual coincidence of the end of the line with the end of the sentence! If the poetry of the next generation was able to resound with the monumental cantilena of Březina's free verse, it was to a large extent because the preceding generation had prepared the way by means of its rhythmic and linguistic achievement. Rhythm and the lyric are an inevitable pair which to a certain extent governs the fate of poetic language in its entire scope, including the language of narrative prose and the drama.

The language of narrative prose also has its own special character given by the tasks which fall to it. Above all, it enters into intensive contact with the theme, which in its cohesiveness places obstacles in the way of linguistic self-orientation. Therefore, narrative expression approaches the very boundary between poetic and communicative language, frequently assuming the appearance of a mere instrument. Even in extreme cases, however, the narrative writer's attitude toward the word is different from that of a speaker who is concerned with a mere message. The writer always thinks "about sentences which have to have their character, their style, their structure and their order and about words and their richness, their triteness, pithiness and staleness and about all the dangers that this material from which he works prepares for him."[14] The central element of narrative language is the sentence, the component mediating between the language and the theme, the lowest dynamic (realized in time) semantic unit, a miniature model of the entire semantic structuring of the discourse. The development of the narrative is, therefore, correlated with the development of the sentence. Thus even the narrative is rooted in

14. M. Majerová, *Pohled do dílny* [A glance into the workshop] (Prague, 1929), p. 13.

the development of poetic language in taking over the conquests
of the lyric and in mediating their transition into communicative
language.

So much for the generic differentiation of poetic language.
What still remains is the question of whether its evolution can lead
to its perfection. If one has in mind an absolute and invariably
obligatory perfection, the answer must be that every period and
each state of poetic structure has its own degree of artistic as well
as linguistic perfection. Artistically the language of Old Czech
literature is not less perfect than contemporary poetic language,
even though it is six hundred years older. There is, however, another possible perfection of poetic expression, a virtual perfection
consisting in the capacity of a given national language to master
the tasks assigned to a particular literature by general literary cur-
rents or immanent developmental preconditions. This capacity increases with the accumulation of solved problems. Even though
the same situation never occurs twice in the course of development, more or less analogous situations often arise, and here
previous experiences in dealing with linguistic devices facilitate
a more complicated and more artificial rather than a smoother and
simpler approach in the new solution. Hence virtual perfection, as
we have characterized it above, does not tend toward an automatic imitation of models but toward a raising of the standard of
the assigned problems and their solution.

Czech literature in particular, especially beginning with the
National Revival which launched a reconstruction of the literary
tradition, offers many interesting examples of "perfecting" in this
sense. Let us compare, for example, the poetry of the
Puchmajerians and the Lumírians. These two schools are linked to
one another by a great similarity in poetic rhythm. Both the
Puchmajerians before the Romantic slackening of the relation between the prosodic scheme and the meter and the Lumírians after
its complete elimination tended toward a maximally precise realization of the meter. A precise realization of meter, however, causes
rhythmic monotony which the Puchmajerians unsuccessfully attempted to veil by various means, whereas the Lumírians almost a
century later chose intonation as an effective device for attaining
this goal; they knocked down all barriers and pushed rhythm into
the background of the overall impression. Here we cannot speak
otherwise than about perfection, especially if we are aware of the

fact that there had already been timid attempts at this solution among the Puchmajerians as well (Šafařík). Then as soon as Czech verse learned to deal with intonation, this linguistic component became more often the object of aesthetic deautomatization. Its exploitation was, however, further elaborated. If the Lumírians had needed a disproportionate violation of both the word order and the syllabic composition of words (consider the Lumírians' "abbreviations": *sledni, hled*[15]) to make the intonation prominent, later schools achieved an uninterrupted intonational line with far fewer means, even without any reshuffling of normal word order (Karel Čapek's translations, Nezval's poems). Hence there is no reason why we should deny the possibility of the perfection of poetic language in the course of development, if only we conceive this perfection as a dynamic factor.

III. The Sound Aspect of Poetic Language

Let us now examine the set of components of the linguistic system in order to ascertain to what extent each of them participates in the structure of a literary work. First we must remember that these components fall into two groups in accordance with the structure of the linguistic sign. The first includes those which can, though they need not necessarily or unconditionally, attain a realization perceptible by the senses; they are, therefore, the "reality" which is the vehicle of the immaterial meaning of the linguistic sign. Saussure, to whom belongs the credit for distinguishing the basic aspects of the linguistic sign, designated them *signifiant*. We shall use the common, though not too precise, designation "sound components" (the precise term "phonological components" does not exhaust the entire range of the sound aspect of poetic language which also includes constituents not belonging to the phonological system, e.g., tone of voice). The second group includes components lacking even merely potential perceptibility. These are semantic—in the broad sense of the word—components, hence even grammatical ones. Saussure uses the term *signifié* for them.

Such a bifurcation does not, however, entail a denial of the essential unity of the linguistic sign. This is attested by the fact that

---

15. *Editors' note.* Analogous, though not identical, abbreviations in English would be, for example, "o'er" and "'tis" in poetic language.

neither of the two groups completely lacks the properties of the other one. "Sound" components are not only a sensorily perceptible vehicle of meaning but also have a semantic nature themselves. Therefore, they do not cease to exist even when they do not attain a sound or, indeed, another (e.g., optical) realization, as is the case in "thought" speech. Above all, they are parts of the linguistic sign and only afterwards an acoustic phenomenon. They can even acquire quite a concrete meaning, for instance in onomatopoeia, when they "signify" non-linguistic sounds. On the other hand, even though the group of semantic components cannot achieve perceptibility, it does not lack a link with reality: the very definition of meaning consists in referring to that reality which the sign signifies. Hence the linguistic sign is actually symmetrical with respect to reality. The sound aspect proceeds from reality, the semantic aspect tends toward it, though only through the mediation of psychic phenomena (images, emotions, volitions evoked by speech).

Saussure's discovery of the foundations of the internal structure of the linguistic sign differentiated the sign both from mere acoustic "things" (such as natural sounds) and from mental processes. New roads were thereby opened not only for linguistics but also, in the future, for the theory of literature. Above all, the study of poetry was forever after freed from an unjustified belief in the direct dependence of the poetic work on an acoustic realization. As a result the claim that a work lives its real life only in an oral recitation was refuted, a fallacious claim, for there are poets (not only readers) in whose minds a written, not spoken, work has its existence. Furthermore, deliberations about the unequivocal onomatopoetic or emotional expressiveness of individual speech sounds became senseless. On the other hand, a perspective on the semiotic character of the literary work in its entirety and in its parts was gained. The literary work was untangled both from a too unequivocal connection with the reality expressed by its content and from an unambiguous dependence upon the mental processes of the author and the reader. Thus attention was directed to the internal organization of the literary work without its being—again, because of its semiotic nature—extracted from the context of surrounding phenomena.

But at the same time it became obvious that the work can "signify" the phenomena which come into contact with it (the poet, the reader, the social reality, etc.) only polysemically and cannot be a mechanically necessary and unequivocal consequence of any of them. For example, one and the same state of a literary structure can "signify" different states of social organization in different milieux. In accordance with the model of the linguistic event, poetic creation was conceived as a cooperation between the author and the perceiver, no longer as the author's unlimited self-expression or as an automatic reaction to a social demand. In the following sections the further influence of modern linguistics on poetics will, we hope, become apparent: linguistics has provided a model for the structural analysis of the *entire* literary work, not just its linguistic aspect. Naturally Saussure's feat has merely the significance of the initiative, albeit an ingenious one; only the further momentous development of linguistics which resulted from Saussure's impulse has revealed and continues to reveal in detail how the linguistic sign is structured. Moreover, only this further development has made possible the application of linguistic methods to the problems of poetics.

Let us proceed to the first of the two large groups of components of the literary work, *the sound aspect*. It is already clear from our preceding statements that this aspect must not be identified with the acoustic realization of the poetic text. Otakar Zich has already differentiated the sound qualities given in the text itself from those which depend on the reciter's decision.[16] Only the first of them comprises the actual "sound" aspect of the literary work. We must not, of course, presuppose, as Zich has already shown, that there is a precise boundary between the "sound" components contained in a work and those which are independent of the text. Each of these components is to a greater or lesser degree given by the text and, again, is more or less independent of it. The characterization of the sound aspect of poetic language has been further facilitated by phonological study, the subject of which is precisely those sound properties of language that are linguistically "relevant" in comprising a component of the linguistic system. But we must add that not all sound properties of the literary text, independent of the sound realization, are phonological in the strict sense of the word, if we consider only

16. "O typech básnických" [On poetic types], *Časopis pro moderní filologii* 6 (1917–18): 1–19, 97–112, and 202–14. *Editors' note.* This study was later published as a book under the same title (Prague, 1937).

the sound aspect of the linguistic *system* (*langue*) as the true subject of phonology. Many of the sound properties in which the theory of poetic language is interested belong to the realm of less abstract norms than are the laws of "language" in the sense of an abstract system—namely, to the realm of so-called speech (*parole*). For example, tone, the coloration of the voice, does not belong to phonology proper. There are, however, poets for whom the text itself predetermines frequent changes in voice coloration; tone thus becomes a component of literary structure and must be an object of poetic study.

We shall now discuss in brief outline the possibilities of the poetic exploitation of the individual sound components of language. Those components are: the speech sound organization of the utterance, intonation, force of exhalation, tone of voice, and tempo. As we have already suggested, each of these is predetermined to a different extent by the text. Thus the speech sound organization is completely provided by the text, and only subsidiary properties of articulation are to a certain degree within the reciter's power. Intonation and force of exhalation are regulated by the text to a lesser extent; still less easily does the text exert an influence on tone of voice and tempo. We must add that the reciter (in dealing with intonation) may frequently claim the right of disposing of these components even beyond the extent defined by the text, of course at the cost of a poor realization of the text and even of physiological vocal "blocks."[17] If we speak about the predetermination of the sound aspect of the text, we have in mind only an adequate, vocally undeformed recitation yielding to the requirements made by the work.

The first of the sound components is the speech sound organization of the text and the speech sound sequence. By speech sound organization we mean the relative representation of individual speech sounds given by the phonological system of the national language in which the text is written. This representation can be different in different utterances, not just literary ones, and can also differ from the average valid for a given language. In literature these deviations must be evaluated as a factor of aesthetic effect, even if the choice of speech sounds happens without the author's

---

17. On this problem see E. Sievers's treatise *Ziele und Wege der Schallanalyse* (Heidelberg, 1924).

conscious intent. Here as well as everywhere else in art it is true that aesthetic intentionality does not necessarily presuppose a conscious intent. In order to ascertain the characteristics of the speech sound organization it is necessary to compare the statistics of speech sounds represented in a given text with the average frequency of the individual speech sounds in a given language in general. In longer works one might pose the question of whether the speech sound organization remains constant or varies in the course of the text.[18]

The speech sound sequence is even more discernibly a factor of the aesthetic effect of a literary work than the speech sound organization. The sound effect called *euphony* results from the intentional organization of the speech sound sequence. Today it is already unmistakably clear that the aesthetic effect of speech sounds has its source in the serial arrangement which attracts attention to them, whereas semantic value adheres only additionally as a consequence of the contact between the euphonic speech sound pattern and the content. Therefore, euphony is not only polymorphous (onomatopoeia, emotional and imagistic expressiveness) but also polysemous. It can never be claimed that this or that speech sound cluster, this or that speech sound, necessarily and of itself expresses an acoustic reality, an optical or other image or in some cases an emotion whose imitation, depiction, or expression it appears to be in a given case. In particular, individual speech sounds are semantically indifferent in themselves: each of them is capable of expressing even mutually contradictory sounds, images, and emotions. The euphonic organization of the speech sound sequence occurs most often in such a way that a certain speech sound is repeated many times or that a certain entire cluster of speech sounds is repeated once or, in some cases, many times either in the same or in a somewhat altered pattern. The qualitative relations among different speech sounds are also exploited sometimes. For example, vowels may be arranged in a sequence according to the height of their overtones (in Czech the scale u, o, a, e, i), or they may be opposed to one another so that a contrast in their height (u – i) stands out. Long vowels in Czech are also euphonic factors. Euphonic intentionality in dealing with lengths

18. For the influence of the speech sound organization upon the artistic structure of the work, see A. Artjuškov, *Zvuk i stix* [Sound and verse] (Petrograd, 1923).

is revealed, on the one hand, by their excessive use which can be ascertained statistically and, on the other hand, by the accumulation of long vowels in conspicuous places in the text, for instance at the end of lines. In its euphonic function, however, length asserts itself much more as a certain articulatory quality than as duration in time; duration attracts the reader's attention only if the temporal difference between long and short vowels becomes the basis of poetic rhythm, as is the case with quantitative prosody.

In all the aforementioned cases, however, euphony usually requires additional support in the rhythmic, syntactic, or semantic articulation of the context. Only a configuration emphasized in this way appears intentional. Even in texts lacking a euphonic, indeed an aesthetic, intentionality, an accidental configuration of the same speech sounds or entire recurring speech sound groups usually occurs because of a limitation of the speech sound repertoire—as, for example, with only five Czech vowels. But such configurations generally escape the reader's attention, just as do accidental, continuous chains of trochaic or dactylic words in prose. The rhythmic articulation of the line is usually the most frequent and most effective support of euphony. In compensation, strongly emphasized euphony in a verse work becomes a significant secondary factor of the rhythm; consider, for example, Mácha's *Máj,* where euphonic patterns as a rule not only emphasize the line as a unit but very often underline its internal articulation.

There are also examples of prosodic systems in which euphony has acquired the function of the basic rhythmic factor: the alliterative Old German *Stabreim* is one. Of course, rhyme and phenomena related to it, such as assonance, lie between euphony and poetic rhythm. In rhyme as well the rhythmic function sometimes prevails over the euphonic, for rhyme is the signal of the closure of the basic rhythmic unit, the line. Though euphony appears to be the most external component of a poetic text, it can acquire, like any other component, the status of the structural dominant, that is, the component which sets into motion the other components and regulates the degree of their deautomatization precisely because it has been made prominent. That is the case with euphony in *Máj.*

We have already encountered more than once the connection of meaning with speech sounds and their sequence, but then we were dealing with a question of meaning or rather an illusion of meaning inherent in the speech sounds themselves. Speech sounds or their sequence, however, can also become an indirect semantic factor as mediators of semantic relations by putting words similar in sound into semantic contact with one another. Certain figures such as παρήχησις, alliteration, and, partially, paronomasia are based on this function. Word plays such as the pun also exploit it; rhyme is a typical example of it. Rhyme has a semantic as well as a euphonic and rhythmic function: to reveal hidden possibilities of semantic relations between words. Baudelaire expresses this semantic relevance when he says that ". . . any poet who does not know exactly how many rhymes each word admits is incapable of expressing any idea whatsoever."[19]

The *syllable* is the next lowest linguistic unit after the speech sound. Still, it belongs completely to the "sound" (phonological) sphere, not being an independent carrier of meaning. A monosyllabic word is precisely a word, no longer a mere syllable. The poetic exploitation of the syllabic composition of words can occur with respect to intonation, expiration, tempo, rhythm, and meaning; it is therefore many-sided, and its investigation is very important for poetics.[20] The syllabic composition of words gains significance for intonation by virtue of the fact that words with a certain constant number of syllables sometimes serve as the basis of intonational cadences in texts with deautomatized intonation. Quite similarly, texts in which expiration is prominently asserted use syllabic patterns of a certain length as the basis of clausulae.[21] The syllabic composition affects tempo by virtue of the fact that an abundance of polysyllabic words necessarily retards pronunciation, especially in Czech, whose rather unemphatic initial stress does not suffice to outweigh the unstressed syllables. The syllable can even become the prosodic basis of poetic rhythm when the number of syllables characterizes the line as a rhythmic unit; verse of this type is called syllabic. But syllables play an important rhythmic role even in strictly metrical systems. Here rhythmical differentiation which eliminates the monotony of the meter is

19. *Oeuvres posthumes et correspondances inédites* (Paris, 1887), p. 9.

20. In Czech poetics Zich has laid the foundation for its study in the article "O rytmu české prózy" [On the rhythm of Czech prose], *Živé slovo* 1 (1920): 66–78.

21. For a discussion of clausulae see F. Novotný's book *Eurhythmie řecké a latinské prózy* [Eurhythmy of Greek and Latin prose](Prague, 1918–21).

often mainly determined by the syllabic composition of the lexical material. Thus, for example, the rhythmic character of the trochaic line is completely different if this line is composed predominantly of tetrasyllabic words than if it is filled mainly with disyllabic words. Finally, the syllabic composition of words has an influence upon the semantic aspect. This is made possible by the fact that some semantic categories of words are characterized by a relatively fixed number of syllables in the words which belong to it. Verbal nouns in Czech, for instance, are often polysyllabic (*předvídání, kupování, odhadování, zakopávání*), temporal and local adverbs frequently monosyllabic (*zde, tu, tam, kam, kde, sem, ted', již, hned, dnes*). Consequently, if a certain type of syllabic composition of words is stressed in a text (e.g., for rhythmic reasons), the semantic category in which words of this type predominate is also emphasized. On the other hand, the emphasis of a certain semantic category can influence the rhythm by means of the syllabic composition.[22]

Intonation is another sound component of language. Linguistics has become accustomed to designating phenomena pertaining to vocal height by this term. These are the relative level in height of the voice (high – middle – low), valid for the entire text or its longer segments, and the oscillation in height on a given level, that is, linguistic "melody," which, of course, differs from real musical melody by not recognizing fixed height values unchangeable in its course, namely, tones bound by a particular system. The function of intonation in language is manifold. Above all, intonation is a syntactic factor, and its role in this function is again multiple: (1) it unifies words and the verbal expressions of which the sentence (the complex syntactic unit) is composed, and thus it is one of the basic features of the sentence; (2) it differentiates declarative, exclamatory, and interrogative sentences from one another; (3) it serves to reveal relations between verbal expressions, in some cases entire sentences, juxtaposed to one another without conjunctions.[23]

As a syntactic factor, of course, intonation is firmly regulated,

22. See our study "Polákova Vznešenost přírody" [Polák's *Vznešenost přírody*], *Sborník filologický* 10 (Prague, 1934): 1–68.
23. A. Peškovskij, *Russkij syntaksis v naučnom osveščenii* [Russian syntax in a scientific light] (Moscow, 1914).

and thus it is a matter of syntactic phonology.[24] Another function
of intonation is the semantic one: for example, a contrast in height
can serve to underline a semantic contrast between words and
sentences. Intonational nuances can be markers of semantic shading. Besides its function in the syntactic articulation, intonation
also supports the semantic division of the sentence. Finally, the
third function of intonation is the expressive and appellative one.
It can, on the one hand, express the emotional coloration of a
word or a sentence, and, on the other, signal the appeal with which
an utterance, though at first glance non-appellative, is addressed to
the listener. In both of the last mentioned functions intonation
does not have the unequivocal regularity that belongs to syntactic
intonation, but nevertheless its form can be determined by the
meaning or the organization of the text.[25]

Poetic language exploits intonation in all three of its functions.
We can even characterize the artistic organization of a given text
merely by determining in which of these functions intonation is
used most often. A more detailed intonational analysis of a literary
text will require in particular the determination of how intonation
affects the other components with respect to their aesthetic
deautomatization and how it is influenced reciprocally by them.
This analysis will also concern the question of its structural
superordination and subordination. The course of the intonational *line* (smooth, unbroken, or interrupted) and its height
required in the performance of the text will also be significant for
a literary work. The steep or gradual ascent of intonational curves
and the density or sparsity of intonational peaks also have an influence on the sound organization of a text. Sievers's well-known
study "On Speech Melodics in German Poetry"[26] deals with all of
these properties of poetic intonation. Unlike Sievers, however, we
must emphasize that only by studying the relations of the particular properties of intonation to the other components of a work
(such as the syntactic and semantic structuring of the sentence,

24. S. Karcevskij, "Sur la phonologie de la phrase," *Travaux du Cercle linguistique de
Prague* 4 (Prague, 1931): 188–227.

25. Cf. the intonational difference between "Pojd' sem!" and "Sem pojd'!", sentences
differing from one another only in word order and, of course, intonation. *Editors' note.*
The English equivalents of these sentences would have the same word order; only the
intonation would change: "*Come* here!" and "Come *here!*".

26. "Über Sprachmelodisches in der deutschen Dichtung," *Rhythmisch-melodische
Studien* (Heidelberg, 1912).

and the choice of lexical material) can we prove and linguistically define how the intonation is determined by the text. Because of its "freeness," that is, its considerable independence from the grammatical structure, word order is an especially effective tool for creating the intonational line in Czech. The Lumírians exploited it most frequently for this purpose; although postwar poetry again deautomatized intonation, it rejected the assistance of inversions in word order (Karel Čapek, Nezval).

Punctuation is the graphic sign which corresponds to intonation in a text. Hence it is very important in the intonational analysis of a literary text to ascertain the relationship between the poet's usage of punctuation and normal usage even when the poet has not consciously emphasized his positive or negative attitude toward punctuation and its regulation. Different kinds of print (cursive, majuscule) can also become graphic signs of the intonational properties of a text if they are used for that purpose in the midst of a normally printed text, as the Symbolists liked to do. The division of a text into lines can acquire the same value if it suggests the rising or the falling of intonation or even some of its other features. In the introduction to his poem *Un coup de dés* Mallarmé specifically talks about the graphic organization of the page as a "score."

Furthermore, the division of a text into paragraphs is relevant to intonation. A sentence standing in a text as an independent paragraph has quite a different intonation (and, of course, meaning, especially semantic relevance) from that it would have if it were merely a part of a longer paragraph. A longer paragraph, however, also represents a certain intonational pattern characterized in particular by a special kind of concluding intonational cadence. Intonation can also play an important role—especially in a lyric poem—in the organization of the overall compositional scheme. In such cases, the text is usually divided by means of a repeated intonational pattern either running through whole segments of the text or at least characterizing the end or even the beginning of a segment in the form of a "cadence."[27]

Finally, we should mention the relation of intonation to poetic rhythm. This is an essential relation, although traditional metrics

27. See V. Žirmunskij, *Kompozicija liričeskix stixotvorenij* [The composition of lyric poems] (Petrograd, 1921).

does not pay much attention to it. If there is no other leading prosodic factor in verse, intonation automatically assumes this function itself (as it does in the "freest" type of modern Czech verse). But even if another sound element, such as stress, is the leading prosodic factor, intonation does not cease to be the background against which the metrical scheme unfolds. The line resembles a sentence. Like the sentence, it is characterized by the unity of its intonational organization, and this "verse" intonation constantly either coincides or intersects with the syntactic intonation in the course of the poem. Thus intonation delimits the basic unit of verse rhythm, the unit without which even the most regular sequence of rhythmic signals does not create the impression of "verse." Hence its basic significance for poetic rhythm. Moreover, it also facilitates rhythmic differentiation, especially in its constant potential clash with syntactic intonation, a clash which can be deautomatized in the form of various kinds of "enjambment."[28]

Of all the sound components the *intensity of exhalation,* expiration, is the closest to intonation. Poetry utilizes expiration for its own purposes. In Czech, expiration is the main sound component of stress. It is therefore the leading vehcile of the metrical scheme in "accentual" verse. At the same time, however, it is a factor of rhythmic differentiation, for the expiratory stream constantly undulates, and the peaks of its intensity are also quite distinguishable from one another. Only rarely are the stresses of two contiguous words equally intensive. The theory of "syntactic" stress, developed for Czech especially by Gebauer and Trávníček, is far from sufficient for grasping this rich variability. The reasons for this variability are manifold. Their character is syntactic, semantic, and rhythmic (we have in mind here the "natural" rhythm of speech in general).

The relation of the undulation of expiratory intensity to intonation is special. In certain ways the two phenomena are concurrent; for example, just as intonation concludes sentences, syntactic units, and semantic segments by cadences, expiration provides "clausulae" with their conclusions. Very often a certain concluding sound pattern, carried by a word unit of a certain number of syllables, is both a cadence and a clausula at the same time. The prevalence of either intonation or expiration in a given text will

28. See our study "Intonation as the Basic Factor of Poetic Rhythm," below.

determine which of these two this sound pattern will more likely appear to be. That is, intonation and expiration counterbalance one another. With the supremacy of intonation there is a prevailing tendency toward an uninterrupted exhalatory flow, toward the obliteration of all boundaries between words, syntactic units, and semantic segments within a sentence. With the supremacy of expiration there is, on the contrary, an effort to emphasize boundaries and thereby to divide the exhalatory flow into segments. Vrchlický's poetry is an example of the first type, Neruda's of the second. An aural impression is the first indication of such differences; however, just as in the case of intonation, an objective determination can be carried out only by a syntactic and semantic analysis that will show which features of the text provide the supremacy of intonation or expiration. This also applies to the determination of nuances in expiration itself.

Let us now turn to another sound component of the literary work, *tone of voice,* which is sometimes designated by the ambiguous term *timbre* (in linguistics this term designates the height of the overtones of vowels as well as voice coloration). In contradistinction to all the aforementioned sound components, each of which achieves phonological validity to a greater or lesser extent, tone of voice is not, at least in Czech, a phonological component. Neither can it be claimed that it could have been predetermined in any way by the structure of the text; the emotional shading of the content is the only means by which it can be rendered implicitly. Not even this means, however, is sufficient in itself. Numerous stage directions in dramatic texts ("angrily," "merrily," "whimsically," etc.), by which the author attempts to convey his idea of changes in tone of voice to the actor, are evidence of this.

Nevertheless, tone of voice is not merely a matter of "sound," for it exerts an influence, often decisive, upon the meaning of the text. It is capable of expressing not only volatile emotional coloration but also such a systematic semantic nuance as irony. Of course, irony also has at its disposal purely semantic means (especially different kinds of ambiguities). Nevertheless, irony in a written text is deprived of an important tool, the ironic tone of the voice. Sometimes irony even exploits this deprivation intentionally for its own disguise (for example, Durych's ironic essays in *Ejhle člověk*). Hence tone of voice expresses not only subjective emotional nuances but also an evaluation which makes a claim for objectivity: it introduces a perspective on people and things into the semantic aspect of a text. Therefore, the determination of changes in tone of voice is important for the analysis of a literary work. But is this possible under the conditions described above? It depends on what our goal is. If we wanted to determine step by step in which places of a text changes in tone of voice occur and what their quality is, we would not, of course, arrive at conclusive and generally valid statements for the very reason that an evaluation whose sound equivalent is tone of voice does not depend— despite its tendency toward objectivity—*only* on the meaning imparted to the text by the author but also on the reader's interpretation and standpoint. But for our purpose we do not require such a detailed investigation. This will be necessary only for an actor or reciter who will, however, arrive at it by a path other than the scientific, the path of artistic creation. It is enough for the theoretician if he can show quite *generally* whether and to what extent a certain text takes into account tone of voice; the place and the quality of *individual* changes need not concern him.

Such an assertion is not impossible. In a written text the very abundance of evaluative expressions and phrases connected with the changeability of the evaluative standpoint, indeed the wealth of volatile and contrasting emotional nuances, prove to the scholar the potential presence of changes in tone. Furthermore, the relation between tone of voice and intonation facilitates the diagnosis. Insofar as intonation dominates in a text, it requires a continuous sound line, whereas if tone of voice is to be felt, it must tend toward sudden changes in this line. Hence if a text is oriented toward intonation, it cannot at the same time be oriented toward the exploitation of voice coloration.[29] This alternative between intonation and tone of voice can facilitate research by excluding in advance texts with deautomatized intonation, which at first glance are more easily recognizable than texts with deautomatized tone. It is natural that tone of voice asserts itself most frequently and most distinctly in dialogue where the participants' evaluative

29. We have attempted to prove this thesis in our study "Próza Karla Čapka jako lyrická melodie a dialog," *Slovo a slovesnost* 5 (1939): 1-12. *Editors' note.* An abridged English translation of this article, "Karel Čapek's Prose as Lyrical Melody and Dialogue," appears in *A Prague School Reader on Esthetics, Literary Structure, and Style*, ed. Paul L. Garvin (Washington, D.C., 1964), pp. 133-49.

attitudes toward things and their emotional interrelations confront
one another immediately. Determining tone of voice and its structural function, therefore, has an especially significant role in the
poetics of drama. Nevertheless, tone of voice does not dominate
in every dramatic dialogue; there are also dialogic forms with predominant intonation. Tone of voice can also manifest itself
markedly in lyric and narrative works; it distinctly predominates
in the sound aspect of Erben's *Kytice*, for example. Julius Tenner
has pointed out the importance of tone of voice for poetry in his
study "On the Melody of Verse." Tenner's basic thesis that "*sound
coloration* is the most decisive factor for the essence and the
nature of the melodics of verbal expression . . ."[30] is, of course,
obviously exaggerated, and this fault has a bearing upon the
author's other comments. Among other things it leads to the confusion of tone of voice with the expressive effect of euphony.

The sound component to which we shall now turn, *tempo,* has a
considerably different character from all of the preceding ones. It
is not a voice quality but the property of duration. Nevertheless, it
indirectly acquires a qualitative character by virtue of the fact that
the tempo of an utterance is primarily a semantic matter for the
listener, and this applies as well to non-poetic language, especially
in speech. A change in tempo can bring about a gradation of
semantic significance, tempo can express the emotional coloration
of meaning, and so on. The possibilities for the predetermination
of tempo by a text are not too considerable. They reach a somewhat higher degree only in rhythmicized texts (verse and rhythmic
prose) because the desired tempo of delivery can be provided by
the arrangement and relative length of the rhythmic segments.
Here basically two matters are involved: tempo in its entirety and
changes in tempo in the course of a text. Tempo in its entirety can
to a certain extent be provided by the sound organization and the
meaning of the text: in an oral presentation a text pervaded by
distinct euphonic schemes will require a slower delivery than a
text with predominant exhalatory intensity. As far as meaning is
concerned, we can assume that a text accompanied by an emotional nuance of joy will compel a faster delivery than a text
colored by sorrow or resignation.

30. "Über Versmelodie," *Zeitschrift für Ästhetik und allgemeine Kunstwissenschaft*
8 (1913): 353.

But much more important for us than tempo in its entirety is agogics—changes in tempo during delivery—insofar, of course, as it can be predetermined by the text. A change in tempo in a poetic work results from the unequal length of contiguous rhythmic segments. This occurs, for instance, if a rather long line follows a very short one in a free rhythm or if polysyllabic "measures" alternate irregularly with short "measures" in tonic verse. An alternation of tempo can even occur in metrically regular verse, for example, when dipodically divided lines are juxtaposed to a line of the same meter lacking the dipodic articulation. The dipodic lines will require a faster tempo than the others in delivery. The utterances of the old woman and the girl are differentiated in this way in Neruda's "Balada horská."

In connection with tempo we should at least mention *pauses*. A linguistic pause can, of course, be rendered by different means, especially by an intonational cadence, an expiratory clausula, or a break. Pauses are a necessary factor of the division of an utterance. Some of them are members of the grammatical system itself, such as those which express the syntactic articulation of a sentence and its conclusion. Other pauses, still less systematized, are a means of semantic articulation. In poetry all kinds of pauses can be de-automatized by means of an accumulation, a strikingly regular repetition, or the use of pauses in unexpected places (for example, the deautomatization of pauses in Mácha[31] or in Dyk). An unusual use of pauses can also be thematically motivated, for instance by the excitement of the speaker. But even if there is not such a motivation, a pause is a carrier of meaning, for in itself it suffices to "signify" emotional excitement. A pause can even become the equivalent of a quite definite meaning, if it is determined by its incorporation into the surrounding context. This happens, for example, in dialogue, where a mere pause can be an answer or, on the contrary, a question. At other times a pause suggests the flow of a semantic current but does not imply its concrete charge. Pauses indicated in a text by several dots which urge the reader to "infer" what was said are of this kind. The lyrical vagueness of a semantic contour can be achieved in this way, and, on the contrary, a quite definite allusion to something that the author does

31. F. X. Šalda, "K. H. Mácha a jeho dědictví" [K. H. Mácha and his heritage], *Duše a dílo* (Prague, 1913), pp. 43–98.

not wish to say directly can also be rendered. In verse there are
rhythmic pauses provided by the rhythmic articulation as well as
syntactic and semantic pauses. These different kinds of pauses
enter into complex positive and negative relations (similarities and
dissimilarities) which are an inexhaustible means of rhythmic differentiation and semantic shading. Pauses can even become tempo-
rarily the only carrier of the rhythmic and semantic context in
verse. This happens when a line or even an entire stanza, filled out
by pauses alone, occurs in the middle of a poem.[32]

The word *pause* comes from musical terminology; however, we
must make a clear distinction between musical and linguistic
pauses. The musical pause is a member of a measurable temporal
sequence of musical rhythm, whereas the linguistic pause, especially insofar as it occurs in non-rhythmicized language, is not, as we
have already said, felt as a measurable temporal quality, even when
it is acoustically realized by an actual break. In verse, of course,
the linguistic pause is somewhat closer to the musical pause than
in unversified language, but even then it is not identical with it,
for poetic rhythm, insofar as it is not "quantitative,"[33] is itself
based more on the periodicity of succession than on the division
of a temporal series into segments comparable to one another in
their duration. It is not, therefore, correct if specialists in metrics
sometimes attempt to introduce the graphic signs of musical
pauses into metrics, for example to mark the difference between
an acatalectic and a catalectic line or to "balance" lines consisting
of a different number of words which alternate in the same
strophe. In this way a shadow of temporal measurability, which is
alien to poetic rhythm in most cases, is introduced into the
scheme. If, of course, it happens that the measurability of pauses
and the distance between them are made palpable in the *acoustic
realization* of even an unrhythmicized literary text, it will be a
matter of an artistically intentional *transposition* of the regularity
of musical rhythm into an utterance. This is, however, already a

---

32. See Ju. Tynjanov, *Problema stixotvornogo jazyka* [The problem of verse language]
(Leningrad, 1924), p. 22.

33. We have put the term "quantitative" in quotation marks because we are not using
it here only for verse based on differences of linguistic quantity but for *all* kinds of verse
defined by the measurability of the temporal distance between individual rhythmic
downbeats, hence, for example, the tonic verse of children's count-out rhymes and
nursery rhymes such as "Píšu, píšu patnáct," and so on.

question of free choice on the part of the artist who realizes the text, not of the text itself.[34]

We have come to the end of our survey of the sound components of poetic language. We should only point out that—with the exception of the incidental references which we have already made and will make below—we are leaving aside verse rhythm, although its sensorily perceptible vehicle is always a set of sound components and in particular the one which is the basic element in the given prosodic system. We cannot possibly burden an already extensive study with a more detailed survey of prosody and metrics. And, further, such a survey has already been published.[35]

IV. The Word in Poetry

The subject of this section and all the following ones will be semantics in the broad sense of the term, beginning with the word and ending with semantic structures of the highest order. For the sake of clarity we shall deal progressively and separately with the word, the sentence, and higher semantic units, then with monologue and dialogue as well as with "unexpressed" meaning. This division, though theoretically not completely precise, seems to be most advantageous because it proceeds from the simplest semantic phenomena to the most complex ones.

The *word,* though the lowest relatively independent semantic unit of language, is not the most basic and simple semantic element of language; this is the *morpheme* which, of course, absolutely lacks independence, for morphemes can occur only as parts of a word. There are root, derivational, and desinential morphemes. A root morpheme is the carrier of the nucleus of lexical meaning. A derivational morpheme places a word in a certain lexical group, thereby introducing into its meaning a nuance common to all the words derived by means of this morpheme. We should add that prefixes as well as derivational suffixes are derivational morphemes. Finally, a desinential morpheme places a word in the morpholog-

34. Cf. E. F. Burian's theatrical work, the principles of which concerning the rhythmical quality of stage speech have been formulated in his theoretical article "Příspěvek k problému jevištní mluvy" [A contribution to the problem of stage speech], *Slovo a slovesnost* 5 (1939): 24–32.

35. See the article "Obecné zásady a vývoj novočeského verše" [The general principles and the development of modern Czech verse], *Československá vlastivěda, III: Jazyk* (Prague, 1934): 376–429.

ical system and at the same time makes it capable of incorporation into the syntactic structure of the sentence. Let us now take a look at the ways in which this internal composition of the word can be poetically deautomatized.

The first consists in calling attention to the "morphological seams" separating the individual morphemes of which a word is composed from one another. This happens, for example, when two words, one of which "contains" the other in its phonetic composition, are juxtaposed by means of a rhyme or a contiguity in a context. The semblance of the composite nature of a longer word and hence the semblance of the corresponding morphological seam in it are thus evoked.[36] At other times two phonetically similar words, each of which has the morphological seam in a different place, are juxtaposed: "dodnes – odnes" ("until today – carried away") (Hlaváček's rhyme). The aesthetically effective uncertainty about the internal division of the word comes about in this way. A similar play, seemingly interfering with the morphological composition of the word, can be made with a word boundary. A single word unit can appear to be split in two because of a juxtaposition (for instance, Hlaváček's rhyme "do karty – oka rty" ["into the card – eyes lips"]), or an apparent shift of a word boundary can occur (Hlaváček's rhyme "plazili se – lysé" ["crawled – bald"]). The illusion of a word boundary in the middle of a word also occurs in a rhyme—most often comically intended—which splits a word: "Mysliveček a je- | ho pes šli do háje" ("A hunter and hi- | s dog were going to the grove").[37]

Now let us characterize the ways of poetically exploiting the individual kinds of morphemes as meaning-creating elements. We shall, however, analyze only derivational and desinential morphemes, because we shall deal independently with the nucleus of lexical meaning, the carriers of which are root morphemes, in another context later.

Derivational morphemes can be deautomatized first of all by excessive accumulation. If a striking number of words derived by

36. Consider Hlaváček's rhyme *natryskla – skla* ("began to spring a little" – "of the glass/glasses") or Deml's sentence: "Ten slavičí klokot opsal jsem z Velkého Přírodopisu jen proto, aby se vědělo, že se v Šlépějích pěje. Šlépěje. Pěje." ("I have copied this nightingale's warbling from *The Great Natural Science Handbook* only so that it will be known that there is singing in *Footprints*. Footprint. Sings.") (*Šlépěje* [Footprints] 1 [Jinošov, Moravia, 1917]: 60).

37. F. Hajniš, "Na veršotepce a rymohonce," *Kopřivy* (Prague, 1853), p. 36.

means of a certain suffix is used throughout an entire text or in one of its segments, not only is our attention drawn to the suffix as a speech sound pattern, but the semantic nuance which this suffix introduces into words is also emphasized. For instance, emphasis of the suffix -*ost* (Eng. -ness) leads the reader to view concreteness non-concretely, namely, from the standpoint of its properties (substantives are often derived from adjectives by means of this suffix). Another way of deautomatizing derivational morphemes, opposite to the previous one, is by clustering together various derivations from the same root. Here the identity of the root may even be only apparent, that is, based upon a mere speech sound coincidence of the root syllables: "spí *myr*ty s *mír*nými lístky i *mír*nými stíny" ("Akord") or "házi vám dolů s oblohy květy *šeři*ku—zvolna se *šeři*" ("Klekání").[38]

We can include the matter of the so-called grammatical categories (noun, adjective, verb, etc.) and verbal aspects with derivational suffixes, even though it does not always belong with them. Both these phenomena are often, though not in every case, expressed by derivational means (in Czech -*ost* is a substantival suffix, -*ný* is an adjectival suffix, verbal aspect is frequently expressed by a prefix). A grammatical category can acquire aesthetic effect by the accumulation of words belonging to it and especially by their accumulation in prominent places in the text. Thus, for example, the clustering of verbs at the ends of lines in Mácha's *Máj* colors the entire text with the semantic nuance of "activity" (Šalda), that is, the property characteristic of the grammatical category of verbs. Verbal aspect is also frequently deautomatized by the accumulation of a certain aspectual type; moreover, the excessive use of less usual aspectual forms adds to the aesthetic effect. Aspect in Neruda is often deautomatized by this means; consider, for example, his favorite aspectual diminutives like *pozajásat* ("to rejoice a little bit") which, of course, have their model in common usage (*povyskočit* ["to jump a little bit"]) but are frequently unusual. We could refer to poetic neologisms as a further case of the poetic exploitation of derivational suffixes; however, these comprise at the same time a certain characteristic "milieu" of the poetic lexicon and will therefore be mentioned below.

38. K. Biebl, *Zlatými řetězy* (Prague, 1926). ("The myrtles are sleeping with peaceful leaves and peaceful shadows"; "He throws lilac blossoms down to you from the sky—it is gradually growing dark.")

In the composition of the word, *desinential* morphemes play the role of grammatical element in the proper sense of the term. Thus it might seem that they are incapable of poetic deautomatization on account of their systematic nature and semantic abstractness. But even they acquire aesthetic effectiveness if attention is drawn to them by the excessive use of a certain grammatical form (for example, the unusual *instrumental* adverbial modifier in Mácha's *Máj*: "A *šírou dálkou* tma je pouhá"—"V kol *suchoparem* je koření líbá vůně"). The poet can also make desinences aesthetically effective by using a particular ending with a word to which the form created by this ending is alien; for example, in Březina's line "a ze stromu tvého slzami horkými *teku*" ("*I flow* in hot tears from your tree")[39] we find the first person singular of the verb "to flow," a form which we are otherwise accustomed to find, if at all, in a grammatical paradigm. The deautomatization of a desinence, of course, calls attention above all to the meaning which the ending introduces into the form. It does not matter that this meaning is only "abstract"; on the contrary, the poetic word can often penetrate right to the roots of the poet's epistemology precisely by means of this semantic abstractness of a desinence. Hence the unusual use of the first person of the verb "to flow" is indicative of Březina's notion of the subject of human activity.

Let us now move from the internal composition of the word to *lexical meaning*. First we encounter the notion of the poet's vocabulary, namely, the set of words used in a certain poetic work. Characteristic of this set, of course, are mainly those words which the poet uses most frequently and most intentionally. A complete list of the lexical material used in a certain work is of more interest to linguistics than to the theory of poetry. Here we need not dwell on the fact that each individual has his own stock of words which represents a particular selection from the total lexicon of a given language. This selection is often governed by the given individual's dispositions (the sphere of his interests, the social stratum and the region to which he belongs, the level of his education, etc.) and by the actual goal of the utterance. Insofar as the individual's predilection for certain words and, in some cases, his aversion to others interfere with this selection, aesthetic intention is always, at least partially, present. This intention is, of course, greatly emphasized

39. The poem "Čas lije se" from *Tajemné dálky* (1895).

in poetic word selection. But in no way do we assert that the poet will always seek a "beautiful" expression; we have already rejected this view at the beginning of our study. We do not even wish to claim that a regard for aesthetic effect in poetic word selection is always exclusive or even decisive; in poetry there is an oscillation between the aesthetic function and the others. We do assert, however, that the choice of vocabulary in a literary work, from whatever considerations it derives, necessarily becomes a part of the artistic organization of the work, enters into complex relations with its other components, and thus must be judged and studied from the standpoint of this structural intentionality. For example, the use of religious terminology as a component of the vocabulary in a certain work can, of course, be genetically explained as a consequence of such factors as the poet's education, his social status, or his profession, and in some cases as a manifestation of his attempt to gain the understanding of particular members of the reading public or to actively influence the reading public.

But insofar as the scholar is concerned with a work of art itself, these and similar considerations can become an object of study only secondarily. It must first be clear what *artistic* task the choice of lexical material performs in a given work. Therefore, the following questions will arise: From what spheres of the general lexicon is the vocabulary of the work drawn? What are the semantic interrelations of these individual spheres? Does one prevail over the others, or do all of them assert themselves to the same degree? And if they are equally represented, do their interrelations appear as an agreement or as a clash or even as a contradiction? Do they somehow color one another semantically? How are their interrelations projected into the structure of the work? Is the choice of lexical material homogeneous in the entire work, or do shifts in its composition occur in the course of the work (e.g., the emphasis of some lexical component in the descriptive parts of an epic work in contrast to the narrative parts)? Is the participation of semantically dependent words (synsemantics) proportionate to the participation of semantically independent words, or, on the contrary, are the semantically dependent words used excessively? Is the poet's vocabulary vast or limited? How are the considerations which govern the choice of lexical material in a literary work related to other components of the artistic structure (to the rhythm, the sentence structure, the theme, etc.)?

This list of questions could be enlarged without, of course, transgressing the boundaries of the artistic structure. Even the very delimitation of the lexical spheres from which a poet draws must to a certain extent be made from the standpoint of poetry itself. Thus, for example, the notions of the archaism and the neologism appear somewhat different to the theory of poetry than to other branches of linguistics. A practical, communicative neologism comes into being from the need to create a name for a new thing or at least a thing heretofore lacking a special designation. A poetic neologism, however, does not spring from this need, but, on the contrary, it often substitutes—completely uselessly, from a practical standpoint—for the common designation of a known thing in order to draw attention to the very fact of the creation of new words. Under these conditions it is obvious that poetic neologization will be governed by quite different rules and will have quite a different appearance from practical neologization. The difference will lie in the fact that the poetic neologism will not make a claim for general acceptance and permanence, for such a claim would conflict with its most intrinsic purpose to oppose the automatization of the act of designation. As concerns the archaism, this term generally means the use of an older, already uncommon but once really valid word or mode of expression. In poetry "artificial" archaisms are also possible, namely, ones that never existed in real usage but that create the *impression* of a bygone mode of expression. In this case it is not a matter of the genesis of the expression but of the function that the expression fulfills in the structure of a given present text.

Which lexical spheres does the poet have at his disposal? One can assert that, more than in any other utterance, all of them are at his disposal for the very reason that poetry is not bound by any practical consideration in its selection. This selection moves along a line of several connections: *referential* (e.g., house – window – roof); *sound* (e.g., *láska* [love] – *máj* [May] – *čas* [time] – *hlas* [voice] – *háj* [grove], etc.); *morphological* (in the broad sense of the word: *dům* [n. house] – *domácí* [n. landlord; adj. home] – *domovní* [adj. pertaining to a house] – *doma* [adv. at home]; *dům* [nom./acc. s.] – *domu* [gen./dat./loc. s.] – *domem* [instr. s.] – *domy* [nom./acc./instr. pl.]); and *lexical* (the vocabularies of various social milieux, various dialects, various functional styles). The "proper" lexical means of poetic language are so-called poeticisms, but these comprise just one of the lexical spheres among which and from which the poet selects, and there are even periods when he avoids them. The very term *poeticism* is not completely unambiguous. Sometimes it means the traditional stock of words felt as "poetic" (*oř* ["steed"]), sometimes the set of words distinctly characterizing the vocabulary of a certain poet or a certain school (e.g., the word *pecen* ["loaf of bread"] is one of the poeticisms of Jiří Wolker and his epigones).

The semantic character of the poet's vocabulary is influenced not only by the lexical spheres from which he draws his words but also by the entire semantic intention by which the selection and application of words is governed in his work. There are poets and poetic schools tending toward semantic coloration which could be called the maximal intensification, either imagistic or emotional. Vrchlický, for example, tended toward such emotional "lexical hyperbole." Others seek the suppression of vivid imagery or emotionality; Machar is thus the antithesis of Vrchlický with respect to emotionality. Among other poets or schools one can detect a general tendency toward the coloration of the lexicon by the semantic nuance of "ordinariness" or "exceptionality," "loftiness" or "baseness." Such a total lexical coloration may be connected with the choice of theme, but this connection is not unconditional or one-sided. Two different elaborations can place one and the same theme in two different semantic "keys" merely because of a different lexical coloration. Moreover, one and the same work can simultaneously have multiple lexical colorations which interpenetrate so that a contrastive effect is achieved. Examples of this lexical technique can be found in Vančura's prose.

We have already encountered more than once—most recently in the immediately preceding lines—the fact that the semantic aspect of a word is not given only by the lexical sphere from which the word comes but also by its confrontation with the other words beside which it appears in the text. But here we do not have in mind the semantic *dynamics* of contexture, about which we shall speak later, but an effect, still *static* in its essence, which we could call a "mirroring" of meanings colliding with one another. The external proof of the static character of semantic mirroring is the fact that it occurs in the smallest possible textual span, namely, that which is occupied by two contiguous words, frequently as closely linked grammatically as possible. The connection of an adjective with a substantive is one type of such a phrase-word. Baudelaire wrote in one of his sketches for the foreword to *Fleurs du mal*, ". . . poetry is connected to the arts of painting, cooking and cosmetics by its ability to express any feeling of sweetness or bitterness, of bliss or horror, *by linking* [italics ours, J.M.] a certain noun to a certain adjective, either analogous or contrary."[40] By means of a paradoxical formulation, mirroring is here characterized as the creation of a *new* meaning which is not contained in either of the two juxtaposed words.

Let us take as an example the phrase-word found in Toman's poem "Aix-en-Provence": *smyslné chrámy* ("sensuous temples").[41] What kind of semantic process occurs in this collision of these two words, both common but originating from such heterogeneous semantic spheres? First of all, the semantic connections contained potentially in each of them emerge. The word *sensuous* will immediately be felt as a member of the semantic spheres of the erotic and sensory perception, and a joyful emotional accent will resound in it. The word *temple,* on the contrary, will be immediately associated with the semantic sphere of a religious cult and will have a serious emotional coloration. These two discordant semantic complexes will then merge into a complicated semantic ambience, for the direct and explicit expression of which many more than two words would be necessary: it might even be an entire cultural-historical essay. The semantic confrontation of words manifests itself in this way: although it originates by a succession of verbal units, its result is a static "semantic ambience." Not even the fact that the encounter of words does not have to be absolutely immediate but can happen at a certain distance—if the semantic correspondence of the confronted words is somehow indicated—changes anything about this. This is the case, for example, with rhyme. One of the most essential semantic tasks of rhyme is precisely to bring the semantic spheres represented by the rhyme words into contact. We could deliberate over Nezval's rhyme "*hruškou - tužkou*" ("pear - pencil," instrumental case) in the same way as we did over Toman's immediate connection of the words "sensuous temples."

40. *Oeuvres posthumes,* p. 9.
41. "Tvé platany a kašny se mnou jdou—tvé chrámy smyslné i modré nebe" ("Your plane trees and fountains go with me—your sensuous temples and blue sky") (*Stoletý kalendář*, 1926).

A special kind of confrontation sometimes occurs in the repetition of the same word, especially immediately (epizeuxis) but even at a certain distance. The same meaning repeated twice is reflected in itself and thus changes from a firmly delimited meaning into an indefinite semantic ambience. Finally, we should mention that a semantic confrontation can result in an aesthetically effective stylistic "abbreviation" (brachylogy) because of its ability to bring together meanings which are very distant from one another. We shall find many examples of its being used in this way in Neruda's poems, for instance "na *zvonivých* jedem *saních*" ("We are riding on a ringing sleigh";[42] that is, on a sleigh pulled by a team which has jingle bells on its harnesses and rings them during the ride). Hence two subordinate clauses consisting of many words are necessary for an elaboration of the abbreviation which in the poet's text is a single adjective—of course, inclined at a particular semantic angle to the adjacent substantive.

We are far from leaving our deliberations over the word as the lowest independent semantic unit; nevertheless, we find ourselves at the divide. From questions of the poetic lexicon we shall now move to questions of *poetic designation,* from the matter of the general selection of vocabulary to the matter of the actual application of a word in a particular case to a particular extralinguistic reality, material or psychic. As a lexical unit a word has only a potential relation to reality: it contains many possibilities for an actual application. As long as it is perceived only as a part of the lexicon, only the *boundaries* of all its possible references[43] are given by the meaning, felt, of course, only as the set of all the possible semantic capacities of the given word, not as the actual semantic equivalent of a particular reality. In an actual application the reference and meaning of the word emerge from their potentiality. Only one of all the possible references of a word finds its application, but as live semantic energy; the meaning also acquires definiteness under its influence. In other words: as long as we

---

42. "Zimní IV," *Prosté motivy* (Prague, 1883).

43. *Editors' note.* Here and elsewhere we have used the word *reference* to render Mukařovský's term *věcný vztah,* which itself is a Czech translation of Husserl's concept *gegenständliche Beziehung.* We prefer "reference" to the more precise "object-relation" (cf. D. Cairns, *Guide to Translating Husserl* [The Hague, 1973], p. 58) because its meaning is immediately accessible even to those unfamiliar with Husserl's work and because phenomenological terminology does not play a significant role in Mukařovský's vocabulary.

conceive of a word as a lexical unit, its meaning is asserted (hence the definition of its meaning in dictionaries); as soon as the word is used for designation, however, it is mainly its reference that comes to the fore. This prevalence of the reference over the meaning becomes especially evident in a figurative designation which assigns the reader the task of discovering the referential relation between the designated reality and the word. The meaning of the word which has been used for the figurative designation often remains in the background. Zich has already called attention to this "secondariness" of meaning in a figurative designation: "If we read in Neruda's 'Romance helgolandská' 'A člunek jeho jako liška běží . . .' ('And his little boat runs like a fox . . .'), only the speed and the predatoriness of the boat or rather of its brigand owner are expressed by this phrase. It would be utterly absurd for a perfect understanding of this figurative phrase to ask the reader to imagine a running fox—perhaps on waves?! Here the term 'poetic figures' or 'images' leads to a fallacious interpretation."[44]

The actual application of a linguistic sign, which is designation, is a sudden *act* by means of which the appropriate word is discovered. The stock from which it is selected is basically the entire lexicon of the given language with all the interconnections and stratifications of the words which run through it. This is, of course, valid in full measure only for an absolutely original designation, namely, one in which the designated fact has just been separated from reality or, in some cases, if it is a question of an "abstract" notion, has just been created by the act of designation itself. Obviously the usual application of words is more or less automatized; there is often an illusion of a necessary and essential connection between a word and a certain reality. Compare the fact ascertained by child psychology that children frequently attribute properties of things to words usually serving for their designation. To the question "Why are clouds called clouds?" a child replies: "Because they are gray"; he attaches a certain power to the word *umbrella* "because someone can pierce our eye with it and kill us with it."[45] Hence one can speak about the whole lexicon being truly set into motion by designation only in the relatively rare cases of original designations or those close to them.

44. "O typech básnických," p. 104.
45. J. Piaget, *La réprésentation du monde chez l'enfant,* 2d ed. (Paris, 1938), p. 51 and p. 31.

We must not, however, forget that there is a wealth of nuances, many of which are very frequent, between the two extreme cases— the absolute deautomatization of the lexicon and the absolute automatization of the act of designation. Looking for a word that does not occur to us quickly enough is not so rare even in the linguistic communication of everyday life, not to speak of cases of responsible formulation, for example scientific, legal, and diplomatic. As a rule, of course, it is not the entire lexical system but only some segment of it that is actually set into motion in such a partially revitalized act of designation.

But there is also the possibility of artificially heightening the revitalization of the act of designation, even of elevating any designation to the level of an original designation by choosing an unusual word for the given thing. There are several degrees here. First of all, a word which is linked to the given thing but which is rarely actually associated with it, namely, a more remote synonym of its usual signification, can be chosen. A higher degree of the revitalization of the act of designation occurs when a word usually associated with another thing is used for the designation; such a designation is figurative. The highest degree of the deautomatization of the act of designation will then occur if a figurative designation is selected from a semantic sphere entirely alien to the appropriate common designation; the image then reaches the level of an original designation. These different degrees of the deautomatization of designation do not, of course, always have to be coupled with aesthetic intentionality and do not have to be used only in poetry; nevertheless, every one of them is more frequent in poetry than elsewhere.

So far we have spoken about the act of designation as a "search" for the appropriate expression; however, we must present a more precise linguistic characterization of it. Karcevskij has done so in his article "On the Asymmetrical Dualism of the Linguistic Sign"[46] when he shows that the search for a linguistic expression for a designation occurs simultaneously in two directions: in the synonymic series (different designations possible for one and the same thing) and in the homonymic series (different possible meanings of one and the same word). In designation, therefore, language

46. "Du dualisme asymétrique du signe linguistique," *Travaux du Cercle linguistique de Prague* 1 (Prague, 1929): 88–93.

is viewed from the standpoint of the designated reality (synonymity), and at the same time the designated reality is viewed from
the standpoint of a given lexical system (homonymity). In this
process the lexical system and reality are, if not actually, at least
potentially juxtaposed and set into motion as wholes, for both the
synonymic and homonymic series are virtually indefinite. Ideally,
everything can be designated by any word, and, on the contrary,
every word can represent any thing. This follows from the basically *conventional* relation between reality and the linguistic sign
which Saussure has already incontestably proven. The designation
for which the speaker opts in the act of designation lies at the
point of intersection of the two series, the homonymic and the
synonymic. This point of intersection is not, of course, especially
in an original designation, provided in advance but comes about
only in the act of designation which establishes a referential relation between the word and reality. This assertion is also important
for a theoretical understanding of the poetic image. That is, it used
to be supposed that a certain "analogy" between the designated
thing and the thing whose name is used was necessary for the
origin of a poetic image.[47] Therefore, a certain preestablished
relation between the word and the thing was presupposed even in
the case of the poetic image itself. In reality, however, this pre-
establishment is a mere illusion, for the "analogy" which the old
poetics presupposed originates only in designation.

Although we have already said much about poetic designation,
we must now elucidate more systematically some of its characteristic features. Above all, we must clarify what we mean by the
term *poetic designation.* At the very beginning of this study we
rejected its unqualified identification with figurative designation.
But we should add that not even "exceptionality," distinctness
from common designation, constitutes a necessary feature of
poetic designation. The most common designations can also be
found in almost every poetic text, and they are components of
poetic structure, too. If the technique and structural function of
designation in a text are to be ascertained, all designations must be
taken into consideration. And it is precisely the quantitative and
qualitative relationship between the common and the exceptional
designations, or between the figurative and the non-figurative

47. See Aristotle's *Poetics,* trans. S. H. Butcher (New York, 1961), p. 99.

designations, in a given text that can indicate the direction for further study. Moreover, we have already shown that the difference between figurative and non-figurative designation is not firmly fixed but that there are degrees and transitions between these two kinds: figurative designation is nothing more than extremely pronounced synonymity or homonymity. We should add that not even in poetry is an image always a "new" and "unusual" designation; there are so-called image clichés which are often more "ordinary" than non-figurative designations.

Although the transition between figurative and non-figurative designation is continuous, we must not overlook the special position of figurative designation in poetry and its particular problems. First of all, there is the moment of selection. Are the figurative designations in a certain poetic text selected from the same lexical spheres as the non-figurative designations or from others? Are they themselves selected from a single milieu or from several contrasting milieux? Next, there is the moment of the relation between the figurative designation and the usual signification of a given thing. Are both from the same lexical sphere or from different ones? Are they of the same emotional accent or of a different one or even a contrasting one? Finally, there is the question of the image type. Do metaphoric or metonymic and synecdochic images prevail in the given text? The metaphoric orientation, for example, prevails among the Lumírians, the metonymic-synecdochic among the Symbolists.

Figurative designation is rarely a matter of a single word. As a rule it "unfolds," that is, it encompasses a larger segment of the surrounding contexture (a figurative subject pulls the verb into its semantic realm, etc.). If there is an intentional emphasis on the development of images, this results in vast image planes which can be particularized to the extent that they appear as an independent image theme. This is the case, for example, in a developed classical simile. Among the Symbolists the development of poetic images into themes occurs under the constant oscillation between the literal and figurative meanings of the words of which the developed image is composed. Thus originates the semantic effect of a verbal "realization" of the poetic image which in later Symbolist poetry was intensified to such an extent that the image as image prevailed over the reality represented by it. Finally, let us add that even higher semantic units than the word can attain a figurative character; a motif (e.g., the motifs of love and May in Mácha's *Máj*), an epic or dramatic figure and, in a certain sense, even an entire work can be figurative.

V. The Semantic Dynamics of Contexture

In dealing with the word and its meaning, we have remained in the sphere of semantic *statics,* although in the case of designation which is an act we have already reached the very boundary of semantic *dynamics.* What do we mean by the antithesis of these two notions in semantics? When is a semantic unit dynamic, when is it static? Let us juxtapose two extreme cases: the word as a type of static unit and the entire utterance as a representative of semantic dynamics. The semantic staticness of a word lies in the fact that its meaning is given to us at once and entirely at the moment that it is pronounced. The "sense" of an utterance, though it also exists—of course, only potentially—at the very moment when the utterance is begun, attains a gradual realization only in time. The utterance is, therefore, a semantic stream which pulls individual words into its continuous flux, depriving them of a considerable part of their independence of reference and meaning. Every word in an utterance remains semantically "open" up to the moment that the utterance ends. As long as the utterance continues, each of its words is accessible to additional shifts in its reference and to changes of meaning caused by further context. For instance, the initial emotional coloration of a word can change under this influence into its very opposite, or the meaning of the word can subsequently contract or expand.

Hence a dynamic semantic unit differs from a static one by virtue of the fact that it occurs as a gradually realized *contexture.* The relationship between a static and a dynamic semantic unit is obviously reciprocal. A dynamic unit, being a mere semantic intention in itself, needs static units for its embodiment; a static unit, on the contrary, acquires an actual relation to reality only in a context. It would be absolutely wrong to conceive of this interrelation according to the model of the pair: composition – compositional material. A dynamic unit not only is "composed" of static units but also reshapes them, and, on the other hand, a static unit does not act passively toward contexture but resists it by exerting pressure through its semantic associations on the direction of its

semantic intention; indeed, it even strives for complete independence. Semantic statics and dynamics are two forces mutually
opposed but nevertheless intrinsically linked, and together they
create the basic dialectic antinomy of every semantic process. The
concrete opposition between the word and the utterance is only
one of many possible examples that we could cite. Not only is a
word—in some cases a lexicalized (i.e., semantically arrested and
perfectly unified) phrase-word—a static unit, but even the smallest
unit of content, a motif, can be a static unit. On the other hand,
not only is an entire utterance a dynamic unit, but a sentence, a
paragraph, and so on are dynamic units as well. The opposition
between semantic statics and dynamics is not even limited just to
linguistic or linguistically expressible meaning but occurs everywhere that a momentary semantic unit and the continuous context into which this unit is incorporated are juxtaposed. In mental
life, for example, it takes the form of an antinomy between an
image and the continuous stream of mental activity; it finds its
application in film in the opposition between a shot and the entire
progression; it occurs in history in the form of an opposition between a "fact" and the "sense of events."

But not even the presence of two semantic units, one subordinated to the other, is necessary for the antinomy between
semantic statics and dynamics to occur. It is omnipresent in the
proper sense of the word, being contained in every semantic fact,
even if taken in itself alone. Let us look, for instance, at the word,
whose semantic structure we analyzed in the preceding section,
and the sentence, about which we shall speak in the paragraphs to
follow. It is quite clear that in moving from the word to the
sentence, we cross the boundary between the statics and the
dynamics of meaning. But in the very application of the word to
reality we used the term *act of designation,* hence a term suggest-
ing dynamism. Indeed, original designation in the proper sense of
the term is most often realized by means of a word that is at the
same time a sentence, such as children's word-sentences like
"Horse!" or "Cart!" An element of semantic dynamics is, therefore, already potentially contained in the word. On the other
hand, the possibility of static meaning is hidden in the sentence.
The lexicalization of such very common sentences as greetings and
formulae ("God bless you!", etc.) attests to this fact. After all,

every sentence that has been completed appears as a static unit in opposition to the semantic dynamism of the following sentence, just begun.

Having made these general remarks, let us turn to the lowest dynamic linguistic unit, the *sentence,* so that we may pose the question of the poetic exploitation of its structure. As a matter of fact, this structure is twofold: both grammatical and purely semantic.

The possibilities for exploiting the *grammatical* structure poetically are relatively simple. The very difference between a minimal and a developed sentence[48] can become a source of aesthetic effect, if the prevalence of one of these possibilities is intentionally established. The difference between sentences with a verbal and a non-verbal predicate can also be poetically exploited. The "marked" member of this pair is the sentence with a non-verbal predicate, and therefore the excessive use of such sentences causes the aesthetic deautomatization of the syntactic structure.[49] Sentences are conjoined into compound or complex sentences; an aesthetic effect can be achieved by the prevalence of one of these two types in a text. When compound sentences prevail, the copulative conjoining of adjacent sentences united into a syntactic whole can be emphasized, or, on the other hand, emphasis can be placed on their other semantically more definite relations (gradation, comparison, cause, condition, adversity, etc.). Syntactic structure is deautomatized by the second of these two means, for example, in Dyk's poetry. If complex sentences prevail, their artistic exploitation can also occur in two ways. Either subordinate clauses linked to a single word of the main clause are used excessively (all kinds of relative clauses), or those types of subordinate clauses that are related to the entire main clause (e.g., temporal clauses) are emphasized. The relative proportion of individual syntactic elements or clauses in compound and complex sentences over the entire span of a sentence can also become an

---

48. *Editors' note.* A minimal sentence (*holá věta*) consists of a subject and a predicate alone, whereas a developed sentence (*rozvitá věta*) has more syntactic units than just a subject and a predicate.

49. Cf. F. Trávníček's assertions about Mahen's nominal non-verbal sentences in "Mahenova básnická mluva" [Mahen's poetic speech], in the anthology *Mahenovi* (Prague, 1933), and in "Však nechci, aby slova šuměla," in his book *Nástroj myšlení a dorozumění* [The instrument of thought and communication] (Prague, 1940).

aesthetic factor without, of course, a norm of perfection being provided a priori. Both the equilibrium and the disequilibrium of the syntactic structure can correspond to the author's artistic intention. Finally, not even the very violation of syntactic structure (e.g., anacoluthon) is deprived of the possibility of aesthetic effect. Merely establishing these or those properties of the syntactic structure of the sentence never suffices, of course. Syntax more than other components requires a juxtaposition with the entire structure of the work precisely on account of its "formal nature."

But what about the *semantic* structure of the sentence? At first glance it might appear that it coincides with the syntactic structure. But even the neogrammarians suspected that the sentence has a semantic context other than just the one which is provided by syntactic relations. Hence the differentiation between the grammatical and the "psychological" subject and predicate which has arisen from the knowledge that the "functional" semantic perspective[50] of a sentence does not always coincide with the formal syntactic division. The "psychological" subject means the semantic complex from which the sentence proceeds and about which the predicate says something; this is not, however, always identical with the grammatical subject (consider the sentence "In a fish pond—there were many fish"). Similarly, neither does the "psychological" predicate have to coincide with the grammatical one (the psychological predicate includes both the main syntactic elements in the sentence "On the moon—there are no living beings").

50. This is V. Mathesius's term; see his article "Funkční linguistika" [Functional linguistics] in *Sborník přednášek, proslovených na I. sjezdu československých profesorů filosofie, filologie a historie* (Prague, 1929).

Editors' note. J. Vachek has rendered Mathesius's term *aktualní větné členění* as "functional sentence perspective" in his book *The Linguistic School of Prague* (Bloomington, Indiana, 1966). According to Vachek, "Mathesius' approach . . . envisages the sentence-utterance from the viewpoint of the information conveyed by it. Now we usually say that this approach establishes the functional sentence perspective. Viewed from this angle, any sentence-utterance is seen to consist of two parts. The first of them, now usually termed the *theme*, is that part of the utterance which refers to a fact or facts already known from the preceding context, or to facts that may be taken for granted, and thus does not, or does only minimally, contribute to the information provided by the given sentence-utterance. The other part, now usually called the *rheme*, contains the actual new information to be conveyed by the sentence-utterance and thus substantially enriches the knowledge of the listener or reader" (p. 89). We, in turn, have followed Vachek's example and have rendered Mukařovský's derived term *aktuální významové členění* as "functional semantic perspective."

Modern linguistics has progressed further in this matter by emphasizing the unity of syntactic meaning.[51] Karcevskij's assertion
about the connection between syntactic meaning and intonation
is also important: "The sentence is a realized communicational
unit. It lacks a grammatical structure of its own. But it has a
particular sound structure which is provided by its *intonation*. It
is precisely intonation which constitutes the sentence. Any word
or group of words, any grammatical form, any interjection can, if
required by the situation, serve as a communicational unit."[52]
V. N. Vološinov's works, especially the article "The Construction
of the Utterance,"[53] have revealed the fact of semantic dynamics.
And we have asserted the polarity between semantic statics and
dynamics in our study "The Genesis of Meaning in Mácha's
Poetry."[54] Proceeding from the premises mentioned, we wish to
attempt an enumeration and a characterization of the main
principles of the semantic structure of the sentence. There are
three in all:

1. The first is the unity of syntactic meaning toward which we
are oriented from the moment that we conceive of some beginning
semantic series as a sentence, even though this total meaning
remains potential for us until the sentence is finished. Karcevskij
has correctly pointed out that any set of words, if it is signaled by
syntactic intonation as a sentence, will be for us a communicational unit (*unité de communication*) to which we will—even
forcibly—ascribe a total meaning. Modern poetry greatly exploits
this basic property of the semantic structure of the sentence in
various ways. On the basis of the postulated unity of syntactic
meaning, Symbolism compelled the reader to look for a connection between several image "planes" which intersected within the
sentence. Some later movements (Futurism, Dadaism) force the
reader to ascribe semantic intentionality to accidental clusters of
words—again on the basis of the semantic unity of the sentence.

2. The second principle of the semantic structure of the sentence can be called "semantic accumulation." It is based on two

51. See Jul. Stenzel's article "Sinn, Bedeutung, Begriff, Definition" in *Jahrbuch für Philologie* 1 (1925): 160-201.
52. "Sur la phonologie de la phrase," p. 190.
53. "Konstrukcija vyskazyvanija," *Literaturnaja učёba* 1 (1930) No. 3: 65-87.
54. "Genetika smyslu v Máchově poesii," *Torso a tajemství Máchova díla*, pp. 13-110.

facts. The first is that the semantic units of which the sentence is composed are perceived in a continuous succession regardless of the complex architecture of syntactic subordination and superordination; thus arises a series that can be schematically represented: a – b – c – d, and so on. But yet a second fact comes into play: every unit following another is perceived against the background of that one and all the preceding ones so that the entire set of semantic units of which the sentence is composed is simultaneously present in the listener's or reader's mind at the conclusion of the sentence. The process of semantic accumulation which occurs in this fashion might be schematically represented as follows:

$$a - b - c - d - e - f$$
$$a \quad b \quad c \quad d \quad e$$
$$a \quad b \quad c \quad d$$
$$a \quad b \quad c$$
$$a \quad b$$
$$a$$

The horizontal alphabetically arranged series of letters in the first line of the scheme represents the succession of semantic units within the syntactic whole. The vertical columns under each letter of the first line schematically express the process of semantic accumulation. At the moment that we perceive unit b, unit a is already in our consciousness; in perceiving unit c, we already know units $a - b$, and so on. We should mention that even in the resulting accumulation of all the semantic units of the sentence the order in which the accumulation has occurred is significant. The sentence "On the table among the books stood the lamp" is not in the total organization of its meaning the same as the grammatically identical sentence "The lamp stood on the table among the books," and both of them are semantically different from the third sentence, again grammatically equal to them, "Among the books on the table stood the lamp." The reason for the semantic differences between them is that the semantic accumulation in each of them has a different order. The theory of the "psychological" subject and predicate does not suffice to explain all of these differences, for the boundary between the psychological subject and predicate is the same in the first and the third sentences. Mathesius's conception of syntactic structure as "functional perspective" is close to our notion of accumulation, because it emphasizes "word order" as a factor of syntactic structure.

The poetic deautomatization of semantic accumulation occurs in such a way that the accumulative process is complicated and retarded by the clustering of very disparate meanings within one and the same syntactic whole. Compare, for example, the sentence-type of Vančura's *Poslední soud* where this tendency became the basis for an experiment: "Smál se potrhuje ramenem, které nosívá střelnou zbraň, jako hospodyně, jež v důvodném veselí roztřese nad zástěrou kličku tkalounu" ("He laughed jerking his shoulder, which usually carried a fire-arm, as a housewife who in well-founded merriment makes the bow of the strings shake over her apron").

3. The third principle is that of the oscillation between semantic statics and dynamics. It is based on the fact that every semantic unit in a syntactic bond (a word, a syntactic unit) tends, on the one hand, to establish an immediate reference to reality which it represents in itself and is, on the other hand, bound by the context of the sentence as a whole, establishing contact with reality only by means of this whole. This is therefore a question of the polarity between designation and contexture, which results in a different solution in different cases. For example, the independence of the reference of individual designations prevails over the cohesiveness of the syntactic contexture in Mácha. This is the source, for instance, of the numerous zeugmas in Mácha's style, and further of the semantic incongruence of word combinations like *večerní máj* ("evening May"), *rozlehlý strom* ("spacious tree") as well as of the syntactic incohesiveness of the sentences. On the contrary, the prevalence of the continuity of contexture over the independence of individual designations occurs in Karel Čapek; hence the gentle undulation of the syntactic intonation and the tendency toward the weakening of the syntactic boundaries. Březina's poetry is a more complicated case; individual figurative designations strive, each out of itself, to produce a special context. They do so by developing into extended image "planes" which collide with one another. The role of coordinating these different partial contexts then falls to the overall context, which itself often remains in a state of mere semantic intention. Hence the ambiguity of the total meaning of some of Březina's poems.

In sum, we can say about the semantic structure of the sentence that, in being less "formal" than the syntactic structure, it mediates between it and the individual semantic charge of every single sentence. But at the same time it obviously has enough general properties to be accessible to scholarly analysis. For both these reasons it is important that the theory of poetic language devote attention to it. In particular, the study of the artistic structure of literary prose and its immanent development is not possible without taking into account the semantic structure of the sentence. This also explains why the scholarly study of prose has hitherto progressed less than the study of poetry, which was content for a certain time with the analysis of the sound aspect, the lexicon, and syntax.

The sentence is not, of course, the last and highest step in the hierarchy of semantic units that fill the span between the word and the whole of an utterance. Units of a higher order are, for instance, the paragraph and the chapter. But are these still linguistic units? They are in the sense that they are components of an utterance. What is given by a succession of linguistic signs cannot exceed the frame of language. If linguistics does not deal with them, it is only because their structure is not governed by grammatical regularity: the highest grammatical unit of language is the sentence. We have seen, however, that the sentence is not only a syntactic but at the same time a semantic structure. All the principles of the semantic structure of the sentence which we have enumerated above can be applied to the structure of wholes higher than the sentence.

The sentence very often refers semantically to a broader context, especially that which has preceded it. For the purpose of explaining the principle of semantic accumulation, we cited above three sentences having the same lexical composition, the same grammatical structure but a different order of semantic units. Here we shall use two of them once more in order to ascertain the way in which a sentence refers to a broader semantic context. They are the following: (a) "The lamp stood on the table among the piled books," and (b) "Among the piled books on the table stood the lamp." The first of them presupposes that the *lamp* has already been mentioned, the second that the *table* was spoken about in a previous context. These two sentences are no longer so unequivocal with respect to the following context. For example, the sentence "Sitting next to it [the lamp] was someone immersed in reading" could very well follow both of them; however, the

sentence "There were a great many books" would more likely
follow the first than the second. Regressive semantic determination
by context is therefore more strongly attested than progressive
determination; this is completely natural. What is instructive for
us about this is the fact that the transition from a sentence to
higher semantic units is continuous, without any substantial break.
Finally, we must mention that there is no fixed boundary even
from the grammatical aspect: the linking of a sentence to the
sentence immediately following can also be accomplished by
grammatical means. For example, the two sentences can be linked
by demonstrative pronouns or adverbs occurring in the second
sentence but referring to some element of the first. A subject can
also be common to two or even several contiguous sentences.

The congruity of the semantic structure of the sentence with
the structure of higher semantic units, indeed, even with that of
the entire text, is a very important working hypothesis for the
theory of literature. That is, it creates a bridge over which we can
pass from the linguistic analysis to the study of the entire semantic
structure of the text. "Compositional analysis" is not doomed to
rigid staticness, if we apply to it the principles of semantic
dynamics, an enumeration of which we presented when we
analyzed the semantic structure of the sentence. In this way
compositional analysis acquires the possibility of leading to the
determination of the "formal" but nevertheless concrete "semantic
gesture" by which the work is organized as a dynamic unity from
the simplest elements to the most general outline. Despite its
seeming "formal quality" the semantic gesture is something completely different from form conceived as the external "garment"
of a work. It is a semantic fact, a semantic intention, though
qualitatively undetermined. And precisely because of its semantic
essence it makes possible the comprehension and determination
of the external connections of a work with the poet's personality,
society, and other spheres of culture. The notion of the semantic
gesture, though it concerns the *internal* structure of the work,
removes the last remains of Herbartian Formalism from the
structural theory of literature.

We must still account for higher semantic units that are semantically concretized, namely, those which are usually called the
thematic components of a literary work. Here we are mainly con-

cerned with the notions of motif, plot, and overall theme. It has been customary to place these elements outside the linguistic context or at least to define the relationship of language to them as a passive one according to the principle that content determines its form. The boundary between them and linguistic elements is, however, far from being so sharp that these two groups can be opposed to one another without reservation as two completely different things. We have already seen (in our consideration of the poetic image) that even linguistic, verbal meaning can be thematicized and that a motif, a unit of content, can often find expression in a single word and thereby merge with verbal meaning. The lexicalization of a motif—its fixation in an immediate conventional semantic unit similar to a word—is also not impossible, as is vividly demonstrated by the lexicalized motifs of which folk tales are composed.

Moreover, modern study has convincingly shown that even a theme, especially a poetic theme, is connected to language bilaterally: not only is linguistic expression governed by its theme, but the theme is also governed by its linguistic expression. Roman Jakobson has provided a very illustrative example of this in his study "Toward a Description of Mácha's Verse."[55] He shows that Mácha's conception of space is different in his iambic lines than in his trochaic lines. In the iambic lines space appears as a unidirectional continuum rendered by the movement from the observer to the background, in the trochaic lines as restless multidirectionality. The concept of space in Mácha is, therefore, closely related to rhythm, and since this is a bilateral relation, it is impossible to say which of the two components predetermines the other. But rhythm is predominantly a linguistic matter based on the sound (phonological) organization of the text; the conception of space, on the contrary, belongs to the thematic aspect. Not even theme, therefore, eludes linguistic analysis, the task and sphere of which is the *entire* structure of the literary work. Here the linguistic approach signifies a methodological orientation, not a limitation of the subject matter of scholarly study.

55. "K popisu Máchova verše," *Torso a tajemství Máchova díla*, pp. 207-78. *Editors' note*. An English translation of this article by P. and W. Steiner will appear in the forthcoming *Selected Writings of Roman Jakobson*, vol. 5 (The Hague).

VI. Monologue and Dialogue. "Hidden" Meaning

We have surveyed the hierarchy of the sound and semantic components of the literary work in several of the preceding sections. This survey does not, however, exhaust all the problems of poetic language. There remains above all the matter of the subject's participation in an utterance, that is, the difference between monologue and dialogue, as well as the question of the "unexpressed" meaning hidden behind the word.

Monologue and dialogue are two basic aspects of the semantic organization of an utterance and at the same time two mutually opposed forms of a linguistic structure in the functional sense; therefore, linguistics often speaks about monologic and dialogic "speech."[56] Nevertheless, monologue and dialogue are more than mere functional languages, for the monologic or dialogic nature of an utterance is determined by whether the utterance comes from one or more subjects. The application of any of the other functional languages is, however, determined by the decision of only one subject. Therefore, the difference between monologue and dialogue is more basic than the other differences among functional languages; this is also apparent from the fact that each of the participants in a dialogue can employ a different functional style. Thus functional differentiation appears to be a secondary superstructure with regard to the difference between monologue and dialogue.

Literature is split into two unequal parts by the difference between monologic and dialogic speech: the lyric and the narrative on one side as monologic forms, the drama on the other as the poetry of dialogue. This does not, of course, mean that dialogue as a mode of linguistic expression can in principle be excluded from the lyric and the narrative (consider lyrical "disputes" and the dialogues of characters in a narrative) or, on the contrary, that monologue can be excluded from the drama (consider narrations inserted into dramatic dialogue). It means only that the lyric and narrative utterances presuppose a single speaker ("the poet"), whereas the drama presupposes several speakers. If this (sometimes only imaginary) boundary is crossed, a lyric or a narrative is transformed into a drama and vice versa; for example, the

---

56. See L. P. Jakubinskij, "O dialogičeskoj reči" [On dialogic speech], *Russkaja reč'*, ed. L. V. Ščerba (Petrograd, 1923), 1: 96–194.

conversation of the quarreling parties in the lyric "dispute" (*The Dispute of the Soul with the Body,* etc.) can also be conceived dramatically. The difference between the monologic orientation of the narrative and the lyric and the dialogic orientation of the drama is, however, manifested not only linguistically but in other ways as well. A dramatic dialogue is bound by two properties of the listener's time, namely, its immediate present and its flow ("transitoriness," according to Zich's terminology[57]), whereas narrative and lyric monologue have only *one* of these properties: the narrative has only the flow but not the present, the lyric only the present but not the flow. Therefore, if the difference between the monologic and dialogic natures penetrates so deeply into the very epistemological basis of the utterance, it is obvious that the opposition of these two orientations is an essential, not just linguistically functional, opposition.

Despite their opposition to one another, however, the monologic and dialogic orientations not only do not exclude one another but they even interpenetrate. We can often discern the presence of a latent dialogue in apparently monologic utterances and vice versa; this is not only true of literary utterances but of utterances in general. Literature, of course, frequently exploits the semantic nuances which arise in this way. Dyk's style, which shows a predilection for compound sentences—not copulative but adversative, gradational, explicative—is full of hidden dialogue precisely because of this feature. E. F. Burian exploited this hidden dialogue dramaturgically when he transformed the poet's monologue in the short story "Krysař" [The Pied Piper of Hamelin] into the dialogue of many dramatic characters almost without changing the text at all. In this case the dramaturgic adaptation did not create the dialogic nature but simply revealed it. It was already present as an element of the semantic structure and as a factor of the aesthetic effect of the work in the poet's narrative version. To illustrate the opposite phenomenon, monologue hidden in a dialogue, we can refer to several passages in Symbolist dramas, especially Maeterlinck's, where the utterances of different characters follow each other so closely that they in fact comprise a continuous monologic contexture divided among several partners.

57. See *Estetika dramtického umění* [The aesthetics of dramatic art] (Prague, 1931), p. 219.

After all, this is only a literary exploitation of a situation rather frequent in intimate conversation in which the speaking persons are bound by common interest and feeling to the extent that the semantic tension which is usually the basis for the division of roles in dialogue is extremely weakened.

Therefore the dialogic and monologic qualities are in fact both present at the very origin of every utterance, whether its apparent form is monologic or dialogic. Indeed, they are even contained in the very mental process from which an utterance arises. The relation between the "I" and the "you" on which dialogue is based does not require two individuals for its activation but only the internal tension, contradictions, and unexpected reversals provided by the dynamics of every individual's psychic life. The apparent and potential dialogic nature of utterances thus has its root in the hidden "dialogic nature" of the course of mental life. For this reason too a psychic process is reflected more immediately in a dialogue among several participants than in a monologue. The "psychological situation" among the participants of a conversation constantly influences the course of the dialogic utterance. Very often the situation intervenes directly in the dialogue to the extent that one of the speakers replies not so much to his partner's words as to the psychic process which accompanies them. A speaker can even take a psychic reaction (expressed by an involuntary rather than a communicative gesture or grimace) as a sufficient reply to which he immediately reacts without letting his partner utter a word ("You don't have to say anything, I know what you want to reply, but I . . .").

Here we find ourselves on the border between language and psychic process; indeed, we even see the psychic process penetrating the utterance as one of its components. The direct participation of the psychic which obtains when the partner's psychic reaction becomes a reply can, of course, occur only under the condition that the psychic process becomes a *communicable* meaning without changing its essence. As far as the semantic natures of mental states and activities are concerned, it is clear from contemporary psychology that all of mental life is saturated with semantic elements even when it is not a matter of communication. All of Gestalt psychology proceeds from the premise that external impulses are spontaneously and immediately arranged in the individual's consciousness in patterns organized by a unified "sense," hence by a certain kind of meaning. There are even scholars (e.g., Vološinov) who believe that the *entire* realm of mental activity comprises a semantic structure; according to them whatever is not meaning is not even a psychic event but a biological process. This opinion is by no means unfounded. Through careful analysis we can discover in a considerable number of perceptions components which, though experienced as inherent to the perceived reality, are in essence the meaning that the perceiving subject ascribes to it. For example, we apparently distinguish a standing table from an overturned one by vision alone, although the recognition of the first position as normal presupposes knowledge of the function of a table. In perceiving a table, we recognize it as an apparatus for eating and working. Therefore, only a position that facilitates these activities appears to us spontaneously as normal. We *see* even the shape of various objects as systematically arranged only if we know what purpose they serve. Objects whose function we do not know may appear to us as formally incomprehensible, even shapeless.

We therefore believe that we are not too far from the truth if we characterize the interrelation of an utterance and the relevant psychic process as the relation of two concurrent and correlated semantic series. The difference between the two series is, of course, that only linguistic meaning is fully communicable, having at its disposal a system of sensorily perceptible symbols, whereas psychic meaning lacks such a possibility of systematic expression. It has at its disposal only symptoms which express it at best very incompletely, namely, *spontaneous* facial expressions, gestures, actions—in sum, "behavior." We emphasize the adjective spontaneous because if the gestures, facial expressions, and so on become conscious and even systematic, a *transposition* of a mental process into a certain system of signs is involved in exactly the same way as when we consciously communicate them by means of linguistic signs.

The study of the relation between language and mental processes is of equal interest to linguistics and psychology. What is of particular interest to linguistics is the question of how the psychic process concurrent with the utterance can reveal its presence or, in some cases, even its concrete semantic quality *immediately* without being deformed by the transposition into a system of linguistic signs with their regularity. The purpose of our study, however, is not to deal with this question in detail and in its entire scope. We want only to outline—and only in the roughest contours—the ways of *poetically* exploiting the correlation between the semantic process of mental activities and that of language.

The first of them is, relatively speaking, very simple. It concerns the *concealment* of meaning that in essence is already linguistic, that is, one that could easily be formulated in words. We have in mind so-called allusion. It frequently occurs even in communicative language if a speaker limits himself to a mere hint of some fact, thought, or evaluation. Such concealment is often motivated by a consideration for the partner's private or ethical feelings, in some cases by a consideration for social, political, or other censorship. What is thus provided by a "practical" consideration in communicative language can become a self-orienting means of aesthetic effect in literature even though this self-orientation does not exclude the genetic influence of the aforementioned practical considerations. Allusion can be developed into a systematic artistic device in literature. For instance, the semantic structure of Dyk's poetry—even that of his intimate lyric where "concealment" has no practical reason—is based upon allusion. Here the technique of allusion is such that utterly concrete facts are expressed in general sentences of a gnomic character; the reader is charged with guessing the concealed concrete meaning from the semantic interrelation of these gnomic sentences. In this case the concrete meaning is literally hidden "between" the sentences.

More complex is another case, namely, the linguistic expression of "inexpressible" psychic meaning. Each of us knows from his own experience that linguistic expression, which masters external reality relatively easily, immediately becomes a weak and insufficient means if it is required to express the course of our mental processes. In such a case we require of it something which is alien to the very essence and purpose of language, namely, that a sensorily perceptible linguistic symbol, the vehicle of *linguistic* meaning, become the vehicle of *psychic* meaning. It was precisely this paradoxical experiment that became the artistic problem of the literary movement called Symbolism. We know how Symbolist poetry, at least in its purest form, represented in Czech literature by Březina in particular, solved this problem. The semantic structure of a Symbolist poem is organized in such a way that *every* word is experienced as a figurative word. If this is achieved, a

special semantic phenomenon occurs. Though the poet speaks almost constantly about the material realities of the external world,
his statements are projected elsewhere than into external reality
because they are constantly figurative. Their "proper" meaning is
placed precisely in the sphere of "inexpressible" psychic meanings.
We have said above that Březina's poetic images are frequently
thematicized. In this process, however—indeed precisely because
of it—the central theme of the entire poem remains indefinite,
often actually inexpressible; not in vain did Březina provide the
title of one of his poems with a question mark: "Zem?" [Earth?].
The proper domicile of "sense" in Březina's poetry is outside of
language in the hidden realm of psychic meanings.

Finally, the third case of the literary exploitation of the correlation between language and psychic processes is even more
paradoxical than the two preceding ones. It arose from the knowledge that a mental process is characterized more distinctly by the
way in which its meanings are connected than by their "lexicon."
Whereas the linguistic ties between the lexical units are syntac-
ticological, it is inherent in psychic life to move from unit to unit
by way of association, which from the standpoint of logic creates
an impression of inexplicable accidentality (of course, only from
the logical standpoint, for from the standpoint of the psychic
process itself—as modern deep psychology has shown—even association has its own strict, though very complex, regularity). Proceeding from knowledge of the associative basis of psychic
semantic links, literature has attempted to make of language as
direct an expression of mental processes as possible by substitut-
ing the associative aggregation of linguistic meanings for their
normal logical connection. Logical relations stand *above* concrete
meanings. Their natural tendency, which almost reaches its goal in
mathematical and logical formulae, is to get rid of concrete
meanings down to the smallest remains. In contrast, associative
links have their source in meanings themselves and let themselves
be determined by them from stage to stage. On account of their
independence from concrete meanings, logical relations have the
possibility of choosing only those aspects of these meanings which
are appropriate for the given, a priori determined logical context,
whereas associative relations, depending on and springing from
concrete meanings, require as great a richness of concrete meanings
as possible for their successful development. Therefore, literature

which is oriented toward a direct rather than an allusive presentation of the course of psychic processes by means of the word strives to record as fully as possible the individual phases of mental processes. An absolutely exact copy is, of course, out of the question because it is by no means possible to purge language of logical relationships, on the one hand, and because an intrinsic precondition of art is the distance between the material and its artistic recreation, on the other. Just as in every solution of an artistic problem, here too we have a mere artistic tendency.

Proof of this is the fact that several solutions have already been presented, and although each of them is valid in itself, they do not represent phases in the perfection of the recording. Edouard Dujardin suggested the first of these solutions as early as the 1880s in the novel *Les lauriers sont coupés*. Dujardin created a so-called interior monologue by working with short compound sentences and unexpected shifts in the semantic connections between them. Since then the course taken by Dujardin has not been abandoned. Its most recent stage is "écriture automatique," emphasizing in particular the absolute mutual remoteness of adjacent semantic units so that their connection on the rational plane is completely impossible. In this way semantic units appear only as symbols, the "proper" meanings of which meet only in the unreachable unconscious. Here the "accidentality" of associative links is heightened to the very limit of possibility. It is characteristic of the interrelation of these different artistic methods that the method of "interior monologue" has penetrated Czech literature (in Milada Součková's novels) at the same time as the method of "écriture automatique," which originated later. Such a development is absolutely unthinkable in science, where every method remains valid only until it has been surpassed by another more perfect one. This is further evidence that these methods beginning with "interior monologue" are facts of artistic development.

We are at the end of our survey of the problems of poetic language. Despite the fact that its elaboration has taken a long time (see the first brief version in the publication of the 1939 Linguistic Congress in Brussels[58]), we do not in the least consider it to be a codification of views about such vital issues. In ten years a similar

58. "La langue poétique," *Rapports du Ve Congrès international des linguistes, Bruxelles, 28 août-2 septembre 1939* (Bruges, 1939), pp. 94-102.

attempt at such a survey would surely turn out completely different, just as the article in which we tried to summarize the current scholarship on poetic language years ago[59] was quite different from our present study. The difference between our present and former way of looking at things calls for caution in the future as well. In this study our sole ambition has been to suggest the direction in which the contemporary study of poetic language is heading and to point out the problems which require a solution most urgently at the present moment. Ten years ago the sound aspect of poetic language was most prominent; among semantic problems only those concerning the lexicon and its poetic usage were within sight. Today the problems of meaning are in the foreground, even in the study of the sound aspect itself, and of these problems the most urgent seem to be the question of the interrelation of semantic statics and dynamics and the related questions of semantic structure. On the one hand, this progression from a foundation to higher levels is natural, and structuralist literary scholarship, like every scholarly movement (after all, it has been in close contact with structural linguistics), has passed it; on the other, it is a product of the pressure of scholarly practice. Since the questions of verse have already attained a certain, at least elementary solution, the turn of prose and its development has come—a problem, as we have mentioned above, unsolvable without a more detailed knowledge of the structure of dynamic semantic units, beginning with the sentence. Moreover, a comparative theory of art is beginning to take shape on a semiotic basis. What is common to various arts is precisely semantic structure and meaning in general, not material substrata (materials) which carry this meaning as sound does in poetry; these are different in different arts, and most often they are incomparable. All the aforementioned circumstances contribute to the fact that the theory of poetic language and poetics in general, especially Czech poetics, is beginning to recognize the problems of semantic structure as the most urgent ones.

As we have said, the definite overcoming of formalism is also characteristic of the present state of scholarship on poetic language. The discovery of semantic dynamics and its opposition to semantic statics has brought meaning closer to the dynamics of

59. "O současné poetice" [On contemporary poetics], *Plán* 1 (1929): 387-97.

psychic processes. Henceforth it becomes possible to study their interrelation without the danger of "psychologism," which threatened as long as static meaning itself was conceived as a passive component of the "formal" interplay of linguistic signs. Today it has become apparent that the immanent initiative belongs to meaning; meaning no longer appears as a mere illusive reflection of reality but as a source of energy, and thus we need not fear its confrontation with man's other life forces. In this, we daresay, lies the most significant virtue of the contemporary theory of poetic language.

2

Two Studies of Poetic Designation

POETIC DESIGNATION AND THE AESTHETIC FUNCTION
OF LANGUAGE

I

The purpose of the present study is to distinguish poetic designation from other kinds. By poetic designation we mean every use of words occurring in a text with a predominant aesthetic function, hence not just figurative designation. Figurative designation very often exceeds the limits of poetry. It also occurs in communicative language, not only in the form of fixed images but also as newly created images (e.g., emotional images). But not every poetic use of words is figurative. There are even poetic schools which restrict the use of the image to a minimum.

What, then, is the characteristic feature of poetic designation if its basis is not figurativeness? It has often been pointed out that the specific nature of poetic language does not lie in its "plasticity." By no means does a poetic expression have to be oriented toward evoking a vivid image. It would be equally wrong to adduce "novelty" as the essential property of poetic designation, for we very often find poets and even entire poetic schools preferring the use of traditional designations, sometimes "poetic" but frequently those belonging to the vocabulary of everyday language.

Thus we must first look for the specific property of poetic designation. As the starting point of our study we can choose any phrase, preferably one which can be taken both as a part of a communicative utterance and as a segment of a poetic text because of the indefiniteness of its semantic coloration. Such is, for example, the sentence "Dusk is approaching," which we involun-

The first of these two studies is translated from "Dénomination poétique et la fonction esthétique de la langue," *Actes du IVᵉ Congrès international des linguistes* (Copenhagen, 1938). Czech version: "Básnické pojmenování a estetická funkce jazyka," *Kapitoly z české poetiky* (Prague, 1941), 1.

The second of the two studies is translated from "K sémantice básnického obrazu," *Kvart* 5 (1946), no. 1.

tarily perceive as a message but which, with a different semantic orientation, we can easily interpret as a poetic quotation from an imaginary text. In each case a different semantic aspect will manifest itself. If the sentence is considered to be a message, the perceiver's attention will be focused on the relation between the designation and the reality signified. It may happen that doubt will arise about its documentary value. In that case we shall ask: Is it really getting dark? Or: Is this statement erroneous or even deceptive? Or: Is it an example from a grammar, unrelated to an actual material situation? The answer to these questions—which can be formulated otherwise or even remain unexpressed—will determine the significance of the message for any eventual behavior. Our attitude toward the utterance in question will, however, completely change when it is conceived as a poetic quotation. The focal point of our attention will immediately become its relation to the surrounding contexture, even if it is only an assumed one. Not knowing this contexture, we will be at a loss: is this sentence the beginning, the end, or the recurring refrain of the poetic text in question? The semantic aspect of the assumed quotation will distinctly change according to the solution for which we opt. If we were to refer to a complete poetic text, for instance a lyric poem, instead of the imagined example, we could ascertain a whole series of interrelations binding its elements (words, sentences, etc.) together and determining the meaning of each of them according to the place which it occupies in this concatenation.

Poetic designation is not, therefore, primarily determined by its relation to the reality signified but by the way in which it is placed in the contexture. This explains the well-known fact that a word or a phrase-word which is characteristic of a certain significant poetic work, when transferred from its own contexture to another one, such as a communicative contexture, takes with it the semantic ambience of the work through which it has passed and with which it is connected in the collective consciousness.

The intimate interaction between poetic designation and contexture can also explain, at least in part, the very tendency of poetic language toward figurative designations, especially toward new and non-automatized images. This is because a radical shift in verbal meaning is possible only on condition that the surrounding contexture alludes with sufficient clarity to the reality for whose designation the given word-image has been unusually and unexpectedly employed. In this way the contexture imposes upon the reader the meaning given to the word through the poet's individual and unique decision.[1] The significance of the contexture for the semantic structure of the poetic utterance is also illustrated by the fact that many of the stylistic devices utilized by poetry serve to establish semantic interrelations among words. Thus, for example, euphony confronts words similar in sound semantically as well as phonologically.

Hence the internal organization of the linguistic sign is quite different in poetic language from what it is in communicative utterances. In the latter, attention is focused primarily on the relation between the designation and reality, whereas in the former the link between the designation and the surrounding contexture comes to the fore. This does not, of course, mean that communicative designation is completely shielded from the influence of contexture or, on the other hand, that poetic designation is totally unrelated to reality. It is merely a question, so to speak, of a shift in emphasis. A decrease in the immediate relation to reality renders the designation a poetic device. For this reason a poetic utterance (insofar as it is conceived as poetic) cannot be evaluated according to the standards valid for the verification of communicative utterances. A poetic fiction is epistemologically quite different from a consciously or unconsciously deceptive "fabrication." The value of poetic designation is provided exclusively by the role which it plays in the total semantic structure of the work.

II

Before we turn to the further analysis of poetic designation, let us recall Bühler's well-known scheme of the basic functions of the linguistic sign.[2] According to this scheme there are three functions deriving from the very essence of language: the presentational, the expressive, and the appellative.[3] Each of these follows from the active relation of the linguistic sign to one of the three instances necessarily present in the utterance. As a presentation (*Darstellung*)

1. B. Tomaševskij, *Teorija literatury* [The theory of literature] (Leningrad, 1927), p. 29.
2. K. Bühler, *Sprachtheorie* (Jena, 1934), pp. 24 ff.
3. *Editors' note.* See footnote 7 to "On Poetic Language," above.

the linguistic sign functions vis-à-vis the reality signified by it; as an expression it appears in relation to the speaking subject; as an appeal it is addressed to the perceiving subject. As long as we have in mind a purely communicative utterance, Bühler's scheme is fully acceptable. In every communicative utterance we can easily distinguish the contours of all three basic functions, especially, of course, those of the prevailing function in the given case.

The situation is, however, quite different in the analysis of a poetic utterance. Even here we can detect the presence of the above functions, but a fourth function, unmentioned in Bühler's scheme, emerges. This function stands in opposition to all the others. It renders the structure of the linguistic sign the center of attention, whereas the first three functions are oriented toward extralinguistic instances and goals exceeding the linguistic sign. By means of the first three functions the use of language achieves practical significance. The fourth function, however, severs language from an immediate connection with practice. It is called the aesthetic function, and all the others in relation to it can be called collectively the practical functions. The orientation of the aesthetic function toward the sign itself is the direct result of the autonomy peculiar to aesthetic phenomena. We have already encountered the aesthetic function in our analysis of the "referential" relation of poetic designation. If in poetry the relation of designation to reality recedes into the background in comparison with its relation to the surrounding contexture, this shift occurs precisely because of the influence of the aesthetic orientation rendering the sign itself the center of attention.

One could, however, object that the phenomena of which we are speaking pertain to poetry alone, where language is usually violently reorganized, but that the poetic application of language cannot be compared with its normal usage: what applies to the language of poetry does not apply to language in general. To these objections we reply: (a) Abuse is a necessary, often even beneficial contrast to the habitual use of every thing. To "abuse" things often means to attempt consciously or unconsciously a new and previously unknown way of using them; (b) The boundary separating the aesthetic function from the practical functions is not always distinct; in particular, it does not coincide with the dividing line between art and other human activities. Nor are the practical functions—in our case the three aforementioned linguistic functions—entirely suppressed in a purely autonomous artistic expression; consequently, every poetic work is—at least virtually—simultaneously a presentation, an expression, and an appeal. Often it is precisely these practical functions which manifest themselves to a considerable degree in a work of art: for example, the presentational function in the novel, the expressive function in lyric poetry. Conversely, not a single practical activity is completely devoid of the aesthetic function. This function participates, at least potentially, in every human act. Even in the most everyday language, for example, every instance in which semantic relations come to the fore by interpenetrating and organizing the contexture evokes the aesthetic function. Every striking phonetic similarity between words or every unexpected inversion of the word order is capable of arousing a thrill of aesthetic pleasure. So powerful is even a merely potential aesthetic function that it is frequently necessary, in revising an intellectual, purely communicative text a second time, to remove the very weakest indications of a deformation of the semantic relations so that the reader's attention will not be attracted to the sign itself. The aesthetic function is omnipresent; not even linguistics can deny it a place among the basic linguistic functions.

There still remains, of course, another possible objection, namely, that the aesthetic function is not per se one of the linguistic functions, for its activity is not confined to language alone. But to this we need only reply that the aesthetic function, being the dialectic negation of every practical function, everywhere and always adopts the nature of that function to which it is opposed in the given case. If it is opposed to the linguistic functions, it becomes a linguistic function itself. The part which it plays in the development of language and the culture of language is also considerable, though we do not overestimate it in the manner of the Vossler school. For example, lexical innovations often penetrate common usage under the pretext of aesthetic effectiveness.

A final possible cause for misunderstanding still needs to be removed. Our thesis would seem to be contradicted by the theory attesting the predominantly emotive nature of poetic language (Bally). It is, of course, true that poetic language bears a considerable external resemblance to emotive language. Unlike intellectual language, both exhibit a definite tendency to assert the subject-originator, the one from whom the utterance proceeds. In intellectual language, the more markedly the intellectual element prevails, the more the influence of the subject-originator on the selection of designations recedes into the background. It would be ideal if this influence were totally excluded and if the relation between the designation and the reality signified by it were rendered definitive, independent of subject and contexture. This is the reason why the meaning of word-terms in science is fixed by definition. Emotive and poetic designations emphasize, on the other hand, the element of choice and thus make the very act of designation performed by the subject the focal point of attention. In this way the feeling is aroused that the chosen designation is only one of many possible ones; the virtual presence of the entire lexical system of the given language is adumbrated behind it.[4] This is especially true in figurative designations in both poetic and emotive language.

These similarities are, however, counterbalanced by essential differences. In emotive language, designation is an expression of the subject-originator's mental state. The listener guesses at the sincerity of the feelings expressed by it, estimates the significance of the volitional elements contained in it, and so forth. In poetic language attention is focused on the sign itself; here an estimation of its relation to the subject-originator's mental life recedes into the background or does not obtain at all. With the loss of its real significance the expression of feelings becomes a mere artistic device. Poetic designation, which is *subjective* in comparison with intellectual designation, appears *objective* when compared with emotive designation; thus it does not coincide with either. And so we have once again ascertained that a poetic designation, viewed from whatever perspective, always appears to be an autonomous sign. The aesthetic function which is the cause of this reflexiveness of linguistic activity has appeared in our analysis as the

4. In essence *every* act of designation establishes a relation between the designated reality and the entire lexical system; cf. the following citations from S. Karcevskij's study "Du dualisme asymétrique du signe linguistique" (*Travaux du Cercle linguistique de Prague* 1 [Prague, 1929]: 88–93): "If signs were fixed and had only a single function, language would become a simple catalogue of labels. . . . The nature of a linguistic sign is to be both stable and mobile at the same time. . . . Every linguistic sign is virtually homonymic and synonymic at the same time. . . . We continually shift the semantic value of our sign. But we notice it only when the variation between the 'adequate' (usual) value of the sign and its occasional value is sufficiently great to make an impression upon us. . . . It is impossible to foresee how far the semantic shifts of a sign can go."

omnipresent dialectic negation of the three basic communicative functions of language, and thereby as a necessary addition to Bühler's scheme.

III

At the end of the first section we interrupted our analysis of the relation between poetic designation and reality after asserting that this relation is weakened on behalf of the attention focused on the sign itself. Is a poetic work, therefore, totally unrelated to reality? If the answer to this question were affirmative, art would be reduced to a game, the sole purpose of which would be aesthetic pleasure. Such a conclusion would, however, be obviously incomplete. We must therefore continue our analysis of poetic designation in order to demonstrate that a weakening of the relation between the sign and the reality immediately signified by it does not preclude a relation between the work and reality as a whole; on the contrary, it is even beneficial to this relation. We have already ascertained above that the active intention of the subject from whom the utterance proceeds manifests itself much more clearly in poetic designation than in intellectual designation. As a result of the close semantic cohesiveness of the contexture characteristic of poetry, this intention is not renewed in each particular designation but remains the same in the course of the entire work, which acquires the nature of a total designation because of this unity of designative intention (Potebnja). And it is precisely this designation of a higher order represented by the work as a whole that enters into a powerful relationship with reality. Does this perhaps mean that a poetic work, even considered as an artistic creation, "signifies" only what it directly communicates through its theme? Let us take as an example Dostoevsky's novel *Crime and Punishment*. It is highly probable that the majority of those who have read or will read this novel have never committed or will never commit murder. It is equally certain that no crime today could be committed in a social or ideological situation identical to the one which gave birth to Raskolnikov's crime. Nevertheless, those who read Dostoevsky's novel react to their reading with the most intimate of their experiences; every reader feels that *sua res agitur*. The psychological associations and the semantic combinations set into motion by reading will, of course, differ from individual to individual. It is also probable that they will have very little in common with the author's personal experiences which gave rise to the work. The existential experiences with which an individual will react to a poetic work will only be symptoms of his own reaction to the poet's attitude toward reality. The stronger this reaction is, the greater the set of experiences it will be able to set into motion, and the stronger will be the influence exerted by the work on the reader's conception of the world.

But because an individual is a member of a collective and since his conception of reality roughly coincides with the system of values valid for this collective, poetry influences the way in which the entire society views the world through creating and reading individuals. The relation of poetry to reality is thus powerful, and this is precisely because the poetic work does not refer only to particular realities but to the total reality reflected in the individual and collective consciousness. Since, then, poetic designation, as we have seen, often sets into motion the entire lexical system of a given language, the thesis which we have adduced may also be formulated in the sense that poetry in the course of its development constantly, and always in new ways, confronts the vocabulary of the given language with the world of things which this vocabulary is supposed to reflect and to whose changes it is continuously adapting itself. We must not, however, believe that the global relation of the utterance to reality which we have just described is limited only to poetry: it is present in every utterance without exception. There is a reciprocal polarity between it and the immediate reference of every individual designation: if one of these aspects prevails, the other necessarily recedes into the background. This polarity is, of course, felt more strongly in poetic utterances than in communicative language, and it is also intentionally exploited for artistic effects.

In conclusion, let us summarize the main theses of our study. Poetic designation differs from communicative designation by virtue of the fact that its relation to reality is weakened on behalf of its semantic incorporation into the contexture. In poetry the practical functions of language—the presentational, the expressive, and the appellative—are subordinated to the aesthetic function which renders the sign itself the center of attention. It is precisely the prevalence of this function that makes the contexture in poetry so important for designation. The aesthetic function, as one of the four main functions of language, is potentially present in every utterance. The specific character of poetic designation, therefore, rests solely in its more radical exposure of the tendency inherent in every act of designation. The weakening of the immediate relation of poetic designation to reality is counterbalanced by the fact that a poetic work as a global designation enters into relation with the *total* set of the existential experiences of the subject, be he the creative or the perceiving subject.

A Note on the Semantics of the Poetic Image

The present study takes up again the problems of our earlier essay "Poetic Designation and the Aesthetic Function of Language" (1938). The starting point of that essay was the rejection of the common opinion that the difference between poetic and communicative expression lies in the figurative character of poetic expression and the non-figurative character of communicative expression. Moreover, neither the plasticity nor the novelty of designation characterizes poetry in general in the entire course of its development. In that essay our conclusion was that the difference between poetic and communicative designation is determined by the specific function of poetry as an art, namely, by the aesthetic function. In poetic designation attention is concentrated on the sign itself, and thus the semantic relation of every word to the surrounding contexture comes to the fore, whereas in communicative designation the main emphasis lies in the relation of the word to the thing which this word specifically signifies, hence in its so-called reference. Even today we insist on this solution, and if we return to the problem of the image in poetry, we do not do so in order to retreat from our former position but in order to attempt to analyze it systematically from the viewpoint of the poetic image.

The problem of the poetic image is not, in effect, completely solved by the knowledge that the image is by no means limited to poetry and that poetry very often uses words in their literal sense. Even if we take this into account, we still have the feeling that as soon as any word appears within the range of poetry, it evokes a "figurative" impression whether it is used figuratively or literally. When used poetically, words and groups of words evoke a greater richness of images and feelings than if they were to occur in a communicative utterance. A word always expresses a richer meaning in poetry than in communication. A communicative word, as scientific language (the most extreme form of communicative language) shows, tends toward a precisely defined meaning, the elements of which can be calculated. Even if a poetic word appears to tend toward intellectual schematization during some developmental stage, it is always directed at a meaning which is not explicitly expressed (an association of images, complex knots of feelings, acts of will), and through the mediation of these not directly expressed meanings a poetic word is also capable of referring to things which lie outside of the narrow path provided by the semantic contexture. Hence the impression of a certain figurativeness in non-figurative expressions of which the famous lines of Toman's "Září" are almost entirely composed:

> Můj bratr dooral a vypřáh' koně.
> A jak se stmívá,
> věrnému druhu hlavu do hřívy
> položil tiše, pohladil mu šíji
> a zaposlouchal se, co mluví kraj.
>   [*Měsíce*, 1918]
> My brother finished ploughing and unharnessed the horse.
> And as it was growing dark,
> he quietly put his head into his faithful
> friend's mane, stroked his neck
> and began to listen to what the countryside was saying.

Let us take the very simple sentence contained in the second line of the citation: "And as it was growing dark . . ." If this sentence occurred in a communicative utterance, it would unequivocally signify a certain natural phenomenon. In the poem it contains, in addition to this message, still other meanings provided by imagistic and emotive elements (the image of the landscape, a certain evening mood) which can, however, differ for each reader according to his own experiences and impressions. But despite this, they appear to him as something provided by the poet's very words. What initiates this semantic change is, on the whole, clear. Above all, it is undoubtedly the verse rhythm and, further, the euphonic clustering of sound elements (e.g., long *í* in the penultimate syllables of three successive lines: *stmívá, hřívy, šíji*). The incorporation of a word into the contexture is emphasized by this means; we have said above that such an incorporation prevails over the referential relation of every word in poetic designation. For example, the linking of words through euphonic resemblance causes the meanings of words connected in this way to be reflected in one another, to be reciprocally enriched by clusters of images which are not proper to any of them if used outside of this given euphonic association. Rhythm, euphony, and other poetic means are, however, only *external* manifestations of the poetic quality which causes every designation within its range to appear to a certain degree as an image.

So far the question of the *internal* connection between the special nature of poetic designation and figurative designation remains untouched. We shall attempt to answer it by proceeding from the well-known fact that the study of the metaphor, the most important category of figurative designations, has frequently encountered difficulty in locating the exact boundary between the spheres of *literal* and *figurative* meaning. Even in particular transitional cases it is sometimes very difficult to distinguish precisely between a metaphoric designation and a synonym, especially in the case of verbs. Thus, for example, in Mácha's lines:

> Tam v modré dálce skály lom
> Květoucí břeh jezera tíží

> There in the blue distance a jagged cliff
> Weighs down the blooming shore of the lake

> [*Máj*]

the designation "weighs down" can be taken equally well as a mere synonym of the verb *lies* (on the blooming shore) and as a metaphor, even a very expressive one. And in fact the boundary between all figurative and non-figurative modes of designation is so indefinite that their fundamental identity has been asserted. Indeed, Winkler declares in his book on stylistics that a designation always expressing a specific prevailing attribute of a thing can be applied to any object with this dominant characteristic, and, consequently, that there is, for example, no difference in the use of the word *rose* for the flower or for the color of the human face. It would be very easy to show the incorrectness of this theory; for us, however, its very existence is a symptom of the difficulties which stylistics encounters in distinguishing figurative from non-figurative designation.

Figurative and literal designations thus change into one another

imperceptibly. Yet it is clear that they are essentially different
from one another in their pure forms. How is it possible to bridge
this contradiction? Only by conceiving the relation between figurative and literal designation as a dialectic antinomy which operates
in every act of designation. Every designation, whether poetic or
communicative, participates in this antinomy and inclines toward
one of its poles. If it inclines toward the pole of literal meaning,
we have more or less the feeling that the designation is intrinsically
connected with the thing (hence, for example, the illusion that the
sound of a word has some necessary relation to a thing—the source
of certain theories about the origin of language and the theory of
the expressive effect of the sound aspect of words in poetry). The
automatization of the relation between an object and its designation thus arises; however, at the same time a precondition for
making this relation more precise is also established. If the designation inclines toward the figurative pole, this tendency is—again to a
varying degree—accompanied by the feeling that the designated
object could have been signified in yet another way and that, on
the other hand, the given designation could signify many other
objects as well. Under these circumstances the designation does
not express an object as a totality of characteristics but emphasizes a certain one of its aspects, a certain one of its characteristics
which it makes the dominant one. If consideration for the subject-
originator (the speaker) is maximally suppressed in non-figurative
designation, this consideration requires a strong, even extreme—in
certain circumstances—emphasis in figurative designation; the moment of *choice* in the act of designation becomes very palpable.

The traditional and common (especially since the period of
Symbolism) evaluation of figurative designation as an intrinsic
feature of poetry would require us now to proceed to identify
the antinomy between literal and figurative designation with the
antinomy between communicative and poetic language. We may
not do so, however, because not only does figurative designation
exceed the limits of poetry by occurring frequently in communicative language as well, but also *the tendency toward imagery
reaches its extreme realization precisely in communicative language and not in poetry*. This happens in so-called emotive
language, the language which serves to express feelings; however,
even the expression of a feeling is a message. With the clair-
voyance of a poet, Vladislav Vančura has shown to what degree

cursing, a typical example of emotive designation, is characterized by boldness in word choice, to what degree one feels the uniqueness of the act of designation which distinguishes figurative designation in its purest forms ("A curse always functions best in its nascent state"), and how strong the subject's participation, his license, and his arbitrariness are in its origin.[5] No doubt Vančura found curses akin to poetry; however, we must draw attention to the difference between a *genuinely* emotive image and a poetic image. A poetic expression can appear subjective only in comparison to a designation tending toward automatization, which we find, for example, in the calm, emotionally undisturbed language of daily contact. It is, however, much less subjective than the spontaneous language of feelings. A subject expressing his immediate feeling speaks for himself and for himself alone, in the extreme case, completely without regard for the listener. The poet, however, speaks both for himself and for the reader; his work is a sign, and his expression has simultaneously a subjective and objective validity.

It is precisely here that we find ourselves at the very heart of the problem. In poetic designation neither the pole of literal meaning nor the pole of figurative meaning prevails in principle; rather an equilibrium is the rule, although this equilibrium is usually strained and oscillates between the two opposed tendencies toward these poles. This also accounts for the special character of poetic designation. On the one hand, as we have already shown, every poetic designation, even a non-figurative one, evokes the impression of imagery; on the other hand, every poetic designation has to a certain extent the character of a non-figurative designation. We have in mind especially the impression of *necessity* which poetic designation creates. Poets are usually credited with discovering the most apt names for objects: for every object precisely that name which expresses it intrinsically. Frequently theoretical reasons also support this impression. We shall not mention them, however, for we are not concerned with criticizing them; we regard the feeling which is their basis as a mere indication of the fact that the tendency toward the pole of the proper literal meaning in poetic designation is at least as strongly present

5. "O nadávkách" [On curses], *Jarní almanach Kmene: Jízdní řád literatury a poesie*, ed. A. Hoffmeister (Prague, 1932), pp. 107-10.

as the tendency toward imagery. In this respect even the boldest poetic image differs from an affective, emotive image. The initiator of Symbolism, the poetry of the image—Stéphane Mallarmé—himself seeks in poetic designation a certain necessity of connection between a word and an object: "I say: a flower! and out of the oblivion to which my voice relegates any contour but the calices on top musically rises the idea itself, sweet, absent from every bouquet."[6] Mallarmé is, of course, speaking about an *idea* instead of an object; this is a question of poetic movement and philosophical view, but what interests us is the fact that he also emphasizes the essential necessity of the referential relation between the word and what the word means. We could never claim about the *emotive* image—and emotive designation in general —what the initiator of the imagery of modern poetry has claimed here; yet genuine literal designation appears necessary for the object signified by it, to the extent that the child whom the psychologist Piaget asked why clouds are called clouds answered, "Because they are gray," attributing the characteristic of the object to the word. Because of the fact that poetic designation is equidistant from these two extreme poles, we can explain its functioning in the development of designation in language in general. In the linguistic consciousness it maintains and refreshes the two forces which govern the semantic movement of the linguistic sign; at the same time it automatizes (viz poetic, imagistic clichés) and deautomatizes, makes objective and sub-jective, and thus prevents the word from being arrested in either of these extremes. Hence the practical import of the aesthetic function is also asserted through the mediation of poetic designa-tion whose special nature is determined by this function.

We must now juxtapose our conception of poetic designation with poetic development. That is to say, it might seem dangerous if we tried to exhaust all the possibilities for developmental changes in poetic designation by means of a single formula. Some-times poetry tends predominantly toward figurative expression, sometimes toward non-figurative; sometimes it seeks a new and unusual image, at other times a conventional image. Here the variations and degrees are numerous. We may, however, suppose that all of them have a common aim, that a restoration of the

6. "Crise de vers," *Divagations* (Paris, 1897), p. 251.

equilibrium between the pole of imagery and the pole of literal meaning, disturbed by the excessively long duration of the previous state, is involved in every developmental variation of poetic designation. After a period in which imagery has been emphasized there can follow a period in which literal meaning will be stressed, not in order to exchange one extreme for another but in order to reach a synthesis through contradiction. Even if the tendency toward literal meaning in the poetic texts themselves were emphasized to the utmost, the reader would conceive it only as a counterbalance to the excessively emphasized imagery of the previous period, as long as the poetry of this previous period was felt as a living tradition which was being resumed. Only when the previous developmental period dies out completely in the readers' memory, as well as in the sensibility with which they approach poetry, will the immoderate emphasis of literal meaning be felt as an excess which should be balanced again. After all, the loss of a direct reference in figurative designations can sometimes achieve, in further development, a dialectic equilibrium, not through a radical return to literal designations but through a change in the semantic structure of the poetic images themselves, as happened, for example, during the transition from the poetry of Čech's and Vrchlický's generation to the poetry of the Symbolists. The real paths of development are, however, much more complex than any generalizing scheme, basically because many more circumstances than the mere internal contradiction contained in designation itself operate in the development of the semantic aspect of the poetic word. The variable relation between poetic language and the development of the standard literary language or, in some cases, other linguistically functional structures, the influence of the development of society, and so forth, operate here. Even with this complexity of influence affecting poetic designation, we could—or so we believe—show that in each individual case their resultant does not tend to disturb the equilibrium between literal and figurative meaning but to strengthen it.

Does any advice for contemporary poetry—or rather for the poetry of the immediate future—follow from this conclusion? Beginning with Symbolism, European as well as Czech poetry has been experiencing an immoderate proliferation of the poetic image in the most varied forms. Today we are definitely growing tired of this stage. Moreover, it would not be difficult to prove on the basis of some contemporary poetic works that the image which has lost the obviousness of literal designation has also lost its poetic effectiveness. Today the risk, the necessary risk, of poetry consists much less in finding a new image—for the paths have already been trod and are entirely accessible to epigones—than in achieving a poetic designation of any kind which has a convincing relation to the reality designated. An image which too importunately indicates the poet's subjective arbitrariness functions as a childish play with words—without the child's freshness; it does not appear, however, as a serious effort to master reality. We do not in the least dare to forecast the solution which poetry will find or the moment at which it will succeed in finding this solution. In this brief essay, inspired by our present feeling for poetry, we have wished to indicate only that in all probability the result will again be the sort of poetic designation which oscillates in an unrestful but, precisely because of this, sharply effective equilibrium between the image and non-figurative designation.

3

Two Studies of Dialogue

DIALOGUE AND MONOLOGUE

I. Introductory Remarks

The problem of the relationship between monologue and dialogue is one of the urgent questions of contemporary poetics and the theory of drama, but it also concerns—in fact, primarily concerns—linguistics itself. In particular, until the relationship between dialogue and monologue[1] has been studied, we cannot successfully conclude, as it will become clear later in this essay, the study of the utterance as an actual application of a linguistic sign. Heretofore linguists dealing with the utterance have generally had in mind a monologic utterance. There are, in fact, only two extensive studies dealing with the interrelation of monologue and dialogue (as well as other questions of dialogue). One of them is Tarde's "Opinion and Conversation," a long chapter in the book *Opinion and the Crowd*,[2] which is devoted to questions of dialogue. The other is L. P. Jakubinskij's "On Dialogic Speech."[3] The methodological difference between these studies lies in the fact that Tarde's considerations are sociologically oriented, proceeding from the extralinguistic circumstances under which dialogue occurs and which influence its development, whereas Jakubinskij as a linguist proceeds from the internal structure of dialogue even though he does not neglect the relation of language to the outside world,

---

The first of these two studies is translated from "Dialog a monolog," *Listy filologické* 68 (1940). The second is translated from "O jeviŝtním dialogu," *Program D*[37], March 31, 1937.

1. Here, of course, we conceive of the term *monologue* in the linguistic sense, not in that sense which theatrical usage attributes to it. In theatrical usage this term means, in fact, a dialogue with an absent or imaginary partner, but for linguistics monologue means an utterance with a single active participant regardless of the presence or absence of other passive participants. A narration, for example, is a typical monologue in the linguistic sense.

2. G. Tarde, *L'Opinion et la foule*, 4th ed. (Paris, 1922).

3. "O dialogičeskoj reči," *Russkaja reč'*, ed. L. V. Ščerba (Petrograd, 1923), 1:96–194.

especially to the material context in which the discourse takes place. In a few of the following paragraphs we shall attempt a critical analysis of those of Jakubinskij's and Tarde's theses which closely pertain to our subject.

The pair dialogue – monologue appears to Jakubinskij as one of the functional linguistic oppositions, as do, for example, literary and colloquial language or intellectual and emotional language. Within this pair Jakubinskij sees dialogue as the basic (in the more recent term introduced by N. S. Trubetzkoj, "unmarked") member, whereas monologue is the "artificial" superstructure of dialogue. Jakubinskij's classification of dialogue and monologue as functional languages represented in its time a decisive turn in the methodological approach of linguistics toward these two phenomena. If up to that time it appeared that the choice between monologue and dialogue was a matter of accidental and linguistically irrelevant circumstances accompanying the application of a linguistic sign, Jakubinskij's thesis showed that this application is a *linguistic* act of choice between two fixed and regular sets of linguistic conventions. The great merit of Jakubinskij, one of the pioneers of the functional view of linguistic phenomena, lies in the fact that he rendered the difference between monologue and dialogue a subject of linguistic interest and study. Today, however, when the functional conception of language is already a methodological matter of course, the need for a more detailed conceptual differentiation has become apparent.

The term *functional language* pertains to the relationship between the goal of expression and the linguistic means appropriate for the attainment of this goal. In each given case a speaking individual determines the choice of a certain set of means ("a functional language") for the actual utterance. The choice between monologue and dialogue does not, however, depend only on the speaker's intention and decision but on the relationship between *both* the parties participating in the discourse, the speaking and the listening participant, the active and the passive subject. An utterance begun as a monologue can in its course change into a dialogue through the interventions of the "passive" participants (this happens, for example, in parliamentary speeches), and, on the contrary, a conversation can shift into a monologue—either for a long time or for its duration—through one participant's prevalence over the others. Nor does just one participant determine the choice of the linguistic means in the dialogue. Proof of this is the fact that each of the participants in a dialogue can use a different functional language: one can use emotional language, the other intellectual, one literary language, the other colloquial. We know what effects can be achieved by such a juxtaposition of functional styles—consider the dramatic dialogue. The difference between monologue and dialogue thus appears as something more profound than the differentiation of language into functional styles, although monologue and dialogue *also* appear as canonized sets of particular linguistic means. But we are dealing with more than a mere functional orientation: monologue and dialogue are two mutually opposed elementary attitudes through one of which every contact between language and extralinguistic reality proceeds with inevitable necessity.

We must still deal with the second of Jakubinskij's theses which concern us: his claim about the priority of dialogue over monologue. Let us point out in advance that Tarde defends quite the opposite thesis; according to him the priority belongs to monologue. We shall cite his statements first:

> Long before it [language] became usable in conversation, it could only be a means of expressing the orders or warnings of chiefs or the maxims of moralistic poets. In brief, it was first and necessarily a monologue. Dialogue came only afterwards according to the law whereby the unilateral always precedes the reciprocal. [p. 91]

And elsewhere:

> It is probable that at the first dawn of speech, in the first family or tribe which heard the first stammerings, it was one individual more gifted than the others who had the monopoly of speech. The others listened, already being able to understand him with effort, but not yet able to imitate him. This special gift must have contributed to elevating one man above the others. From this one can conclude that the monologue of the father speaking to his slaves or his children, of the chief giving orders to his soldiers, preceded the dialogue of the slaves, the children, the soldiers among themselves or with their master. [p. 92]

And finally:

> In contrast to the Classical epics and also the *chansons de geste*
> in which conversations are so sparse, modern novels beginning
> with those of Mlle de Scudéry are characterized by the ever
> increasing abundance of dialogues. [p. 99]

Jakubinskij, on the contrary, convinced of the priority of dialogue, quotes Ščerba's assertion about linguistic practice with
respect to dialects from the study *Vostočno-lužickoje narečije*
[The east Lusatian dialect]:

> Recalling the time which I spent among these half-peasants
> and half-workers, I realize with surprise that I *never* heard
> monologues but only *fragmentary* dialogues. There were occa-
> sions when people rode with me to Leipzig to an exhibit or to
> surrounding cities on business, and so on, but *no one ever*
> narrated his impressions: the matter was usually limited to a
> more or less lively dialogue. And this was not because of a lack
> of culture but rather, on the contrary, perhaps because of too
> much "culture," the constant quest for new superficial impres-
> sions and a certain impatience which distinguishes workers
> from real peasants. . . . All these observations once again show
> that monologue is to a considerable degree an *artificial* lin-
> guistic form and that *language reveals its genuine essence only
> in dialogue.* [pp. 131–32]

Jakubinskij himself then provides an even more emphatic formulation:

> There is no linguistic interaction *in general* whenever there is
> not dialogue, but there are certain interacting groups of people
> who know *only* the dialogic form and not the monologic. . . .
> In essence, every human interaction is precisely an *inter*-action;
> it actually strives to avoid one-sidedness, seeks to be bilateral,
> "dialogic," and avoids "monologue." Every unilateral action,
> insofar as it belongs to human perception, evokes in us a num-
> ber of more or less strong reactions which strive to reveal
> themselves. The same is true of the effect of monologic speech
> whereby the reactions arising in the process of perception (our
> attitude, evaluation, etc.) naturally strive to manifest them-
> selves in *speech.* . . . Not without reason is it said that one must
> *know how* to listen to someone else, one must *learn* to listen—

one does not have to *know how* to interrupt someone else, for it is natural. . . . In order for people to listen to a monologue certain secondary conditions are usually necessary, for example, the *organization of a meeting* with the order of the speakers, the yielding of the floor, the chairman, and nevertheless "voices from the audience" are always heard. . . . Dialogue which is without doubt a "cultural" phenomenon at the same time appears to be a more "natural" phenomenon than monologue. [pp. 133-39]

Hence we have before us two opposing opinions, one of which grants primacy to monologue (Tarde), the other to dialogue (Jakubinskij). With which of these should we agree? Obviously, each of them is partly true. We can, however, object that the "orders of fathers and chiefs" to which Tarde refers can hardly be considered monologue. They are dialogues in which the replies are extralinguistic acts—compliance with the commands. We can also raise an objection to Jakubinskij by pointing out that milieux where the basic form of linguistic discourse is monologue are known from everyday experience. Such is, for example, the school milieu, where the teacher's monologue prevails in his presentation. Even the pupils' answers at an examination tend toward a monologic reproduction of the teacher's presentation. If the examinee is interrupted, that is, if the examiner makes an effort to substitute dialogue for monologue, the pupil feels that the exam is being made more difficult. It is therefore impossible either to presuppose the priority of monologue or to prove the general priority of dialogue. The relation between monologue and dialogue can be characterized rather as a dynamic polarity in which sometimes dialogue, sometimes monologue gains the upper hand according to the milieu and the time. In the following sections of our study we shall attempt to show that the bond between them is even closer than it might appear on the basis of the preceding citations and deliberations.

II. On the Basic Aspects and Types of Dialogue

Some of the rather paradoxical differences between Tarde's and Jakubinskij's views follow from the fact that each of these scholars has in mind a different nuance of dialogue. Whereas Jakubinskij thinks, as is evident from his explanations, primarily about the dialogue of everyday life merging directly and closely with man's

activities,[4] Tarde has in mind primarily "conversation," artificial
dialogue deprived of an immediate dependency upon everyday
life, carried out as a rule under circumstances specially adapted
for talk (such as the gathering of company *only* for the purpose of
talk). Such a difference in notions, of course, necessarily leads to
the disagreement in the scholars' results. It is therefore not a good
idea to use the term *dialogue* without being aware in advance of
the entire scope and heteromorphism of the phenomenon designated by it. Thus, even though we are primarily interested in
defining the relation between monologue and dialogue, we cannot
avoid enumerating the essential aspects of dialogue in general.
Only in this way can we hope to reach a complete and undistorted
notion of dialogue.

What, then, are the necessary and thus omnipresent aspects of
the linguistic phenomenon commonly called dialogue? There are
three:

1. The first of these aspects is provided by the relation between
the two participants, which from the standpoint of the one speaking can be designated as the relationship between "I" and "you."
Even in a monologue, of course, two parties participate in the
discourse, but in no way does a monologue have to be "addressed"
by the speaker in a particularly striking manner. Indeed, even if
such an "addressing" of a monologue (by such means as apostrophe
or second person personal pronouns) occurs, it colors the monologue dialogically. The reason why the polarity between "I" and
"you" in a dialogue is so emphasized is that the roles of the speaker and the listener are constantly alternating. The interrelation of
the participants in a dialogue is therefore felt as a tension not
bound to either of the two speaking persons but actually existing
"between" them; it is thus objectified as the "psychological situation" of the dialogue. This is illustrated by the fact that even
though a certain mood has originated in the mental state of one of
the participants in the dialogue, it often quickly takes hold of all
the other participants and sets the tone of the entire emotional
coloration of the dialogue.

2. The relationship between the participants of a discourse and
the real, material situation which surrounds them at the moment

4. See his reference to the incorporation of dialogue into the context of everyday
life, pp. 174 f.

of the discourse comprises the second basic aspect of dialogue. The material situation can penetrate the discourse both indirectly, when it becomes its theme, and directly, when it influences the direction of the dialogue by its changes (for example, the theme of the discourse changes as a result of an event which attracts the speakers' attention, such as a shout overheard from the street), or even when a reference to the material situation replaces individual words or even sentences and entire replies (someone enters a room where a dead man is lying without seeing him and without being informed of his fate; he asks the other person present: "Where is X?", and this person answers without speaking, merely by means of a demonstrative gesture). The influence of the material situation upon the discourse can, of course, be extremely limited. This happens, for example, when the conversants meet in a room particularly designated for talk or when they are isolated from the surrounding material context by the theme of the discourse, which is very remote from it. Even in such cases, however, a negligible impulse arising from the material situation is often enough to exert its influence on the discourse. The material situation is therefore omnipresent, if not always actually, then at least potentially, in a dialogue.

3. The specific character of the semantic structure of dialogue constitutes its third necessary aspect. If both of the preceding aspects are provided by the external circumstances which accompany the discourse, this third aspect lies in the discourse itself, for it pertains to its contexture. Unlike monologic discourse, which has a single and continuous contexture, several or at least two contextures interpenetrate and alternate in dialogic discourse. Not even dialogue, of course, can do without semantic unity, but this is furnished primarily by the subject of the discourse, the theme, which must be the same at a given moment for all the participants. Dialogue is impossible without the unity of a theme. Consider the derisive folk saying "já o voze a on o koze" ("I'm speaking about a cart and he about a goat") or a folkloric parody of a dialogue with a dual theme, a talk with a deaf person: "Tetka, jdete z funusu?"—"I ne, prodala jsem husu."—"Teta, hodně plakali?"—"I ne, málo mi za ni dávali, atd." ("Auntie, are you coming from a funeral?"—"Why no, I sold a goose."—"Auntie, did they cry a lot?"—"Why no, they didn't offer me much for it," etc.). The contexture is different from the theme in that it is

provided by the meaning which the speaking person ascribes to the theme—by the point of view which he adopts toward it and by the way in which he evaluates it. Because there is more than one participant in a dialogue, there is also a manifold contexture: although each person's utterances alternate with those of the other person or persons, they comprise a certain unity of meaning. Because the contextures which interpenetrate in this way in a dialogue are different, often even contradictory, sharp semantic reversals occur on the boundaries of the individual replies. The more vivid the dialogue, the shorter the individual replies, and the more distinct the collision of the contextures. Thus arises a special semantic effect for which stylistics has even created a term: stichomythia.

Such are the three main and essential aspects of dialogue. Dialogue is impossible without any of them, for two of them follow from the necessary real premises of a discourse, and the third constitutes the semantic difference between dialogue and monologue. Each of them also manifests itself in its own way in the linguistic organization of dialogue:

1. The opposition between "I" and "you" has its linguistic correlate in the semantic opposition between the pronouns—personal and possessive—of the first and second person, further in the opposition between the first and second person of the verb, then in the imperative, the vocative, and to a certain extent in the interrogative sentence. This can also be projected into the opposition between affirmation and negation (yes – no) and into certain syntactic relations between sentences, especially the adversative (however, but) and the concessive relation (despite, nevertheless). All of these linguistic means are capable of emphasizing the demarcation of the speaking subjects of a dialogue from one another and of stressing the variety of their opinions, feelings, and volitions.

2. The speaking subjects' relation to the actual situation in which the discourse takes place, to the "here and now," finds its linguistic expression in the spatial and temporal deixis represented by demonstrative pronouns (this, that, etc.), local and temporal adverbs (here, there, now, in the morning, in the evening, today, tomorrow, etc.), and verbal tenses (the present in opposition to the preterit and the future).

3. The semantic reversals which, as we have said, occur on the

boundaries of the individual replies in a dialogue as a result of the interpenetration of several contextures have their linguistic correlate in lexical oppositions of an evaluative character, such as good – bad, beautiful – ugly, noble – base, important – insignificant, useful – harmful. An evaluation can, of course, be projected into qualitative oppositions, such as big – small, young – old. The nuances of semantic reversals possible on the boundary of replies are, of course, much richer than these strict contrasts. Often they are based on a mere play with meaning, as, for example, in the exploitation of ambiguity and in various kinds of paradox. Phonologically semantic reversals in dialogue find their expression in differences of intonation (for example, in the contrast of intonational height between two contiguous replies), expiratory intensity, tone of voice (for example, the ironic repetition of a partner's words), and tempo. Even these phonological means, of course, have a semantic import, for they often express semantic shifts inaccessible to verbal expression. The more a discourse is based on semantic reversals, the greater demands it makes on the speakers' ability to control their voices with respect to these qualities. For this reason, too, social discourse can attain real cultivation only in those milieux which have at their disposal a perfect vocal culture; on the other hand, the development of social discourse supports the differentiation of intonation, expiration, tone of voice, and tempo into subtle nuances.

The three basic aspects of dialogue that we have just enumerated and characterized are, as we have said, necessary and therefore omnipresent: no dialogue completely lacks a single one of them. In spite of this there are cases in which one of them predominates and thus colors the discourse with its characteristics. In this way mere aspects of dialogue turn into *types.* In a few of the following paragraphs we shall attempt to characterize these pronounced forms of dialogue corresponding to its individual basic aspects.

A discourse of the first type emphasizes the opposition between "I" and "you." Emotional and volitional elements come to the fore especially distinctly in a dialogue oriented in this way. Its most extreme case is therefore the *dispute,* which is only a step away from physical interaction. The more cultivated a certain collective is, the more strongly is this extreme result of "personal" dialogue subdued in it. But as Tarde shrewdly demonstrates, this "personal" aspect of dialogue has, nevertheless, an elementary significance: "The pleasure of disputing corresponds to a childish instinct, that of kittens, of all young animals. . . . But the proportion of dispute to conversation diminishes with growing up" (p. 108). Hence from the ontogenetic standpoint Tarde sees the dispute as a primal form of dialogue. But according to Tarde philogenetic development also follows the same course. He explains that a gradual diminishing of the impulses for disputes and hence of disputes themselves occurs in the development of society. Bargaining in commerce was eliminated by fixed prices; the collective vanity of corporations, families, and churches, which had frequently provided the impulse for disputes, disappeared; knowledge of foreign lands, the indefiniteness of which had often provoked disputes, became more precise. "It is true that if the advancement of reliable and certain information has solved problems once debated, it has raised new ones and has provoked new disputes, but these are of a more impersonal and less harsh nature, and all violence is excluded from them: philosophical, aesthetic, moral discussions which stimulate the adversaries without injuring them" (p. 109).[5]

Let us now take a look at the second basic aspect of dialogue, the relation between the speaking persons and the actual material situation. How and when does this aspect manifest itself in a pure form? It occurs most distinctly in a "business" talk. Let us imagine, for example, two engineers exchanging views in the countryside, or even just over a map of the countryside, about building roads or making rivers navigable. As long as their talk does not turn into a discussion, it will be full of deictic references to the individual details of the countryside, its overall formation, and so forth. Many substantives will be replaced by demonstrative pronouns; syntactic members or even entire sentences will often be replaced in the discourse by demonstrative gestures; the discourse will also be bound to the countryside situation by numerous local adverbs. A discourse conducted in this way will be as pure a representative as possible of dialogue bound to the material situation. Similarly, other talks during work will approximate the "situational" discourse. Sometimes in manual work a talk will

_____

5. We must add to Tarde's remark that, according to our conception, discussion constitutes a linking member between predominantly "personal" dialogue (type 1) and dialogue based on the opposition of semantic contextures (type 3).

become only a fragmentary accompaniment of the work actions. Talks of this kind lack strong emotional coloration; there is no tension between the speakers; these talks do not turn into physical interaction but into action with respect to the situation. We must still add that the situation to which they are related can even be remote from the actual "here and now," can be located elsewhere in space and time. Take, for example, a foreman's talk with a worker in a workshop about the job that must be done in another place known to both or about a job that has already been done.

Let us now turn to the third aspect of dialogue and thus, of course, to its third type. We shall focus our attention on dialogues based predominantly on semantic reversals provided by the inter-penetration and alternation of several contextures. The boundary which we are crossing here is more significant than that between the first type (the "personal") and the second (the "situational"). This is because dialogue of the third type is, relatively speaking, removed to a considerable degree from a direct dependence on external circumstances, both on the interlocutors' emotional and volitional interrelation and on the material situation. A pure play of meanings is both its aim and its extreme limit. Its prerequisite is a concentration of attention on the dialogue itself as a chain of semantic reversals. External circumstances are also adapted to this requirement. People gather for the sole purpose of talk, often in special rooms, and if there are more than two conversants, there is usually one (the host) who sees to it that the talk remains re-moved from both emotional and volitional interrelations among the individuals as well as from the actual material situation. A *conversation,* a talk for the sake of talk itself, to a certain extent self-oriented and hence quite strongly colored aesthetically, as Tarde has correctly grasped, occurs under the following condi-tions:

> By conversation I mean every dialogue without direct and immediate usefulness in which one talks primarily in order to talk, for pleasure, for play, out of politeness. This definition excludes from our concern both judicial inquiries and diplo-matic or commercial negotiations, councils and even scholarly conferences even though they abound in superfluous talk. It does not exclude flirtation or amatory talks in general despite the frequent transparency of their objective which does not

prevent them from being pleasing in themselves. . . . If I were
concerned only with urbane conversation cultivated as a special
art, I should hardly date it earlier, at least since classical
antiquity, than the fifteenth century in Italy, the sixteenth
or seventeenth century in France, somewhat later in England
and the eighteenth in Germany. But long before the full
bloom of this aesthetic flower of civilization its first buds began to appear on the tree of languages; and though less fertile
in visible results than the conversations of an elite, the unin-
spired talks of the primitives nevertheless have a great social
importance. [pp. 83-84]

Hence, unlike the first two types of dialogue, conversation is
not an existential matter of course but a cultural conquest, and
there is, consequently, quite a lot of artificiality in it, even the
very choice of the theme. In the first two types of dialogue, the
theme is generally predetermined to a certain extent or even
provided completely from outside by the psychological or material
situation, whereas in a conversation the theme is a matter of the
speakers' free choice. It is well known how often the theme of a
conversational dialogue must be sought in several common attempts before one suitable for all the participants is found. Concern that the theme remain as far as possible from the actual
psychological and material situation plays a very important negative role in this search. Sometimes conversation, or at least the
semblance of it, is even intentionally used to divert attention from
this dual actual situation, to "talk around" the situation.

It is, of course, impossible that consideration for the surrounding external and internal reality be completely suppressed. Here
there is just a tendency toward the self-orientation of talk, and
this tendency reaches its ultimate goal only in extreme cases of
"subjectless" discourse. Such cases are usually created only artificially for the purpose of a special effect, most often comic—here
we have in mind especially the "subjectless" discourses of comic
clowns on stage.[6] Sometimes, of course, it happens that even a

6. See R. Jakobson's article "Dopis Romana Jakobsona Jiřímu Voskovcovi a Janu
Werichovi o noetice a semantice švandy" [A letter from Roman Jakobson to Jiří
Voskovec and Jan Werich on the epistemology and semantics of fun] in *Deset let
Osvobozeného divadla: 1927-1937* (Prague, 1937), pp. 27-34. *Editors' note.* This
article has been reprinted in R. Jakobson, *Studies in Verbal Art* (Ann Arbor, 1971), pp.
299-304.

"real" conversation comes quite close to the very boundary of subjectlessness, as, for example, in the discourses of strangers who, being compelled by some external circumstance to remain face to face for a long while, talk only in order to avoid "awkward silence." In such cases the talk consists almost entirely of formal "synsemantic" phrases which could mean something only in connection with a particular theme but mean almost nothing without it ("I'm of the same opinion as you, but I think that nevertheless . . ."–"Of course, this matter must be considered from a broad perspective"–"But nevertheless this will become clear" etc.). Even these cases, however, are merely peripheral. The relation to reality, as we have already said, cannot be completely suppressed, but the main emphasis in the conversation is not placed on it. Hence the tendency toward the variability of the theme during a conversation in contrast to dialogues of the first two types which usually stick to the original theme or at least stubbornly return to it.

But if conversation is thus disengaged from an immediate relation to actual reality, though not completely detached from it, the question arises whether we may attribute to conversation "great social importance" as Tarde does in the above citation. Well, despite all its independence from the actual situation, or perhaps rather precisely because of it, conversation is very closely incorporated into the general social situation. The very influence which the social situation, in the broad sense of the word, exerts upon conversation is evidence of this, as Tarde points out.[7] Thus in certain periods *religion* limits conversation by forbidding particular themes and by imposing silence upon particular groups (monastic orders), and, on the other hand, it may provide certain themes. *Politics* leads to talk about public affairs in a democracy; on the other hand, it compels the priority of literary themes and psychological observations in a totalitarian regime. *Economic conditions* influence conversation in the sense that their favorable state provides enough free time for talks and facilitates their cultivation by satisfying at least the most urgent material needs. Such is the passive connection between conversation and the social reality. An extensive discussion of the active influence of conversation upon the creation of a general consensus in the most varied matters of public concern is not necessary because of its

7. *L'Opinion et la foule*, pp. 99 ff.

obviousness. For the mere sake of example let us mention the influence of conversation upon the creation of a common opinion about literary matters: "Especially wherever literature has been the constant subject of talks in a certain milieu, people have, without knowing it, been collectively elaborating a poetics, a literary code accepted by all and capable of supplying ready opinions, always consistent with one another, on all kinds of creations of the mind."[8] The relation of conversation to reality is therefore of a special kind: even when conversation concerns some concrete case, what "is meant" by it is a generality. In this respect conversation resembles, *mutatis mutandis* of course, the work of art whose reference also goes beyond the concrete theme.[9]

We should add that conversation is not the only kind of dialogue based on the interpenetration of several semantic contextures and the semantic reversals deriving from it. Forms of dialogue akin to conversation but not identical with it can often be found in poetry, especially dramatic poetry; such a form is the "lyrical" dialogue. After all, though drama exploits all three aspects of dialogue and all the types based upon them for its own purposes, it always focuses the spectator's attention more sharply—because of its very artistic nature—on the semantic aspect of the discourse than is the case in practical dialogues.

We have analyzed in more detail the three characteristic types of dialogue which are quite distinct from one another: "personal" dialogue and "situational" dialogue and conversation. We must not, of course, forget the basic homogeneity of dialogue. The types analyzed by us are only the extreme limits which a prevalence of one of the three basic aspects of this fundamentally homogeneous linguistic phenomenon attains. There is, however, a vast, almost endless number of nuances of dialogue arising from different combinations and different "dosages" of its basic aspects. In this study we cannot attempt a more detailed enumeration and typology of the nuances of dialogue; nevertheless, we would like to point out the transitional types comprising links between the third type (dialogue of a conversational character) and each of the first two types ("personal" and "situational" dialogue). This would seem necessary in order to show that the apparently very deep

8. Ibid., p. 147.
9. See our study "Poetic Designation and the Aesthetic Function of Language," above.

divide which separates conversation from the other two pronounced types of dialogue does not affect the essence of the
phenomenon called dialogue.

The first of the transitional types that we wish to analyze
mediates between conversation and "personal" dialogue based on
the opposition "I" and "you"; this is *discussion*. We have already
quoted Tarde's observation that the discussion largely replaced
disputes in the course of civilization because it was less personal.
This fact historically substantiates the transition from "personal"
dialogue to dialogue based on the interpenetration and alternation
of contextures. We can, after all, recall the fact that the degree of a
personal emotional relation among the participants was much
stronger in medieval disputes than it usually is in modern scholarly
discussions. Gradually it came about that an opposition of *theses,*
that is, semantic contextures, replaced an opposition of *persons,*
and thus discussion approximated conversation without merging
with it completely at any time. The surprising semantic reversals
on the boundary of contiguous replies which sometimes lead us,
indeed even lure us, to paradoxes sharply elucidating the difference of opinions also bring discussion close to conversation.

The transition from "situational" dialogue to dialogue with a
predominant semantic aspect, hence conversation, has an even
more interesting appearance. In speaking about conversation, we
emphasized that the influence of the material situation upon it is
usually carefully removed by the very nature of the place where
the talk occurs. It might therefore seem that we are dealing with
an uncrossable boundary. But Tarde's observation shows that there
has been a close connection between situational and purely semantic dialogue for a long time:

> Quite often, and much more often the closer one is to primi-
> tive life, men and women, particularly women, converse only
> while doing something else, whether it be performing some
> easy task, as do the peasants who during evening get-togethers
> shell legumes while their wives spin, sew or knit. . . . [pp.
> 101-02]

The transitional type of dialogue between situational and purely
semantic dialogue is therefore a talk which is usually called a *chat.*
A purely semantic (most often associative) linking of the replies
connects it to conversation; an obligatory, though only formal,

bond with the material situation connects it to situational dialogue.

The divide between purely semantic talk and the remaining two types of dialogue, epistemologically very significant, is therefore very easily crossable in practice precisely because dialogue in its very essence is a single and indivisible phenomenon. Dialogue must not, however, be conceived as an isolated fact, even from the overall viewpoint. We have already explained in our introductory remarks that monologue is its indispensable companion and constant competitor. In the following sections we want to attempt to prove that their interconnection is even closer and more substantial than it might appear at first glance, that monologue and dialogue are simultaneously present in the speaker's consciousness in every speech act and are still struggling for dominance in the very course of this act. In order to prove this we must first look at the psychology of language.

III. The Question of the Psychic Subject in Dialogue and Monologue

Every utterance presupposes at least two subjects between whom the linguistic sign mediates: the subject from whom the linguistic sign proceeds (the speaker) and the subject to whom this sign is addressed (the listener). We have already indicated that in monologue one of these subjects is constantly active, the second constantly passive, whereas in dialogue the roles constantly change: each of the two subjects is alternately active and passive. At first glance it seems that the notion "subject" here is necessarily a synonym of the notion "concrete psychophysical individual," but this is not so. The phenomenon called "soliloquy" in which an individual addresses an utterance, thought or even pronounced aloud, to himself is known from the most common linguistic experience. In a soliloquy, therefore, a single psychophysical individual is the vehicle of *both* subjects necessary for an utterance, the active and the passive. If the utterance is of dialogic nature, the two subjects, realized by the voice of a single individual, can alternately address one another as "I" and "you." The origin of the medieval literary theme called "The Dispute of the Soul with the Body" is to be found in such a split of one and the same individual consciousness into the two subjects of an utterance. Here the duality of the subject in a single psychophysical individual is projected into a biunial bond of the body with the soul. It is natural that the relation between "I" and "you" is very fluid in a soliloquy. Thus we shall find, for example, in Březina's lyric poems several cases in which it appears as if the first and second person pronouns have changed places. This is the case, for instance, in the poem characteristically called "Slyším v duši" [I hear in my soul], the first and last stanza of which read:

> Když slunce zpívalo, *tys* na svůj nástroj nesáh',
> jen pod *mým* bodnutím krev tryskla tónů *tvých*!
> *tvá* ruka v křečích jen zahřměla na klávesách
> jak v noci úzkosti na dveře umdlených.
>
> A zpupný roj *tvých* včel, jenž z *mého* ulét' úle,
> ze stromu dutého jsem kouřem vyhnal zpět;
> *tvé* dni jsem uvěznil a suggescí své vůle
> *tvých* písní zahořkl jsem mízu, dech a květ.
>
> [Svítání na západě]

> When the sun was singing, *you* didn't touch your
>   instrument,
> only under *my* piercing did the blood of *your* tones
>   spring!
> *your* hand in convulsions only thundered on the keys
> as anxieties at night on the door of weary ones.
>
> And the audacious swarm of *your* bees, which flew
>   away from *my* hive,
> I chased back from a hollow tree with smoke;
> I imprisoned *your* days and through the suggestiveness
>   of my will
> I made the sap, breath and blossom of *your* songs
>   bitter.

Who is speaking here? The one who addresses the other by the pronouns "you" and "your" or the other who is addressed in this way? This is left in uncertainty, for nothing would be easier than to reverse their interrelation by interchanging the pronouns ("When the sun was singing, *I* didn't touch my instrument, only under *your* piercing did the blood of *my* tones spring," etc.). Here the reversal of the grammatical persons is used simultaneously as a poetic and an epistemological device.

These considerations alone suffice to indicate the complexity of the question of the subject in the utterance in general. However, we are concerned with testing our hypothesis that the oscillation between an orientation toward "I" and an orientation toward "you," and hence the oscillation between dialogue and monologue as well, manifests itself at the very origin of an utterance. Let us therefore see what Victor Egger says in his famous treatise *The Interior Word*: ". . . tormented by insomnia, we cannot *silence* our thought; we hear it, for it has a voice . . . ; not only do we hear it, but we listen to it, for it is contrary to our wishes . . . , it astonishes us, it troubles us; it is unexpected and hostile. . . ."[10] Elsewhere in the same work the author says, "It even happens sometimes in the hypnagogic state [i.e., on the boundary between the waking state and sleep, J.M.] that we do not attribute the words which we hear either to ourselves or to others" (pp. 77–78). In such cases, therefore, "I" remains completely undistinguished from "you." I myself remember an event which I experienced when I was tired after a long journey. A friend said a few words to me that stuck in my memory; however, I still do not know to this day whether these words were actually spoken or whether I just thought them up myself at the time. The story of a dream which Georg Christoph Lichtenberg tells contains very striking evidence of the oscillation between "I" and "you" in the individual's consciousness:

> It was at the end of September 1798 when I told someone in a dream the story of the young and beautiful Countess Hardenberg that had moved me and everyone else very much. She died in September 1797 during the time of her confinement, in fact during parturition, which failed. She was cut open, and her child was put next to her in the coffin, and in this way they were brought by torchlight at night by an enormous crowd to a nearby town where the family tomb was. This was accomplished by means of the Göttingen hearse, a very unwieldy vehicle. The result was that the corpses were tossed about a great deal. At the end several people once more wanted to see her before she was put into the crypt. The coffin was opened, and she was found lying on her face in a heap with her child. . . . At that time my mind was often preoccupied by this scene, because I knew her husband, who was one of my most diligent auditors, quite well. Now in a

10. *La Parole intérieure: Essai de psychologie descriptive* (Paris, 1881), p. 4.

dream I was telling this sad story to someone in the presence of a third person who also knew the story, but I forgot (strangely enough) the circumstance with the child which, after all, was the major fact. After I had finished my story, as I believed, with great energy and with the listener greatly moved, the third person said: "Yes, and the child was lying next to her, all in a heap." Yes, I almost blurted out "and her child was lying in the coffin with her." That was the dream.

What makes it noteworthy for me is the following: Who reminded me of the child in the dream? Was it I myself to whom the fact occurred? Why didn't I myself recall it as a memory in the dream? Why did my fantasy create a third person who had to surprise me and almost embarrass me? Had I told this story while awake, this poignant fact could certainly not have escaped me. Here I had to omit it to let myself be surprised. . . . An event, not unusual for me, was dramatized here. But on the whole there is nothing unusual for me about being instructed in a dream by a third person, which is nothing but dramatized recollection.[11]

We have cited this rather extensive passage almost completely because it is so instructive. The story which the dream reproduced in the narrative form was evidently preserved in the author's mind as a monologue bound to a single narrator. However, the dream allows the narrator to omit an important moment and attributes it to another person. It is interesting that in the story itself, the unexpected semantic reversal, the pivotal point of the story, is found where the subject of the narration is split from the main narrator's person. We have said above that semantic reversals at the boundary of contiguous replies are characteristic of dialogue as a semantic structure of a particular kind. Therefore it may be supposed that to a certain extent the dialogization was already latently contained in the monologic version of the story and that the dream only revealed the potential dialogic quality hidden in the aforementioned place of the monologue. This assertion is important for the further course of our deliberations.

The problem of the so-called interior monologue with which the practice and theory of narrative prose has been concerned for

11. "Die 'Bemerkungen'" in *Gesammelte Werke* (Frankfurt am Main, 1949), 1: 112–14.

the last few decades, beginning with the 1880s, provides us with an even more detailed insight into the psychic event from which the utterance originates. The aim of writers who are artistically involved with interior monologue is to render an equivalent of the psychic event in its actual appearance as it takes place in the deep strata of mental life on the boundary between consciousness and subconsciousness. Several successive artistic schools, beginning with the Symbolists and ending for the time being with the Surrealists, have tried to solve this problem. The Surrealists have even given it a new name: "automatic writing" (*écriture automatique*). The difficulty of artistically mastering interior monologue consists—as Jean Cazaux has correctly recognized[12]—in the fact that a transcript of the individual phases of a psychic event is not enough to evoke an illusion of a direct insight into an inner life. This requires a different mode of presentation than that which offers itself spontaneously to the author during self-observation: here too, as always and everywhere, the necessity for an artistic reshaping lies between reality and art. This is the source of the theoretical interest of artists themselves in the problems of interior monologue. Their deliberations concern us as far as we find in them mention of the psychological connection between monologue and dialogue. In the following paragraphs we shall cite several passages from the most comprehensive discussion of interior monologue, the poet (and historian) Edouard Dujardin's book *The Interior Monologue*.[13]

The author's very conception of monologue is interesting for us. We would have expected that precisely "interior" monologue

12. *Surréalisme et psychologie* (Paris, 1938).

13. *Le Monologue intérieur: Son apparition, ses origines, sa place dans l'oeuvre de James Joyce et dans le roman contemporain* (Paris, 1931). By way of introduction to these quotations we should note that Dujardin, one of the Symbolists, published in 1887 the novel *Les Lauriers sont coupés,* which is considered by many and, of course, by the author himself as the first attempt at an artistic exploitation of the interior monologue. After its publication the novel almost sank into oblivion, and memory of it revived only at the beginning of the 1920s with the resounding success of *Ulysses,* the author of which referred to Dujardin as his precursor. At the same time, however, there were some like André Gide, for example, who denied Dujardin's priority by claiming that older authors, especially Dostoevsky, had already known the technique of interior monologue. Thus, in order to defend himself, Dujardin was compelled to attempt a theory of interior monologue, especially a definition of the difference between this technique and the former "indirect" descriptions of the inner life of characters in novels. Like every serious polemic, this one also led to a series of shrewd observations.

would appear to the author as a matter of only a *single* subject, the one who experiences the psychic event. Instead, however, Dujardin links his conception of interior monologue to dramatic monologue, which is in its essence a dialogic utterance. Charles Le Goffic, whom Dujardin quotes, says that "to give an exact and detailed description of all the feelings, ideas and sensations that can pass through a human brain from seven to ten o'clock in the evening [would be] a monologue [worthy of such a great actor as was] Coquelin the younger" (p. 98). And Dujardin himself dedicated his novel to the memory of a dramatic author, Racine. He explains, in a characteristic manner, how this dedication came about: "Such a dedication was not only a reaction against the injustices of the Romantics; it was not only the affirmation of my extreme admiration for classical beauty; it indicated my determination, against winds and tides, to connect my attempt to tradition; it signified above all my ambition . . . to continue Racine's poetic conquest by other means and on another level. This is what was not at all understood. There was too great a distance between the rational order within which the seventeenth century had evolved and the irrational order that I was trying to penetrate. Most of my friends asked why I had dedicated my book to Racine" (pp. 104-05).

Hence young Dujardin, creator of the technique of interior *monologue,* was consciously following the tradition of *drama,* dialogic poetry, and wanted to transfer this tradition to "another level" and continue it "by other means." Just as all the Symbolists, he yielded to the paradoxical temptation to express what is hidden and inexpressible in human mental life, but in contrast to his poetic comrades, he keenly sensed the potential *dialogic nature* of mental activity; his discovery lies in this. From the linguistic standpoint the objective which Dujardin had in mind can be formulated as the transposition of dialogue into monologic speech.

At the same time it was a matter of another transposition, equally instructive for us. Dujardin, again as a good Symbolist, yearned to transfer the artistic devices of Wagner's music into poetry:

> I undertook the novel *Les lauriers sont coupés* with the foolish ambition of transposing into literature Wagnerian devices which I defined as follows: the expression of mental

life by means of the incessant thrust of musical motives which
come to express one after the other, indefinitely and succes-
sively, "states" of thought, feeling or sensation; one realizes
or rather attempts to realize this device by means of an indefinite succession of short sentences, each of which presents one
of these states of thought and which follow one another without logical order, rising from the depths of the being or, as
one would say today, from the unconscious or the sub-
conscious. . . . [p. 97]

It begins to become apparent to us why mental life strikes
Dujardin as dialogue. The "randomness" of succession in which
its individual phases follow one another causes a constant semantic
variability resembling the semantic variability of dialogue. This
will become even clearer from the following passage:

. . . a psychologist would, I think, say that not only do we
think on several levels at once but that our thought races from
one level to another with a rapidity which may later seem to
be simultaneity but really is not; interior monologue gives the
impression of precisely this racing "in fits and starts"; Joyce's
"continuous line" is actually a broken line. [pp. 61-62]

Here Dujardin describes what we have called one of the basic
aspects of dialogue, the interpenetration and alternation of several
contextures. As the poet shows, this essential feature of dialogue
is already contained in the mental event from which the utterance
originates and which therefore has priority over the utterance.
Now it is also clear where the source of the oscillation between
the unity and the multiplicity of the subject in the individual's
consciousness, about which both Egger and Lichtenberg speak, lies.
The variety of semantic contextures into which mental events are
incorporated can be very easily attributed to the variety of subjects. What follows from these deliberations is that the monologic
and dialogic qualities are simultaneously and inseparably present
in the psychic event from which the utterance originates and that
monologue and dialogue must not be conceived as two mutually
alien and hierarchically graded forms of the utterance but as
two forces which always struggle with one another for predominance, even in the very course of the utterance. In our next and
final section we shall attempt to prove this thesis on the basis of
discourse itself.

IV. Dialogue in Monologue and Monologue in Dialogue

Let us first attempt to discern the dialogic quality potentially contained in monologue. For our purposes the most suitable material, which literally was the authority of a scientific experiment, is the dramatization of Viktor Dyk's short story "Krysař" [The Pied Piper of Hamelin] undertaken by E. F. Burian and presented in January 1940 by the theater D⁴⁰. In this dramatization Burian proceeded in a manner very different from the usual one. He did not limit himself to the extraction and dramaturgic modification of the dialogue contained in the poet's text but, instead, dramatized the entire text, even its monologic sections, maintaining as literally as possible its original reading. Such a modus operandi is the most suitable for revealing the potential dialogic quality concealed in the monologic parts of Dyk's story.

Let us begin with an example:

V. Dyk:

On Sunday after the solemn mass it was lively and tumultuous in the pub "At the Thirsty Man."

The pub "At the Thirsty Man" was the most famous and most popular of what the Hanseatic Town of Hamelin had to offer. One couldn't drink better wine anywhere else for miles around, and the cook at the tavern, the black Liza, could measure up to any other cook. Neither did the heads of the community spurn the entrance to the vaulted hall of the pub; they had their own table carefully guarded against intruders. They were the first to taste the newly arrived barrels; they uttered the important and decisive word in matters of cuisine and public opinion.

Business deals were made in the pub "At the Thirsty Man" because it was only here that the cautious and prudent citizens of the Town of Hamelin warmed up. Marriages were contracted here because it was only here that the cautious and prudent citizens of the Town of Hamelin began to think about something which could resemble love, perhaps in the same way that a sparrow resembles an eagle. If sadness afflicted a citizen of the Town of Hamelin, he went to drink at Konrad Röger's (this was the name of the stocky proprietor, a good fellow who didn't shun the treasures of his own cellar!). But if something joyful happened, one also drank at Konrad Röger's.

No one else knew how to share joy so exuberantly; christenings were celebrated, and it seemed that the baptism was taking place in Röger's family. Name-days were celebrated, and it appeared that Röger himself was celebrating.

E. F. Burian:

First guest: And it is most lively and tumultuous at "The Thirsty Man" on Sunday after the solemn mass, stranger.

Second guest: The pub "At the Thirsty Man" was always the most famous and most popular of what the Town of Hamelin had to offer.

Stranger (indifferently): Hm . . .

First guest: You can't drink better wine anywhere else for miles around. . . .

Second guest: And the cook, the black Liza, can measure up to any other cook.

Röger (serves them another glass of wine).

First guest: It's true, friend . . . that neither do the heads of the community spurn the entrance to your pub. . . .

Röger (majestically): Over there—they have their own table carefully guarded against intruders. And they taste the newly arrived barrels. . . . They utter the important and decisive word in matters of cuisine and public opinion. . . . Over there—at their table. . . . (He hurries off.)

Second guest: Business deals are made at "The Thirsty Man."

First guest: . . . because it is only here that the cautious and prudent citizens of Hamelin warm up. . . .

Second guest: Marriages are contracted here!

Stranger: Even!

First guest: . . . because it is only here that the cautious and prudent citizens of the Town of Hamelin begin to think of something which could resemble love, perhaps in the same way that a sparrow resembles an eagle. . . . (He starts laughing and the others after him.)

Second guest: Yes . . . that's the way it is at "The Thirsty Man," stranger. . . . You must know all of this if you come to Hamelin.

First guest: If sadness afflicts a citizen of the Town of Hamelin, he goes to drink at Konrad Röger's.

Stranger: Röger is the name of that stocky proprietor?

First guest: Oh, he's a good fellow! He never shuns the treasures of his own cellar.

Second guest: But if something joyful happens, one also drinks at Konrad Röger's.

First guest: No one else knows how to share joy so exuberantly!

Second guest: No one else knows how to celebrate christenings in such a way.

First guest: Many times it has seemed that the baptism has been taking place in Röger's family.

Second guest: Name-days have been celebrated, and it has appeared that Röger himself was celebrating.

Here the monologue has been transformed into dialogue almost without a change in its wording. Moreover, it is not a monologue dramatic in itself but rather a calm narrative monologue. The narrator of the monologue was the poet himself; the participants of the dialogue are the characters derived from the realization of the material situation which the monologue only narrated. These characters are the guests of the pub "At the Thirsty Man," but they are not provided in the text of the monologue itself. The monologue has, therefore, actually generated its dialogization from itself, from its structure, not from its theme. How did this happen? First, there was Dyk's predilection for using main clauses, coordinate with one another. The joining of these clauses into compound sentences is usually achieved copulatively in Dyk, even though their real semantic relation is other than copulative ("christenings were celebrated, and it seemed" instead of "if christenings were celebrated, it seemed" or "whenever christenings were celebrated, it seemed"). Thus even in its original state the monologue is divided into independent semantic segments, each of which can to a considerable extent stand alone regardless of the fact that the polyfunctionality of the copulative connection renders their syntactic and hence also their semantic interrelation potentially ambiguous. The possibility of semantic reversals at the boundaries of the replies is indicated in this way, even though in this passage of dialogue the replies follow one another calmly without striking semantic shifts.

Another circumstance which accommodated a future dialogization of the original monologue is the multitude of words and

phrases overtly or at least implicitly evaluative. Such are, for example, the superlative "the most famous and the most popular,"
the conjunction "neither" in a comparative meaning ("neither did
the heads of the community spurn"), words that in their very
meaning contain an evaluative nuance such as "important and
decisive," "cautious and prudent," and finally the evaluative
simile "which could resemble love, perhaps in the same way that a
sparrow resembles an eagle." With few exceptions the evaluations
in the text are uniformly positive, and they thus seemingly lack
the contradictoriness desirable for dialogue. This contradictoriness
is, however, rendered possible by the fact that some of these
evaluations are obviously intended to be ironic ("the cautious
and prudent citizens"), while others at least admit an ironic interpretation. These two circumstances—the predominantly copulative
character of the syntactic connections and the multitude of partly
positive, partly ironic evaluations—have made it possible for the
dramaturgist to loosen the continuous structure of the monologue
with a single pull and turn it into a series of dialogic replies. Hence
the dialogic quality was already potentially present in the monologic text, which only substantiates our thesis of the preceding
section. What is important here is that the means by which this
dialogic quality was provided are *linguistic* in nature and that thus
the very linguistic aspect of the text appears to be oscillating between monologue and dialogue.

The dialogic nature of the passage cited manifested itself even
more distinctly in the stage presentation than in the written
dialogue, for the director had at his disposal the differences of
phonic properties: intonation, tone of voice, expiration, and
tempo. And it was precisely Burian the director who greatly exploited these properties. This is even evident from the script of *The
Pied Piper of Hamelin,* which contains a conspicuously large
number of stage directions requiring, either directly or indirectly,
the actor to change his voice with respect to one of these phonic
properties. The brief first scene (corresponding to the first chapter
of Dyk's text), for example, has such a stage direction with almost
every reply, sometimes even several in the course of a single reply.
We shall cite them in order to make apparent, at least from their
wording, the extent of the scale, which is, of course, far richer in
vocal reality: *Agnes* with light laughter. with laughter, a tone of
laughter, urgently in a feminine manner, light laughter, sighs

enraptured, barely breathing, very seriously, whispers, laughs in a caressingly childish manner, after awhile sighs quietly, very deeply; *Pied Piper* ardently, with passion, quietly, darkly, but vehemently. Even nuances of this kind are already contained in the original monologue, although they are unwritten. They are provided by the content of the sentences, by the meaning of the words, by their emotional coloration, by the sentence structure.[14] And thus sound changes also constitute a component of the latent dialogic nature of Dyk's monologue.

The "dialogic nature" of an utterance does not, therefore, begin only by its division into individual replies. We can even find—again in Burian's dramatization of "The Pied Piper of Hamelin"—evidence which directly proves the secondariness of this division in the dialogue itself. Dyk's text, in this case dialogic, reads:

> "Yes," laughed the woman in the doorway. "Quite a rat appeared at Katherine's wedding. The groom was white as a sheet, and Katherine fell into a swoon. People can't stand anything as little as what spoils their appetite; then they decide to call a rat-catcher."
>
> "Are you preparing a wedding or a christening?" asked the Pied Piper suddenly, without transition.

Burian takes over this dialogue word for word but shifts the boundary between the replies:

> *Agnes* (with laughter): Quite a rat appeared at Katherine's wedding. The groom was as white as a sheet, and Katherine fell into a swoon.
>
> *Pied Piper*: People can't stand anything as little as what spoils their appetite. Are you preparing a wedding or a christening?

One of the two sentences which Agnes utters in Dyk's text has been allotted to the Pied Piper in Burian's play. Hence a dialogic

14. Burian the director, as a matter of fact, often takes expressive intonational motifs from poetic texts and then creates—independently of the original texts—from them a lexicon of sound signs for certain dramatic situations. Here is some anecdotal evidence overheard at a rehearsal. An actress is supposed to utter the words "Pied Piper!", the tone of which Dyk's text describes in the following way: "'Pied Piper,' whispered Agnes appeasingly and beseechingly." Burian pronounces the words himself and adds: "This is how [they] must be said; Šrámek has discovered this intonation once and for all for the Czech theater (thus a poet in a written text)."

reversal which struck the dramaturgist as a more desirable boundary between the two utterances than the boundary chosen by the poet occurred *within* the first of the original utterances. But this has in no way suppressed the semantic reversal between the sentence "People can't stand anything as little . . ." and the following question "Are you preparing a wedding . . ."—although the dramaturgist has shifted it into the reply; rather it has emphasized this reversal, for in a live presentation it will necessarily manifest itself by a sudden change in tone of the Pied Piper's voice.

What follows from this case for us? The fact that the "dialogic quality" of the dialogic speech itself is not concentrated only at the boundaries between the replies, but, just as in a monologue, it uniformly saturates the entire speech. In order to verify this assertion even more distinctly, we shall provide one last example from *The Pied Piper of Hamelin.* This time the dramaturgic adaptation alone will suffice; the poet's text will not be needed. This is a scene between Agnes and the Pied Piper; the setting is Agnes's room; the time is the morning after a night of love. The Pied Piper paces back and forth across the stage restlessly, while Agnes sits on the bed:

> *Agnes* (quietly after a moment of anxious observation): How handsome he is in his anger! His eyes are burning with alarming fire. All of his movements have become beautiful. As if he were growing. . . . (She huddles fearfully in the corner of the bed.) Grow, Pied Piper, beautiful Agnes is waiting. . . . I'm afraid, Pied Piper, of your unknown power. I don't understand it very well, but from time to time I yield to it. I'm afraid, and I love my fear. I also love you, Pied Piper. . . . (She rushes to him and embraces him. Beseechingly:) Pied Piper . . . .

What we read here is, to be sure, a longer continuous utterance; nevertheless, it has been inserted into a dialogue and addressed to a partner. Hence it is a dialogic utterance. In three places we read stage directions which prescribe a change in gestures and facial expressions as well, of course, as a change in voice. There will probably be even more vocal changes in a performance. But since these changes are signals of semantic reversals, which are also obvious in this case from the changes in the emotional coloration of the text (admiration, fear, love), their presence proves that even the inner structure of the utterance quoted is in constant motion. The more "dialogic" the dialogue is, the more densely it is saturated with semantic reversals regardless of the boundaries of the replies. This thesis concerning dialogue as a special kind of semantic structure oriented toward a maximum of semantic reversals has followed from our thesis about the potential dialogic nature of every utterance. In this light the breaking up of the dialogue into replies appears as a secondary sign.[15] Even from this aspect, therefore, functional linguistics was right in introducing the term *dialogic speech,* meaning a special kind of linguistic (and thus, of course, semantic) structure to complement the term *dialogue,* meaning a certain external form of an utterance. We must add only the term *dialogic quality,* designating a potential tendency toward the alternation of two or more semantic contextures, a tendency which is manifested not only in dialogue but also in monologue.

We must now turn the problem around in the sense that we shall pose the question of the *monologic quality* in dialogue. The presence of the monologic element in dialogue is most evident when monologue (a speech delivered without the interventions of the second participant of the talk, though he is present, hence not a "dramatic" monologue) is inserted into dialogue. Such is the old man Peter's narration in Stroupežnický's *Naši furianti* about how he acquired his memorable thalers. In such cases, however, it concerns the encounter of two clear-cut linguistic forms. We are concerned rather with the *monologic tendency* penetrating dialogue without violating its specific character.

We can observe this tendency in almost every discourse. Let us only recall the well-known fact that as a rule one of the speakers

15. On the basis of the tendency of dialogue toward maximal and continuous semantic variability one may explain the undying adherence of drama to verse, an adherence that has even been able to withstand the crushing blows of Realism and Naturalism. At first glance it might seem that precisely drama, which anticipates a performance in a material milieu through the assistance of real people-actors, has the least reasons for maintaining a literary convention as remote from real speech as is poetic rhythm. But instead drama has preserved the possibility of a verse presentation right up to the present, whereas the epic has largely abandoned it. The explanation for this is to be found in the fact that a line of verse is not only a rhythmic but also a semantic unit and by means of this property increases the possibility for semantic reversals which are so desirable for dialogue. Every verse boundary in a versified dialogue is a potential location of a semantic reversal. The text itself in a given case can exploit or disregard this possibility. Thus arises a certain syncopal relation between the rhythm and semantic structure of a text, and this makes possible an unusual wealth of nuances.

makes an effort to dominate the talk: ". . . ordinarily the influence exerted by one of the speakers over the other or others is
predominant and reduces that of the latter to almost nothing."[16]
Plato's dialogues are a good example of this. The predominance
of one speaker over the others happens for various reasons: because he is better informed, because of his intellectual or social
superiority, because of his seniority. But the one who gains this
predominance always embodies the tendency toward the monologization of dialogue, and this tendency also acquires linguistic
expression (in the sentence structure, in the choice of words, etc.).
It also, of course, affects the semantic structure of the predominant utterance which begins to exhibit a tendency toward an
uninterrupted logical continuity without semantic reversals. There
are still other cases of the monologization of dialogue. It occurs,
for example, in a peaceful chat between participants close and
equal to one another by virtue of the fact that one of the speakers
forgets his partner and speaks "to himself" by indulging in recollection or by becoming absorbed in himself. A greater number of
participants in a talk almost necessarily causes monologization, for
the division of roles in the talk can hardly be equal. In such cases,
as a rule, one of the participants automatically becomes the main
speaker, the others are almost reduced to passive listeners. Sometimes it also happens that a chain of monologues arises instead of
a dialogue: the individual speakers take the floor in succession for
uninterrupted utterances. This mode of "talk through monologue"
is, as is well known, a favorite and very old compositional scheme
of short story cycles.

A special kind of monologization occurs when the consensus of
the interlocutors reaches such a degree that the multiplicity of
contextures necessary for a dialogue completely vanishes. In such
a case the dialogue as a whole turns into a monologue uttered
alternately. A fragment of a dialogue from Maeterlinck's drama
Intérieur can serve as an example. The situation in this scene is
that two people, an old man and a stranger, while standing out-
doors, observe a family in a room through a window. The talk goes
as follows:

> *The Stranger*: See, they are smiling in the silence of the
> room. . . .

16. Tarde, *L'Opinion et la foule*, p. 146.

The Old Man: They are not at all anxious—they did not expect her this evening.

The Stranger: They sit motionless and smiling. But see, the father puts his finger to his lips. . . .

The Old Man: He points to the child asleep on its mother's breast. . . .

The Stranger: She dares not raise her head for fear of disturbing it. . . .

The Old Man: They are not sewing anymore. There is a dead silence. . . .[17]

The degree and the nuance of monologic quality in a dialogue can thus be extremely varied, and only an analysis of a number of concrete cases could show the significance of the monologic quality for a dialogue in its entire import and scope. A detailed differentiation of monologic from dialogic speech must, however, precede such an analysis. These two tasks exceed the limits of our essay, the purpose of which is to present the epistemological premises of such studies. Let us cite the poet Dujardin's words, intended, of course, only with respect to dramatic dialogue but essentially valid for dialogue in general, as a preliminary characterization of the variety of the possible combinations of dialogue with monologue:

> If so many poets have been attracted by the dramatic form, it is not because this form offers them the rather crude (and generally dearly paid) delight of embodying their conceptions in an atmosphere of painted cardboard but because it enables them precisely to let the voices that they hear in the depths of their hearts speak. Such is, in fact, the interest not only of those rather rare monologues which we encounter in the theater but also of sections of dialogue in which a character speaks as if he were speaking to himself, whether in a reply that seems to be but actually is not addressed to his interlocutor, whether in a sentence uttered in the middle of the discourse or in a simple syntactic member where the cry of the subconscious rises like a puff of smoke, and which are nothing but fragments of concealed monologues. In this sense, the true

17. M. Maeterlinck, "Interior," in *Fifteen International One-Act Plays*, ed. J. and M. Gassner (New York, 1969), p. 181.

dramatic dialogue is a continual combination of concealed
monologues expressing the character's soul and dialogues in
the proper sense of the word. . . . [p. 35][18]

We have reached the end of our deliberations about monologue
and dialogue. We have attempted to prove the thesis that the
monologic and dialogic qualities comprise the basic polarity of
linguistic activity, a polarity which reaches a temporary and always renewed equilibrium in *every* utterance, whether formally
monologic or dialogic. It was not, however, our intention to
answer the question of monologue and dialogue by means of this
assertion. It was simply a matter of posing it.

ON STAGE DIALOGUE

E. F. Burian is right in saying that the Wagnerian conception
of theater as a synthesis of several arts is reviving again in the contemporary theater.[19] The difference between the Wagnerian conception and the present state or, better, the present orientation of
the theater, is, of course, likewise evident. Modern art has revealed
the positive aesthetic effect of the internal contradictions among
the components of the work of art too distinctly for us to be able
to conceive the interplay of the individual elements of a drama as a
mere complementing of one another. The modern stage work is
an extremely complex structure (more complex than any other
artistic structure) which eagerly absorbs everything that the contemporary development of technology offers and that other arts
provide, but it does so as a rule in order to exploit this material
as a contrastive factor. The modern stage work takes hold of the
film in order to juxtapose corporal reality and an immaterial picture, of the megaphone in order to confront natural sound with
reproduced sound, of the reflector in order to sever the continuity
of three-dimensional space with its sword of light, of the statue in
order to heighten the antithesis of a fleeting and petrified gesture.
All of this renders the artistic structure of the contemporary stage
work a protean process which consists in a constant regrouping of
components, in an agitated replacing of the dominant one, in an

---

18. We must, of course, add, as has been said above, that the hidden monologic
quality is not always an "expression of the soul" but often the result of the external
circumstances of the talk.
     19. "Divadelní synthesa" [A theatrical synthesis], *Život* 15, nos. 3–4.

obliteration of the boundaries between the drama and kindred forms (the revue, the dance, acrobatics, etc.). This situation is, of course, more interesting for the theory of theater than ever before, but it is also consequently more difficult, for the old certainties have vanished, and so far there are no new ones. Today it is even difficult to find the very point of the easiest access into the labyrinth of the theatrical structure. Whenever we attempt to declare some component of the drama as basic and indispensable, a dramatic expert, a historian of the theater, or an ethnographer can always point his finger at some dramatic form lacking this element. There are nevertheless certain components which are more characteristic of the theater than others and to which therefore falls the role of the unifying cement in a stage work. One of the most basic is dialogue; we devote the following remarks to its function in theater.

First, what is dialogue? From the linguistic viewpoint it is one of the two basic patterns of speech, the opposite of monologue. By monologue we do not, of course, mean dramatic monologue but an utterance that—though addressed to a listener—is in its continuity largely freed from a consideration for his immediate reaction and from a close bond with the actual temporal and spatial situation in which the participants of the utterance find themselves. Monologue can either express the speaker's subjective mental state (in literature, the lyric) or narrate events severed from the actual situation by a temporal distance (in literature, the narrative). On the other hand, dialogue is closely bound to the "here" and "now" valid for the participants of the talk, and the speaker takes into account the listener's spontaneous reaction. As a result, by a sleight of hand the listener becomes the speaker, and the function of the carrier of the utterance constantly jumps from participant to participant.

This is, of course, valid as well for stage dialogue, which has yet another factor: the audience. This means that to all the direct participants of the dialogue is added another participant, silent but important, for everything which is said in a dramatic dialogue is oriented toward him, toward affecting his consciousness. We can even speak about well or poorly played theater, about a comedy, in normal nondramatic talk, if it happens that the interest of all the participants but one is concentrated—on the basis of a secret agreement—on influencing the consciousness of precisely this one so that every word of the talk has a different meaning for the conspiring participants than for him. Stage dialogue is hence semantically much more complex than normal talk. If character *A* utters a certain sentence, the meaning of this sentence is determined for him (as, after all, in every talk) by a consideration for character *B*. But it is not at all certain that character *B* will understand this meaning as character *A* has wished. With respect to this the audience can be subjected to the same uncertainty as character *A,* but it is also possible that the audience has been informed of character *B*'s state of mind by some previous talk about which character *A* does not have to be aware so that character *A*'s surprise at his partner's unexpected reaction will no longer be a surprise to the audience. The opposite case can also occur: something about which the audience still does not know will be known to the characters onstage. The audience can share the semantic context that provides the uttered words with sense with only some of the characters, this complicity with the audience can alternately shift from character to character, or finally the audience can understand the semantic orientation of all the characters, even though these characters do not understand one another. Moreover, the entire preceding semantic context of the play, of which not all of the characters by far need be aware, is always in the audience's consciousness. There can also occur cases in which the audience is more extensively informed about the situation onstage than the characters of the drama (e.g., when the audience sees a spy, listening to the talk, about whom the characters onstage are not aware). Finally, everything that is said onstage can collide in the audience's consciousness or subconsciousness with its system of values, its attitude toward reality. All of these circumstances make possible an immensely complex interplay of meanings, and it is precisely this complex interplay taking place on several horizons that constitutes the essence of the dramatic dialogue.

Since dialogue is incorporated into the whole of the dramatic work, it need not, of course, be free to the extent that it can develop all its infinitely changeable possibilities, for it can be limited in its fluidity by some other component. Thus, for example, the realistic theater, whose conception of dialogue has still not been completely abandoned even today, bound dialogue closely to the scheme of the play, that is, to the interrelations of the dramatis personae as constant characters. Here dialogue serves to make the characters' interrelations more and more distinctly pronounced during the course of the play and hence to define each character through his relationship to the others more and more clearly. The unexpectedness of semantic reversals is therefore permitted only as far as it does not interfere with this main purpose but rather serves it. Another possible restriction on dialogue can be found, for example, in medieval plays where dialogue serves to illustrate the plot.

To these two restrictions we must oppose the tendency of contemporary stage practice toward dialogue freed of all bonds, dialogue as a continuous play of semantic reversals. Dialogue freed from restrictions becomes stage poetry: at any moment just as final as it is continuous. Again and again, without an obligation—though, of course, not without a latent relationship—to what has preceded, the word seeks a relation to the characters, the actual situation and the audience's consciousness and subconsciousness. There is no semantic context which dialogue conceived in this way cannot reach from any direction, but neither is there any to which it has to adhere. The Aristotelian law of regularly increasing tension cannot be valid for free stage dialogue; on the other hand, it is not impossible that precisely this form is capable of renewing the feeling of the tragic emanating from the classical tragedies, which indeed terminate in a quarrel forcibly concluded but actually unresolved and potentially continuing ad infinitum.

4

Intonation as the Basic Factor of Poetic Rhythm

Until recently the concept of isochronism (the same or at least exactly commensurate duration of rhythmic segments) has been accepted, either expressly or tacitly, as the starting point in the analysis of poetic rhythm. Therefore, most theories of verse examine mainly the smallest rhythmic segments, the durations of which are easily comparable to one another and are even accessible to experimental verification. We do not want to deny the fact that a tendency toward isochronism is intrinsic to some modes of the rhythmic organization of verbal expression. Besides quantitative prosody (with which we shall not be concerned in this study) there are verse forms in which this tendency stands out quite distinctly. For example, in folk poetry there are nursery rhymes and count-out rhymes which must be scanned in recitation. On the other hand, however, there are verse types in which isochronism, at least objectively ascertainable isochronism (since "subjective" isochronism characterizes only the perceiving subject's attitude rather than the perceived object), plays almost no role at all. Thus if a general theory of verse is based on isochronism, the scope of our study is dangerously narrowed, and our perspective is distorted from the very beginning.

It is, of course, true that a rhythmic series elapses in time. Our attention is not, however, inevitably attracted to the measurability of the temporal flow but rather is drawn first to the configuration (*Gestalt*) of its sequence. Benussi says about this:

> As soon as a rhythmic phenomenon comes into play, it is no longer primarily the perceivable duration (i.e., an object of extensive nature, whose relatively most conspicuous feature consists in its magnitude) which obtrudes itself upon our attention, but something entirely qualitative which remains in close relationship to the given, quantitatively determined foundation

This essay is translated from "Intonation comme facteur du rythme poétique," *Archives néerlandaises de Phonétique expérimentale* 8-9 (1933). Czech version: "Intonace jako činitel básnického rytmu," *Kapitoly z české poetiky* (Prague, 1941), 1.

(noises following one another at given temporal intervals) yet differs from it as much as a melodic figure differs from the manifold tones that provides its foundation. Just as the melody can divert attention from the tones and the tonal intervals themselves, so the rhythmic *Gestalt* can almost completely suppress the conspicuousness of the time intervals between the vehicles of the *Gestalt*.[1]

Hence we must pose the question of the essence of poetic rhythm in the following way: Which factor can be designated as indispensable and basic for the formation of the verse configuration?[2] Only if we answer the question posed in this way can we grasp the feature common to *all* verse types, at least as far as it concerns the linguistic and prosodic systems from which we have drawn our material. Traditional metrics could lead us to believe that in prosodic systems founded on stress the contour of a verse form is given only by a fixed number of icti, in syllabic systems only by a fixed number of syllables, and hence that there is not a common structural feature which interconnects the internal organization of the line in different prosodic systems. We can, however, find in syllabic systems (e.g., French poetry) as well as in tonic systems (e.g., Czech or German poetry) a certain type of free verse which lacks any kind of internal organization provided by the means of the relevant prosodic systems and which, nevertheless, retains the character of verse.

A Czech example:

Má touha mne vodí jak vzdalující se bubeník
Stromy podobné plynovým plamenům gestikulují jak ramena v
tanci
Připojuješ své kroky k prodavačům preclíků
Líbezná eskadrona[3]
[Nezval, "Procházky," *Praha s prsty deště*]

1. V. Benussi, *Psychologie der Zeitauffassung* (Heidelberg, 1913), p. 420.

2. Permit us to refer to Meillet (*Origines indoeuropéenes des mètres grecs,* Paris, 1923) and several Russian theoreticians (e.g., B. Tomaševskij, *Russkoe stixosloženie* [*Russian versification*], Petrograd, 1923), who developed the notion that verse must be understood principally as a rhythmic unit before it is broken down (theoretically) into secondary rhythmic segments.

3. My desire leads me like a departing drummer
    The trees resembling gas flames gesticulate like shoulders at a dance
    You fall into step with the pretzel vendors
    A pleasing squadron

A German example:

Zu meinem fünfundzwanzigsten Jubiläum als deutscher Dichter
lade ich mir alle Götter.
Auch Timur, den Esel Bileams, sowie den Oberhofmarschall ihrer
                       Majestät der Kaiserin v. Mirbach.
Kurz
sämtliche Notabilitäten.
        [A. Holz, "Drachenmotiv," cited according to the
        International Symposium on Free Verse, Milan, 1909]

A French example:

    Maintenant tu marches dans Paris tout seul parmi la foule
    Des troupeaux d'autobus mugissants près de toi roulent
    L'angoisse de l'amour te serre le gosier
    Comme si tu ne devais jamais plus être aimé
                 [Apollinaire, "Zone," *Alcools*]

Even though all three examples come from three different
prosodic systems (not even the prosodic principle of the Czech and
German line is the same, though both systems are "accentual"),
they have the same principle of rhythmic organization, a very
simple one: their special intonation characterized above all by a
very expressive melodic formula at the end of each line. A
metrical scheme is completely lacking, unless we want to so
designate this special intonation. With its concluding intonational
formula, verse of this type is reminiscent of liturgical recitatives,
such as "Vere dignum et iustum est," the concluding syllables of
which are sung. It is interesting to note that, in reciting his own
verse, Nezval emphasizes the intonational conclusion of each line
by means of an almost pure musical cadence.

Hence if we ask about the most basic vehicles of verse rhythm,
we must turn our attention to intonation. We have just ascertained
that in different prosodic systems there are verse types in which
intonation alone fulfills the task of the rhythmic vehicle. First we
must take note of syntactic intonation, for it is evident that its
scheme does not cease to exist and function even in the verse line;
this follows from the very fact that syntactic intonation is closely
bound to the semantic structure of the sentence. Intonation interests us here, of course, only as a phonological element. This
means that we do not intend to take account of the accidental

nuances of its acoustic realization. We want to deal with intonation only as a component of a poetic text, not as a declamatory quality. We must also call attention to the fact that what we shall say about intonation in the following paragraphs applies only to languages in which intonation is limited to the phonology of the sentence and does not participate in the phonology of the word (i.e., languages without "melodic" stress). We shall borrow the characteristics of syntactic intonation from Karcevskij's study "On the Phonology of the Sentence," For our purposes we have compiled a selection of relevant citations:

> The sentence is a realized communicational unit. It lacks a grammatical structure of its own. But it has a particular sound structure which is provided by its intonation. It is precisely intonation which constitutes the sentence. Any word or group of words, any grammatical form, any interjection can, if required by the situation, serve as a communicational unit. Intonation causes the *realization* of these virtual semiotic values, and from this moment we encounter a sentence. . . . Here we are not, however, concerned with the modulations of the voice which express emotions. Likewise we are leaving aside the volitional sentence type. We are interested only in . . . syntactic intonation in its two variations: question : answer. The question and the answer are the two broadest dynamic schemes capable of encompassing the most diverse attitudes and fitting into the most varied situations. . . . Even if intellectualized and impoverished in this way, intonation nevertheless constitutes an integral part of the linguistic mechanism. Even internal speech always has intonation, though only psychological, and only a little attention is necessary to notice that internal speech also has the form of a dialogue: we converse with ourselves, we ask our "interlocutor" questions, and we answer him. In brief, we make sentences. . . . Every intellectual sentence, provided that it is not too short, tends to divide into two parts or syntactic members. Thus arise two phonological peaks separated from each other by a pause, the first surpassing the second in expressiveness as well as in intensity. The [intonational] line rises in the first part and falls in the second. . . . The structure of the sentence . . . is the synthesis of a question and an answer. . . . The division of the sentence

(we are using this term here only to designate the division of the sentence into two parts) has nothing to do with the distinction between a subject and a predicate, nor with any other grammatical opposition in general. Likewise we prefer to avoid such terms as "psychological subject" and "psychological predicate."[4]

According to Karcevskij, therefore, the main properties of syntactic intonation are the following: a division into two parts,[5] the correspondence of the relationship between these parts to the relationship between a question and an answer, the relation between this division of the sentence and the organization of the semantic plane of the sentence.

Now let us take a closer look at the intonation of verse. If, in reading a poem aloud, we devote our attention to the intonation, we shall discover even at first hearing the persistent repetition of a certain intonational scheme, which always returns with every line regardless of the diversity of the syntactic and semantic organization. We do not claim, of course, that the details of this scheme will not change throughout the poem; nevertheless, its total contour remains constantly the same. But if we extract a certain line from a given poetic context and attempt to pronounce it as prose (which we can often do without any difficulty whatsoever), what will be especially affected by this change in orientation is precisely the intonation. First, let us give a French example:

Et que je suis plus pauvre que personne

[Verlaine, *Sagesse* II, 1]

4. S. Karcevskij, "Sur la phonologie de la phrase," *Travaux de Cercle linguistique de Prague* 4 (Prague, 1931): 188–227.

5. Phonetics has also asserted the intonational bipartition of the sentence as an acoustic and articulatory phenomenon. See Jespersen's *Lehrbuch der Phonetik* (Leipzig and Berlin, 1904), where the rising of the beginning of the sentence and the falling of its ending are linked to the physiology of expiration (p. 228). See as well J. Chlumský's *Česká kvantita, melodie a přízvuk* [Czech quantity, melody and stress] (Prague, 1928), where he shows in diagrams that "an affirmative sentence is divided into two parts, of which the first maintains a higher tonal level than the second" (p. xxxiii). Interesting materials on the bipartition of the sentence can be found in L. Martin's *Les symétries du français littéraire* (Paris, 1924). Finally, let us mention Zwirner's lecture at the Second Congress for the Phonetic Sciences (Amsterdam, 1932), illustrated by a graphic record of the speech of an aphasiac who retained only the ability to articulate vowels and consonants connected by an intonational line; nevertheless, the intonation of his "sentences" turned out to be distinctly bipartite.

We can very easily imagine this sentence in a prosaic context, for example, "Vous savez que je n'ai rien et que je suis plus pauvre que personne." The poetic context in which we find it in Verlaine is the following:

> Vous connaissez tout cela, tout cela,
> Et que je suis plus pauvre que personne,
> Vous connaissez tout cela, tout cela.

If we compare the intonation of this sentence read in a prosaic manner with the intonation which it acquires if it is apprehended and read as verse, we shall discover a remarkable difference: the divide between its two intonational segments will be in a different place in verse than in prose. In the prosaic context the intonational split will come after the word *pauvre,* in the verse context after the word *suis.* The explanation is simple. In the verse line *suis* occupies the fourth syllable, after which the caesura of the French *décasyl-labe* has its fixed place. Hence a metrical reason has determined the intonational divide in the verse. But the semantic bisection (which, as we have seen, has its divide in a different place from the rhythmic bisection in the given sentence) cannot be completely suppressed in the verse line, for the semantic structure of the sentence has not changed—at least not substantially—as a result of the fact that the sentence has been conceived as verse. Therefore, we can infer that a syntactic intonational divide is potentially present even in verse, and this is true even if it falls in a different place from the rhythmic intonational divide. Indeed, we shall actually find its traces in the acoustic realization itself. Hence we may say that two virtual intonational schemes occur simultaneously in verse but do not always coincide. One of them is bound to the semantic structure of the sentence, the other to the rhythmic structure of the line. The first of them can be designated as linguistic intonation, the other as rhythmic intonation. Both of these schemes are bipartite. The intonational line which we hear during the recitation of the verse is the resultant of these two scheme-energies, existing and functioning simultaneously. And it is precisely the superimposition of these two schemes and their tension that determines the contour of the rhythmic configuration of the verse.

As a further example we shall cite a German line written by A. Holz ("Weihnachten," *Buch der Zeit*):

> Ihre grossen, blauen Augen leuchten

Just like the preceding line of Verlaine, Holz's line can also be conceived as prose, if we change the original context, which reads as follows:

> In den offenen Mäulerchen ihre Finger
> stehn um den Tisch die kleinen Dinger,
> und um die Wette mit den Kerzen
> puppern vor Freude ihre Herzen.
> Ihre grossen, blauen Augen leuchten,
> indes die unsern sich leichte feuchten.

This context can be transferred into prose—without changing the cited line—as follows: "Die Kinder stehen am Christbaum. Sie sind glücklich; ihre grossen, blauen Augen leuchten." If this sentence is read as prose, it has an intermediate intonational divide after the word *Augen;* if, however, it is conceived as verse, it is split by a divide after the word *grossen.* Even in verse, however, the articulation that we have detected in prose is not completely obliterated.

A Czech example:

> Ze tvé krve zbyl tu | malý pohrobek
>
> [Nezval, *Edison*]

Here we have a trochaic hexameter with a caesura after the sixth syllable, hence after the word *tu.* The context is the following:

> Nevím kde a máš-li jaký náhrobek
> ze tvé krve zbyl tu malý pohrobek
> hled' už slabikuje v Kanadě tvé knihy
> hled' už těší se jak půjde na dostihy[6]

We may, however, pronounce this line by itself as prose, if we put the intermediate intonational divide in a different place:

> Ze tvé krve | zbyl tu malý pohrobek

The disagreement between the rhythmic and semantic bisections of the sentence-line is therefore not only perfectly possible but even very common, as the above examples show. If this disagreement becomes striking, we usually speak about "internal enjamb-

---

6.   I don't know where and whether you have any grave stone
       of your blood is left here a little posthumous child
       see, he's already starting to read your books in Canada
       see, he's already looking forward to going to the horse races

ment" (*rejet a l'hémistiche*). We shall cite several examples of this phenomenon borrowed from Grammont's book *French Verse*[7]:

> Le plus vil artisan eut ses dogmes à soi
> Et chaque chrétien | fut | de différente loi
>   [Boileau, *Satire XII*]

The rhythmic divide (the canonized caesura of the alexandrine) is found in the second of these lines after the word *fut,* the semantic boundary after the word *chrétien.* Their disagreement acquires emphasis by virtue of the fact that the rhythmic divide severs from itself words closely related semantically and syntactically. Another example:

> Comme si de ces fleurs ayant toutes une âme,
> La plus belle se fût | épanouie en femme
>   [V. Hugo, "Le sacre de la femme"]

During an oral reading, the second of these lines manifests very distinct traces of a dual intonational articulation: the rhythmic divide is after the word *fût,* the semantic after the word *épanouie.* The four-syllable word *épanouie* separates them from one another to the extent that they can both assert themselves, counterbalancing one another, in the acoustic realization of the line.

All the lines which we have cited so far have contained disagreements between the dual intonational articulations—the rhythmic and the semantic. Despite their abundance, however, cases of this kind do not represent the only possibility of the relation between the sentence and the line as intonational wholes. Frequently the intonational schemes of the sentence and the rhythm coincide. The question is whether in such cases the virtual duality of the intonational scheme ceases to exist in the line. Were it to disappear, our assertion that precisely the superimposition of a dual intonational scheme determines the basic rhythmic contour of verse would be incorrect. It is not difficult, however, to detect the existence of this duality even in such cases where the two intonational schemes coincide. Here too it is enough to consider lines which can easily be inserted into a prosaic context; on the basis of these we shall see that even with the complete agreement of the verse intonational articulation with the prosaic, verse is intoned

---

7. *Le vers français,* 3rd ed. (Paris, 1923).

differently in a poetic context than in a prosaic one. We shall
begin with an example from book 3 of Hugo's collection
Contemplations:

> Shakespeare songe; loin du Versailles éclatant,
> Des buis taillés, des ifs peignés, où l'on entend
> Gémir la tragédie éplorée et prolixe
> Il contemple la foule avec son regard fixe,
> Et toute la forêt frissonne devant lui.

We are interested in the penultimate line of this passage, which
can be transferred, without doing violence to it, into a prosaic
context, such as the following: "Il arrive; il contemple la foule
avec son regard fixe; puis il s'en va à pas lents." Both in verse and
in prose the intonational divide will occur after the word *foule*,
hence in the same place. During the acoustic realization, however,
the intonation will be different in each of the two cases. In what
this difference will consist is of little importance for us here; we
are interested only in ascertaining its existence.

This proves to us that the virtual duality of the intonational
scheme in verse endures even if the verse intonation coincides
with the syntactic intonation. Otherwise there would be no reason
for the verse realization to differ from the prosaic realization.

An analogous German example:

> So heimlich war es die letzten Wochen,
> Die Häuser nach Mehl und Honig rochen,
> Die Dächer lagen dick verschneit,
> Und fern, noch fern schien die schöne Zeit,
> Man dachte an sie kaum dann und wann.
>   [A. Holz, "Weihnachten," *Buch der Zeit*]

The last line of this fragment can also be conceived and read as
prose, for example, in the context: "Die schöne Zeit war schon
vorbei und man dachte an sie kaum dann und wann." Here, too,
the intermediate divide of the line does not change its place (after
the word *sie*) in the shift into prose, but the realized intonation
will, nevertheless, be different.

We shall find a Czech example in Březina's poems. Since it is
free verse, we will not even have to fabricate a prosaic context. We
need only imagine the given line by itself, extracted from any kind

of context, and the reader will be able to recognize it as prose or verse according to the attitude that he adopts toward it.

Nedočkavé hlasy všech vůní | zmateně vyvalily se z nížin,
Žíznivé klasy prohnuly se s bolestnou rozkoší | pod sesutím
                                                    světla[8]
                                        ["Ranní modlitba"]
            Okna naše ukáží nám barvy | umyté nebeskou bouří[9]
                                        ["Víno silných"]

In both a rhythmic and a non-rhythmic recitation the intonational divide will be in the places indicated by the perpendiculars, but the character of the realized intonation suffices to make apparent to the listener when the reciter conceives the given sentence as verse and when as prose.

Thus the intonation of verse is always carried by a dual, virtual intonational scheme, and therefore it is always the resultant of the tension between two forces, the relation of which is characteristic for a given line, whether they disagree or agree. The intonational tension is also reflected in the state and organization of the other components of verse, and it even intervenes in its semantic structure. In some cases the relation between the intonation and the semantic structure manifests itself very palpably; for example, in French verse with "internal enjambment" (*rejet a l'hémistiche*), of which we spoke above. A word which falls between the intonational divides of the line and the sentence is usually emphasized semantically by this position, is foregrounded.[10] Even if the reciprocal effect of the meaning and the intonation is less striking, however, it never ceases to exist and function. At this point we should mention the very subtle analysis of the semantic import of poetic rhythm presented in Jurij Tynjanov's book *The Problem of Verse Language.*[11] Of course, both syntactic and rhythmic intonation are factors of the semantic structure of a poetic work only insofar as both are phonological, that is, insofar as they are

8.   The impatient voices of all the fragrances poured out of
                the lowlands in confusion,
            The thirsty spikes sagged with painful pleasure under an
                avalanche of light
9.   Our windows will show us colors washed by the heavenly storm
10. See Grammont, *Le vers français,* pp. 43-52.
11. *Problema stixotvornogo jazyka* (Leningrad, 1924).

independent of the accidentalities of a sound realization (a recitation). If in the preceding paragraphs we have, nevertheless,
appealed to the acoustic realization so often, we have employed
it only as a symptom, being aware at the same time that the
duality of the intonational scheme in verse and the tension within
this dual scheme exist independently of empirical sound and are
the concern of the work alone.

We have stated our thesis in its main outlines; however, a detailed proof is still lacking. Against the assertions which we have
made someone might object that there are cases in which one or
even both of the intonational articulations of verse are missing. In
general we could reply that the tension between the two virtual
intonational schemes is not a matter of an isolated line (which,
extracted from its context, can sometimes appear as prose) but of
the entire context so that because of rhythmic inertia the intonational tension can function even in such lines where one of the two
virtual intonational schemes is absent. But in order to be perfectly
clear, we shall explicitly mention all the possible cases of irregulari-
ties.

First of all, there are the types of free verse that we cited at the
beginning of this study. Since they are characterized only by a
concluding formula, one might object that a rhythmic intonational
bipartition is completely absent in them. But this is not so. Here
the rhythmic-intonational articulation is only strongly asymmetrical in the sense that the first segment encompasses an entire,
often very long line except for the syllables bearing the concluding
cadence, and the other is then given by this very cadence. This
articulation, then, enters into relation (and tension) with the
syntactic intonational scheme; if this tension disappeared and if
the syntactic intonation alone asserted itself, the verse would be
conceived and would sound as prose in recitation. Nor is it incon-
clusive that if we read free verse, organized only by intonation,
properly, that is to say precisely as verse, we are compelled to read
the first, longer segment much faster than the concluding cadence.
The reason for this is that we feel the cadence and what precedes
it as values comparable to one another and rhythmically counterbalancing one another; if we read the same verse as prose, the
acceleration of its first part would disappear.

Another seeming contradiction of our thesis consists in verse lines that from the semantic (and syntactic) standpoint are not simultaneously sentences but either only parts of sentences or, on the contrary, complex syntactic units. Such lines can provoke the objection that verse can do without the intonational bipartition of the sentence. We must, however, take into account that as a rule such lines have, nevertheless, a certain semantic or even syntactic boundary (between coordinate syntactic members) which suffices to take over the function of the syntactic intonational division. As regards lines containing two sentences, it is natural that the boundary line between these sentences takes over the role of the syntactic intonational divide.

We must also mention lines which are too short to contain any bipartition. Often a single word becomes a line. Thus, for example:

> Pod mými okny člověk pad.
> Stařík—
> Tváře vyhloubeny,
> raneček v týle[12]
> [Theer, "Milosrdenství," *Všemu na vzdory*]

Here a special intonation compensates for the absent bipartition in recitation: the word *stařík* can be pronounced with three different intonational cadences according to whether we conceive it as a lexical unit, as a one-member sentence, or as a line. If an excessively short line is a component of a poem written in metrically regular verse, it will frequently be conceived in comparison with adjacent lines as an incomplete rhythmic unit, as a mere fragment of verse, which is completed by a pause, and also, occasionally, as a mere reduplication of the concluding cadence of the preceding line. This is usually the case in strophic forms, especially, for example:

> Dříve nežli rozkvěte,
>   z poupěte
> na tebe se z dálky dívá,

12.   A man collapsed under my windows
             An old man—
             Hollowed cheeks,
             A little bundle on his nape

> krade tobě polibky,
>   z kolíbky
> tvého děcka tiše kývá[13]
>   [Vrchlický, "Smrt," *Kytky aster*]

Moreover, there is also the problem of tripartite lines, a problem most obvious in French metrics. We have in mind the tripartite alexandrines (*alexandrins tripartis, trimètres*). It is, of course, true that their tripartition can sometimes be only illusory; nevertheless, the existence of tripartite alexandrines is undeniable, and the role which they play in the development of French verse, especially Romantic verse, is not insignificant.[14] An extreme case of tripartition is the kind of *trimètres,* all three parts of which are parallel from the syntactic standpoint:

> Gardiens des monts, gardiens des lois, gardiens des villes
> Malheur à vous! Malheur à moi! Malheur à tous
> L'homme est brumeux, le monde est noir, le ciel est sombre
>   [V. Hugo, cited after Le Dû, *Les rythmes dans
>   l'alexandrin de V. Hugo,* Paris, 1929]

But parallelism is not necessary for the origin of even a quite distinct tripartition:

> Où je l'ai vu | ouvrir son aile | et s'envoler
>   [V. Hugo, cited after Grammont, *Le vers français*]

Although the existence of *trimètres* is well attested, they are, nevertheless, not an autonomous rhythmic form but are always felt as a deformation of lines which are rhythmically and intonationally bipartite. It is characteristic that some critics, like P. Stapfer, C. Tisseur, and E. Rigal have claimed "that a stress, though sometimes very weak, is always perceptible after the sixth syllable of Hugo's *trimètre.*"[15] Whether this opinion is correct or not, it is evidence of the spontaneous evaluation of the *trimètre* as a

13.   Before it blossoms,
                   from the bud
           it looks at you from a distance,
           it steals kisses from you,
                   from the cradle
           of your child it nods quietly
14. Cf. Grammont, *Le vers français,* pp. 59–77.
15. Le Dû, *Les rythmes,* p. 162.

deformation of bipartite verse. *Trimètres* must be interpreted only as cases of a very strong tension between the syntactic and the rhythmic intonation. Lines which are halfway between the *trimètre* and the bipartite alexandrine with internal enjambment are proof of this. The tension between the syntactic and rhythmic intonational bipartitions is still quite palpable here:

> Cet andalou | de race arabe | et mal dompté
> [Heredia, cited according to Grammont]

In this line the syntactic intonational divide is after the word *andalou;* the rhythmic divide, the traditional caesure of the French alexandrine, would then fall after the word *race.* This place, however, is hermetically sealed by the close semantic and syntactic connection of an adjective with a substantive (*race arabe*). The rhythmic divide is thus pushed beyond the two next syllables and falls after the word *arabe.* In recitation this divide actually occurs here, and it thus results in a uniform tripartite line (4–4–4 instead of 6–6).

Thus the existence of tripartite lines does not conflict with our thesis about the basic intonational bipartition of the verse contour. It is not, after all, difficult to offer direct evidence of the fact that a *true* tripartition, which is not merely a masked bipartition, obstructs the verse rhythm. Here we must, of course, resort to free verse where a fixed metrical form does not compensate for tripartition—that is, free verse can be semantically and syntactically tripartite. Let us take as an example Péguy's line

> Tout était consommé. Ne parlons plus de cela. Cela me
> > fait mal.
> ["La nuit," cited according to *Morceaux choisis*
> > *de Ch. Péguy,* Paris]

If we want to read these three sentences as a single line, it is absolutely necessary that in recitation we emphasize the second of the concluding syntactic cadences, which is borne by the word *cela,* more distinctly than the first, which is given by the word *consommé;* the third cadence, carried by the word *mal,* will be the most expressive of all. In other words: the second cadence acquires the role of the intermediate intonational divide of the line, and the third then becomes the conclusion of the whole line. If we pronounced all three cadences with equal expressiveness, the verse would turn into prose; only the intonational bipartition of recitation can preserve the verse rhythm.

Březina's Czech verse will also lead us to a similar conclusion:

Vření jeho odívá zvukem písně hlasu nesmrtelného,
| jenž hovoří v duších.[16]
["Polední zrání"]

Although we are dealing with a very free verse (because it is long and is rhythmized only by intonation), its rhythm will be preserved in recitation as long as the intonational bipartition with the divide after the word *nesmrtelného* is preserved. If, however, we introduce—by means of regular word order—tripartition (a main clause in two segments, a subordinate clause as a third segment), the verse will turn into prose, albeit rhythmic prose:

Vření jeho odívá zvukem | písně nesmrtelného hlasu,
| jenž hovoří v duších.

The rhythmic effect will then be identical with the impression which rhythmic prose creates, such as the following:

Znám ještě mlčelivé roviny | dalekých rozloh | v zapadlých vévodstvích své duše, | neznámé, neohraničené | a zašeřelé od věků | v podmračné, večerní šero agonie . . . .[17]
[K. Hlaváček, "Rêverie," *Pozdě k ránu*]

It therefore seems possible to define the difference between the rhythm of verse and that of prose in that there is no superimposition of a dual intonational scheme in rhythmic prose but only a simple sequence of intonational segments, similar to one another, provided by the syntactic intonation, and following one another without any tension whatsoever.

We must still say something about the hierarchy of the other rhythmic values of verse with regard to intonation. We have expressed the opinion that all these values are secondary with respect to intonation, but by no means do we want to claim that they will be less important nor that intonation will necessarily be

16.   His turmoil arrays in sound the songs of an immortal voice,
                     which speaks in souls.
17.   I still know the silent plains of distant spheres in the remote
       duchies of my soul, unknown, unbounded and darkened
       by the ages into the gloomy evening twilight of agony. . . .

the immediate vehicle of rhythm in every given type of verse. We claim only two things: (a) that intonational bipartition suffices as the sole vehicle of rhythm in those kinds of verse with a very weak rhythmic organization; (b) that even in verse with a distinct rhythmic organization, intonational bipartition provides the basic framework of this organization.

If intonation alone frequently bears the burden of rhythmic organization in very free verse, we may say that in verse with a traditional and regular metrical scheme it simply plays the role of a factor of rhythmic variation because other factors fully suffice to mark the rhythmic contour of the line. It is enough, however, that if a loosening of poetic rhythm occurs after a period of very regular and rule-bound versification, intonation will reclaim its full rights.

If we are to realize fully the role which intonation can acquire in the internal organization of verse, we must devote attention to intonational bipartition as a means of relating the two halves of the line. We shall begin with a citation from Karcevskij's aforementioned study. In the section treating the bisection of the sentence by intonation, Karcevskij says:

> The second part of the sentence exists only as a complement of the first. It cannot however be said that it is "subordinate" to the first: our examples show clearly enough that this notion is not appropriate here. It would be more precise to consider the second part as the function [in the mathematical sense, J.M.] of the first. In effect it is the first part which to a certain extent determines the character of the intonation of the second, thus, for example, the heightening or the weakening of the tension of the first part will entail modifications in the intonation of the second. [p. 207]

So it happens in the verse line as well: here too the second segment is evaluated with respect to the first. Whether the first segment is long and richly articulated and the second is short and rhythmically simple or whether the opposite is true, the first segment will always be the measure of the second. In recitation the lengthiness of the first segment will compel us to retard delivery of the short second segment, or, on the contrary, the shortness of the first will cause us to accelerate delivery of the second, especially if it is much longer than the first. Only if the two segments are equal will the supremacy of the first not be felt. We can observe the same thing from a semantic standpoint. If the second segment is considerably shorter than the first, the semantic values which it contains will be emphasized because fewer semantic units will be found in the relatively equal semantic range of this segment.

The internal organization of each of the two segments of the line—which is provided by the number and grouping of the syllables in syllabic verse, by the number of icti in purely accentual verse, and by the number of feet in syllabo-tonic verse—serves as a gauge in their confrontation with one another. Common opinion attributes to the metrical factors discussed here the role of serving as a basis of isochronism, which is uniformly spread over the entire line; however, this opinion is valid only insofar as it concerns a line not only metrically homogeneous in its entire course but also symmetrical with respect to intonational bipartition. But as soon as we look at a line, the intonational segments of which are unequal, we shall discover in recitation that its isochronism is deformed by this intonational asymmetry: syllables, icti, feet will follow one another more quickly in the part which is longer, more slowly in that which is shorter. Let us take as an example two lines from Neruda's "Romance helgolandská" (*Ballady a romance*), both written in iambic pentameter:

> Bouř žene koráb | u divokém běhu
> A koráb k světlu žene se | a v trysku[18]

As in the preceding examples, we have indicated the intonational divides by perpendiculars. In the first of the two lines the first segment includes two feet, the second three; hence the line is divided equally as far as is possible with an odd number of feet; in the second line the first segment contains four feet, the second only one. In recitation it will not be difficult to detect by ear alone that the tempo of delivery in the first segment of the second line is faster than the tempo of delivery in the first segment of the first line as well as the tempo of the second segment of the second line. The isochronism of the feet is thus deformed by the inequality of the intonational segments.

Let us summarize. The role of intonation in the rhythmic

---

18.   The storm drives the ship in a wild course
             And the ship rushes toward the light and at a gallop

organization of verse consists in the superimposition and tension of a dual intonational scheme, syntactic and rhythmic (verse). Each of these two schemes is bipartite, articulated by an intermediate divide; these divides can coincide or disagree with one another, but both are always virtually present, and it is precisely their interrelation that causes the tension between the syntactic and rhythmic intonation and characterizes the verse as a unified configuration. This tension, constantly felt, is the basic characteristic which distinguishes the rhythm of verse from the rhythm of prose. The dual intonational bipartition of the line is the foundation of its rhythmic organization; other means of this organization are secondary with respect to intonation in the sense that intonation alone is capable of characterizing the line as the highest form of linguistic rhythm; other rhythmic factors, if present, manifest themselves only against the background provided by the intonational bipartition.

Finally, we must add that our intention in this study has not been to discuss the question of verse intonation in its entire scope. We have attempted to examine it only in relation to the internal organization of the line as the basic rhythmic unit and have left aside everything which exceeds the limits of this unit; this means that enjambment and the intonational structure of the stanza have remained beyond the scope of our study.

5

A Note on the Czech Translation of Šklovskij's *Theory of Prose*

Šklovskij's treatise comes to us after a considerable delay, and it thus enters quite a different scholarly, literary, and general cultural context from that in which it originated.[1] Moreover, the difference between the Russian and Czech milieux is of consequence. Hence approaching this work is difficult, even for those who wish to deal honestly with it, out of a sense that it cannot be overlooked regardless of whether it is evaluated positively or negatively. There are, however, others whose childish lack of judgment and humility lead them to dismiss Šklovskij and "formalism" without hesitation by citing arguments from textbooks, but it is better to disregard them. If we are to be fair to Šklovskij's book and if we wish to reap the benefit which this work is still capable of rendering today, we must be aware of its two identities: that which it had for the author's audience and the state of scholarship at that time and that which it is acquiring today in our country as the result of a changed environment and a different developmental context of scholarship.

Therefore let us first try to outline the work's original appearance. *The Theory of Prose* was published in 1925, but all of its studies originated and were printed long before this date, beginning as early as 1917. The scene of its origin was thus Russia during the period of the Revolution and its immediate aftermath, when that country was full of unrest and ferment. Movements whose common denominator was a disregard for the significance of the artistic aspect of the work had had almost unlimited sway in European literary studies up to that moment. Some of these movements conceived the history of literature as a mere reflection of the history of ideology or culture in the broad sense of this

This essay is translated from "K českému překladu Šklovského Teorie prózy," *Čin* 6 (1934).

1. *Editors' note.* This essay is a review of the Czech translation of Viktor Šklovskij's *Teorija prozy* [The theory of prose] by B. Mathesius, published in Prague in 1933. Accordingly all page references in Mukařovský's article are to the Czech edition.

134

word; others interpreted the literary work as a document of the author's internal and external life; still others accorded validity to the work only as a mere commentary on social or economic events. In Russia, with her long tradition of interest in artistic composition, Potebnja's school, which had developed from a scholarly orientation parallel to the Symbolist movement in poetry and which interpreted the work of art as an image, enjoyed, of course, a strong position. By interpreting the work in this way, Potebnja's school had also reduced the artistic aspect to something secondary, had rendered the work of art a passive reflection of something which was outside of art, had not differentiated sufficiently the specific function of poetic language from the function of the communicative utterance. Šklovskij, on the other hand, was a member of a group of young scholars, primarily interested in linguistics, who—in a tightly-knit community with their artistic contemporaries—defended the principle that the feature which renders a literary work an artistic creation differentiates it substantially from any other communicative utterance and that it is precisely this that must be the central interest and the axis of the scholarly study of literature.

The Theory of Prose is a bellicose challenge addressed to those who do not differentiate between poetic language and the communicative utterance. It is an aggressive book written in such a way that its voice would not be drowned out in the general turmoil of its day. Nevertheless, it is the fruit of careful preparation. Any bibliography of the Russian "Formalist" movement will show that this work had been preceded and was followed at the time of its origin by a number of specialized and detailed studies by the entire group of scholars mentioned above. At the moment that Šklovskij wrote his book, one could risk a certain popularization, though intellectually quite a demanding one, of the results of specialized studies. The total array of basic principles, therefore, had the appearance of a barrage of paradoxes whose angle of incidence had been precisely calculated in advance. The author addresses himself to the literary public rather than to specialists. At the same time, however, he requires the public to figure out the total plan and direction of his attack from fragmentary allusions. Instead of full-blown proofs he provides only synecdochic illustrations. Šklovskij has chosen literary material for these illustrations without tactful consideration for conventional taste but rather with an effort at placard expressiveness. He prefers those works—both older and contemporary ones—which provoke and surprise to those whose rough edges have been smoothed either by their creators' hands or by a lengthy pilgrimage through handbooks and anthologies. Nor does Šklovskij coddle his opponent. He does not hesitate to push an opposing idea *ad absurdam*. He says in as clear-cut and challenging a way as possible that art has no other purpose than to be art; he enthusiastically tells an anecdote about a prince who preferred dancing to the hand of a beautiful bride. The composition and style of *The Theory of Prose* are based on a loosely linked coordination rather than a smooth subordination of sentences and entire paragraphs. Both Šklovskij's predilection for paradox and his fragmentary formulations can be disorienting in the Czech context, where the very character of the language leads to explicit formulation allowing for restrained objections and careful limitations.

Yet the main difficulty which stands in the way of our understanding Šklovskij's book adequately today is its "formalism," better called the phantom of formalism. We are not forgetting that this label was a militant slogan during the rise of the group to which Šklovskij belonged and thus that it has the right to the honor paid to flags which have gone through battles. But if it is detrimental in its one-sidedness to the cause itself, especially in the eyes of our public, for whom the association of the word *formalism* with Herbartian aesthetics is still alive, it must be exposed for what it is—a mere word. We must show that it did not correspond to reality even at the time when it was accepted as a formulation of a program.

It cannot be denied that *The Theory of Prose* contains several passages at which the hearts of orthodox Herbartian Formalists would rejoice. Such is, for example: "A literary work is pure form, it is not an object, it is not a material but a ratio of materials. Like any other ratio, this ratio has no dimension. Therefore the scale of a work, the arithmetic value of its numerator and denominator, is irrelevant; what is important is their ratio. Comic works, tragic works, world-renowned works, chamber works, the relation of world to world, or that of a cat to a stone are equal to one another" (p. 223).

We must, however, take into account that Šklovskij was primarily concerned with sniffing out in the "material" work the contours of the aesthetic object (structure), which is, to be sure, connected with the work but which exists in the collective consciousness; hence the statement that "the literary work is not an object." In doing so, he reached for terminology and concepts which were at hand; he used Herbartian Formalism as a springboard.[2] In essence, however, his work is the first step toward overcoming formalism, and its seeming one-sidedness derives from its polemical character. An unconditional emphasis on "content" had to be countered by a radical antithesis stressing "form" so that a synthesis of the two, structuralism, could be achieved. Šklovskij tended toward structuralism from the beginning. Thus, for example, the statement that the content of a work equals the sum of its stylistic methods (p. 225) is important and characteristic. The notion of "form" which usually includes stylistic methods (devices) preserves its genuinely "formalist" character only insofar as form and content are differentiated as a shell and a kernel. As soon as we cease to place them in opposition, that is, as soon as we declare everything in the work as form, the notion of form changes, and so should its verbal denotation. But if matters stand as we have said, we should not criticize Šklovskij for limiting himself to only a part of the work, even to the less substantial one (for the shell is regarded as less important than the kernel which it encloses).

We are not saying that the standpoint advocated in *The Theory of Prose* is above criticism. We are aware that the thesis "Everything in a work is form" could, even should, be countered by the antithesis "Everything in a work is content," which likewise refers to all the parts, and that then a synthesis of the two should be sought, as contemporary structuralism attempts to do. We are, however, trying to show that the superstition of formalism veils from critics the most important contribution of Šklovskij and his friends. This assertion is important because the majority of objections addressed to Šklovskij in our country attack not his specific ideas but a phantom—and even a vulgarized phantom—of aesthetic Herbartianism.

As proof that Šklovskij's conception of "form" deals with the entire scope of the literary work, we could cite numerous passages

2. By "Herbartian Formalism" I mean a certain type of conception of artistic structure. I am, however, leaving aside the question of whether there was a real, immediate connection between Šklovskij's and Herbart's aesthetic ideas.

from the articles in his book, but we shall limit ourselves to only a
few examples. Emotional reevaluation is introduced (p. 117) as a
compositional element in the novel (in an analysis of Cervantes's
Don Quixote). Well, if the term *composition* is understood in a
genuinely formalist sense, it means the architecture of a work, that
is, the ratio and composition of its parts provided by the relative
scope of those parts, by the regularity or irregularity of their succession, and so on. But if emotional evaluation is designated a
compositional element, form ceases to be the proper term: emotional evaluation is obviously one of the attributes of content. In
other passages Šklovskij discusses the compositional utilization of
time or mystery in the epic plot (p. 120) or even the compositional
explanation for the choice of theme. On page 225, for example,
we find the explanation that in the succession of literary schools,
themes preferred by the previous school are prohibited for the
newly arising school, obviously not because the situation corresponding to these themes ceases to occur in "life," but because
it is a matter of the renovation of the composition of the work.
Elsewhere (p. 110) the illusion of reality is dealt with as a compositional factor. Through all of this the notion of composition
acquires a non-formalist coloring. It is no longer a matter of
architecture (the proportions and the succession of parts) but of
the organization of the semantic aspect of the work. Following
Šklovskij, we could introduce a definition: "Composition is a set
of means characterizing the literary work as a semantic whole."
Even according to the usual notion, however, meaning is part of
content rather than of form. We can therefore call Šklovskij's
book, which infuses the notion of composition with new meaning,
a first step toward the evolutionary overcoming of the contradiction between "form" and "content" conceptions of art.

The importance of the overcoming of the traditional notion of
form as a mere envelope will become quite clear in a comparison
with the theory (and history) of the visual arts. This discipline
realized much earlier than the theory and history of literature that
what renders an artistic work art, namely its special structure, must
not be overlooked. The theory of the visual arts has, however,
adhered too much to the Herbartian conception of form and
therefore has up to the present—despite the splendid results it has
attained—lacked an understanding of the function of the theme as
a meaning in the overall structure of the work as well as an

appreciation of the semantic value of those components usually called formal. This insufficiency is less discernible in studies of non-thematic art, such as architecture, than in the study of distinctly thematic painting, especially some of its genres, like the illustration or the portrait, the specific character of which is furnished precisely by certain semantic features. By understanding the structure of the work of art as a complex semantic composition, literary studies have not only caught up with but have even surpassed the theory of the visual arts.

We had to say this much in order to elucidate Šklovskij's controversial and disquieting book and also, in part, the entire period of literary theory and history which is usually called "formalist." We have tried to depict how Šklovskij's book functioned in the milieu for which it was written and at the stage of scholarship to which it belongs. Now, however, we must confront this book with the results of further developments in scholarship. By saying "developments," we are indicating in advance that today we cannot or need not accept without reservation and discrimination all of Šklovskij's assertions, even if we agree with his basic orientation. The merit of his book lies not only in what is permanently valid in his statements but also in what he has formulated with intransigent one-sidedness as an antithesis to the contrary one-sidedness of his predecessors. Only a radical emphasis of the antithesis makes possible a transcendence of them.

We shall proceed from Šklovskij's words at the end of his foreword: "In the study of literature I am concerned with the investigation of its inner laws. To give a parallel from industry, I am not interested in the situation on the world cotton market, or in the policy of trusts, but only in the kinds of yarn and the methods of weaving." The difference between the viewpoint of contemporary structuralism and the formalist thesis cited could be expressed in the following manner: Even today the "method of weaving" is, of course, the center of interest, but at the same time it is already apparent that we may not disregard the "situation on the world cotton market" either, since the development of weaving—in the non-figurative sense as well—is governed not only by the progress of textile technology (the internal regularity of a developing series) but at the same time by the requirements of the market, by supply and demand. The same is valid *mutatis mutandis* for literature.

This opens up a new perspective for the history of literature.

It becomes possible for the history of literature to take into account at the same time both the continuous development of literary structure furnished by the constant reshuffling of elements and the external interventions which, though they are not the vehicles of development, nevertheless unequivocally determine each of its phases. From this viewpoint every literary fact appears to be the resultant of two forces: the internal dynamics of structure and external intervention. The mistake of traditional literary history lay in the fact that it took into account only external interventions and denied literature autonomous development; the one-sidedness of formalism, on the other hand, consists in the fact that it placed literary activity in a vacuum. The standpoint of formalism, though one-sided, was an essential conquest, for it revealed the specific nature of literary evolution and freed the history of literature from a parasitic dependence upon the general history of culture or, in some cases, upon the history of ideology or society. Structuralism as the synthesis of these two opposites, on the one hand, retains the postulate of autonomous development but, on the other hand, does not deprive literature of its relations to the outside world. It therefore lets us grasp the development of literature not only in its entirety but also in its regularity.

Let us return once again to the quotation about the production of materials in order to make clear that even the "situation on the cotton market" (that is, what is outside of literature but is realted to it) is not a chaos in itself but that it is governed by a fixed order and has its own regular development just as does the "method of weaving" (the internal organization of the literary work). The sphere of social phenomena to which literature belongs is composed of many series (structures), each of which has its autonomous development. These are, for example, science, politics, economics, social stratification, language, morality, and religion. Despite their autonomy, however, the individual series influence one another. If we take any one of them as a starting point in order to study its functions, that is, its effect upon other series, it will appear that even these functions constitute a structure, that they are constantly regrouping and counterbalancing one another. Therefore, none of them must be made dominant a priori over the others, for the most diverse shifts occur in their interrelations because of development. But neither should the basic importance and special character of a specific function of a given series (in the case of literature it is the aesthetic function related to the literary work as an aesthetic object) be overlooked, because if it were completely suppressed, the series would cease to be itself (for example, literature an art). The particular function of any series is not defined by its effect upon other series but, on the contrary, by its tendency toward autonomy. Here we cannot explain in detail the principles which the structural conception brings to the study of functions; we have attempted only to suggest that even the field of literary sociology is fully accessible to structuralism.[3]

Thus structuralism does not limit literary history only to an analysis of "form," nor does it clash at all with sociological studies of literature. It does not restrict the scope of the material or the wealth of problems, but it insists on the postulate that scholarly study not regard its material as a static and atomized chaos of phenomena but that it conceive every phenomenon as a resultant and source of dynamic impulses and the whole as a complex interplay of forces. Finally, let us point out that structuralism in literary theory and history is not an isolated exception. In arriving at structuralism, literary studies simply join the general tendency of contemporary scholarly thought. Throughout almost the entire realm of contemporary scholarship the discovery of the dynamic relations which pervade its material has proven to be an effective modus operandi—for example, in the disciplines of the arts and in general aesthetics, in psychology, sociology, linguistics, economics, and even in the natural sciences.

In speaking about structuralism, we have seemingly digressed from Šklovskij's book and formalism. Indeed, Šklovskij intentionally limited his view to literary structure and categorically forbade himself to transgress these boundaries. This was quite natural and necessary. First, all attention had to be focused on the point which was most remote from the interest of previous literary history, namely, on the internal structure and specific function of the literary work, for only with this limitation and from this point

3. Let us not forget that Šklovskij himself had already written the article "V zaščitu sociologičeskogo metoda" [In defense of the sociological method] for the journal *Novyj Lef* in 1927 and that he had presented a sociological analysis of Tolstoy's *War and Peace* and of several eighteenth-century Russian works in special monographs. *Editors' note.* The reasons for Šklovskij's embracing the sociological approach and its impact upon his theoretical work are discussed in detail by Victor Erlich in *Russian Formalism: History - Doctrine,* 2d ed. (The Hague, 1965), pp. 118-25.

was it possible to loosen the entire system of scholarly concepts. Only later, when the new epistemological orientation had been fixed, was it possible to return gradually to the traditional problems of literary study without the fear that the previous automatized way of understanding them would entice a scholar into a compromising methodological eclecticism. Šklovskij's book and the work of his colleagues completely fulfilled their pioneering task: they discovered—in parallel with the literary scholarship of other countries, including ours[4]—a new field of study, and, moreover, they assumed an epistemological stance from which the material of literary study, as well as all of its problems, appeared in a new light.

4. I have in mind especially the works of Šalda (articles in the collection *Duše a dílo* of 1913) and Zich ("O typech básnických" [On poetic types], *Časopis pro moderní filologii* 6 [1917-18] and "O rytmu české prózy" [On the rhythm of Czech prose], *Živé slovo* 1 [1920-21]).

6

The Poet

A poet is the originator of an utterance with a predominantly aesthetic orientation. A more specific definition of the poet and his task changes with time: the prophet, the hero, the professional eulogist, the specialist, the producer, the special psychological or social type, and so on. *The poet's life and works* influence one another. The influence of a life upon a work is sometimes apparent (in works of an autobiographical nature), sometimes veiled. The correspondence between a life and a work can also be, however, a merely artistic device without any claim on the documentary validity of the work. On the other hand, the question of this correlation does not lose its significance even when the relationship between a work and its originator is concealed.

The poetic work is always a *sign*, sometimes direct but more often figurative with respect to the poet's life. Even if actually experienced facts are rendered as they happened, they can acquire a completely different meaning in the context of a work from the one which they had in the context of the poet's life. What is transferred from the poet's life into a work are: (1) events in which the poet directly participated or facts which he directly perceived (events relevant to the course of a life will sometimes remain without an echo in a work, and, on the contrary, events of negligible existential import, affecting the poet only subconsciously, will manifest themselves in a work—hence the difficulty of comparing a work with a life); and (2) facts which the poet learned from hearing or reading them. These transferences are therefore a matter of immediate or mediated experience acquired in part involuntarily, in part by an intentional search for the purpose of creation. The intentionality involved in the search for experience manifests itself in a different way and to a different extent in different literary movements. Immediate experience is, of course,

This essay is translated from "Básník," an article for the unrealized *Literární encyklopedie;* delivered as a lecture at the Prague Linguistic Circle on March 24, 1941; published in *Studie z estetiky* (Prague, 1966). Supplementary notes to the essay, which were supplied by Dr. Jaroslav Kolár after the book was in page proofs, are printed in an appendix on p. 235, below. They are cued in the text by * or †.

more relevant for the poet's attitude toward reality than mediated experience, whether it involves a presentation that reproduces or reshapes the experience or one that completely disguises it figuratively (consider the remote reflection of Mácha's experiences in his poetic works).

The attitude toward an experienced reality does not as a rule depend only on the poet's personal inclinations but also on the contemporary tendency of literature. It is frequently even impossible to differentiate precisely what has entered a work from reality and what comes from the thematic tradition of literature. Karolina Světlá's short story "Skalák," for example, reflects the relationship between herself and Neruda, but the first elaboration of its theme occurs in the author's writing ("Líbánky koketiny") before the establishment of this relationship as the fruit of "that rebellious social tendency which is close to the titanism of the contemporary Byronic poets" (Arne Novák).* It is precisely experience mediated by reading or hearing that brings the poet into contact with the written and oral (folk verbal art) literary traditions. Sometimes such a mode of experience is simulated in a work for an artistic purpose. The work acquires a special semantic nuance because the poet presents, for example, the plot of a narrative work as adopted from old chronicles or an eyewitness's narration.

The actual share of the mediated experience can be determined only by studying the sources. A direct experience and a mediated experience often interpenetrate indistinguishably. For example, in the novel *Povětron*, Karel Čapek depicts exotic and regional cultural milieux which he could only have known from reading, but the very source of Čapek's exoticism is to be sought—according to some autobiographical allusions of the poet himself—in direct impressions from his childhood. The exotic milieu of *Povětron* is therefore simultaneously adopted and experienced. Not only does the poet's life influence his work, but his work also influences his life. The very success or failure of a work can change the course of a poet's life (and thereby his future creation). Poetic creation imposes certain requirements upon his way of life, such as the preparation of a "productive mood" or the intentional acquisition of experiences. Sometimes the creative process in a poet prepares a psychological situation in life which is able to imitate creation: the anticipation of an experience through creation. A poetic fiction can be experienced by the poet himself as part of his existential reality (a poet's sympathy for the fictitious characters of a work, for which there is ample evidence), and, on the other hand, the course of life is sometimes conceived by the poet as a part of a poetic fiction.[1] Therefore even writings of a non-literary nature (such as memoirs), indeed even mere papers, can be perceived by their author, the poet, as a part of his works. Vilém Mrštík used his love letters as the utterances of a character in the novel *Pohádka máje*.

The question of *the relationship between poetic creation and the poet's age* also belongs to the correspondence between a life and a work. Considerable attention has already been devoted to the connection between creation and childhood.[2] Some literary and theoretical movements consider the connection with childhood experiences as one of the basic features of literature in general (Surrealism, psychoanalysis). But nor are other periods of human life unrelated to literary creation. In some poets the creative process is equally distributed over the entire course of life; in others it is completely or predominantly concentrated in a certain period (youth in Březina and Bezruč, advanced age in Čapek-Chod); in still others it exhibits periodicity (Neruda's lyric creativity in his youth, then again at a relatively advanced age; the case of the seven-year periods in Goethe's creativity is well known). The connection between the creative process and age has been considered up to now especially from the psychological and physiological points of view. More important, however, is the question of the structural differences between the individual periods within the writings of particular poets.

But with respect to his creation the poet is not only a living and creating individual; he is also a *personality* which is the "common denominator" of all the works that he has created (Julius Petersen). The poet and his works are in a relation of polarity to one another. Sometimes the work prevails over the personality, at other times the personality prevails over the work (see Schlegel's statement that Lessing was more than all of his talents), and at

1. See Roman Jakobson, "Co je poesie?" [What is poetry?], *Volné směry* 30 (1933–34): 229–39. *Editors' note*. This article has been reprinted in Jakobson's *Studies in Verbal Art* (Ann Arbor, 1971), pp. 20–32.

2. See, for example, the frequent uses of childhood experiences in the works of Svatopluk Čech, verified by the documentary autobiography *Druhý květ*.

other times the personality and the works are in equilibrium, which makes their tension felt most strongly (Mácha, Němcová).

The term *work* can mean a single book but also the sum of all the poet's writings, the temporal succession of which traces the line of his development. In this developmental context individual writings can acquire a different meaning and a different value from that which belongs to each of them in itself. The poet's first works are thus subsequently elucidated and revaluated by later writings which complete what was before merely embryonic in them. The poet's personality is related to the work in a complex way; nevertheless, it is a relation that is inevitably necessary. An originator is felt to be behind the work even if he is not known. The work in itself sometimes suffices to generate the poet's personality: consider the *Chronicle* of the so-called Dalimil or Bezruč's *Slezské písně* until the author was known. This property of poetic creation is sometimes used intentionally to produce a *fictitious* poet (for example, the poetess Žofie Jandová feigned by Čelakovský).

The work always presents a certain *image of the personality* of its author both through direct statements which can be related to the creator's personality (the knowledge and views expressed in the work, etc.) and also through its entire structure. Even if the image acquired in this way is as complete as possible, it must not be identified with the actual poet without further verification. Here, too, it is valid that the literary work is a sign, not necessarily a true cast of the poet. Nor do the unity of a work and the unity of the poet's personality stand in a one-to-one relation. Šalda rightly notes: "If a poem is extensive, there are so many bounds and rebounds in imagery that it creates an impression of not originating from a single person."* On the other hand, Ivan Olbracht admits his anonymous collaboration with his father, Antal Stašek, on *Na rozhraní,* hence two poets in collaboration on a single work by a single author: "When Antal Stašek was writing *Na rozhraní,* at a time when I myself still hadn't published anything, and once was unhappy that he couldn't finish a certain part of his book (my father was a very busy man), I told him with youthful impudence: 'I'll write it for you.' He looked down at me a little, he smiled a little, 'Write it!'" He didn't change one word in my manuscript. *Na rozhraní* was published, it was reviewed, my contribution wasn't exactly small—none of the critics and philologists recognized a thing."†

There is a difference in a poet's attitude toward a *finished* and an *unfinished* work. As long as the work is not completed, its total and partial structure and meaning can always be changed by further interventions. An unfinished work is therefore more closely connected with the author than a finished work. If a sketch gets into the hands of the reading public, it evokes more easily than a finished work the impression of the poet's intimate confession (note the interpenetration of Mácha's diary entries and literary sketches). This property of a sketch can also be exploited intentionally if the completed work is presented in such a way that it produces the impression of a sketch. In contrast, a *completed* work becomes common property, disengaged from a direct connection with the author. The notion of "completeness" is, of course, quite relative, as is evident from the fact that poets sometimes reshape and complete in succeeding editions an already published work (for example, the genesis of Čapek-Chod's *Antonín Vondrejc,* which grew into an entire novel from several previously published novellas). Sometimes a new work arises from a reelaboration of an already completed and published work (as in the reelaboration of Růžena Svobodová's first books, which in one case led to a change in title). Finally, sometimes the poet is already so alienated from his work that in reelaborating it he upsets its artistic structure.

The relationship between the poet and a work does not, of course, pertain to his personality as an undifferentiated whole but to all of its individual components and their interconnection. All of the *poet's inherited and acquired dispositions* (character traits, abilities, his psychology) and the set (typology) of these manifest themselves in a work. The degree and the manner of the manifestation of these psychic factors are, of course, dependent on the present state of literary structure. A strong personality, to be sure, transforms the suprapersonal structure of literature which is the property of an entire collective, but this process is largely facilitated by the fact that the dispositions of this personality are in accord with the developmental tendency of literature at a given moment. If, for example, this tendency requires that intonation assume the role of the leading component, then at this moment the road is especially open to personalities whose feeling for language is based on intonation. At a moment when literature tends toward a "lowering" of its vocabulary, access to literature is made easier for individuals coming, for example, from the urban lower

class and intimately acquainted with its manner of expression
(such as Neruda).

Nor is the *individuality of a poetic work* unequivocally related
to the poet's personality. It is therefore impossible to claim without reservation that the pronounced individuality of a work is a
necessary indication of a strong personality and vice versa. There
are periods which emphasize individuality in creation, which require it in evaluation (Romanticism, contemporary poetry); there
are others which suppress it (classicism). After all, not even the
notion of individuality persists without changing: sometimes the
originality of the theme is emphasized, sometimes the uniqueness
of the artistic structure. Besides intentional individuality there is
spontaneous individuality created especially by individual linguistic
habits which can occur in any utterance, even a non-poetic one.
In literature they are foregrounded much more distinctly, often
regardless of whether or not the literary structure of a given period
tends toward individuality.

The question of "a model," a literary personality which influences other poets through the individual features of its creation,
is also related to individuality. The functions of a model are various. Sometimes it almost completely absorbs the individuality of
its imitators (its "epigones," like the so-called Vrchlický school or
Bezruč's imitators); sometimes, on the other hand, it is an impulse
for the formation of an imitator's own personality—the "overcoming" of a model (for example, young Bezruč's attitude toward Čech's poetry). In the last case the choice of the model is not
a passive assimilation but a feat. By virtue of the fact that the
young poet enters into a dialectic polarity (which in later development can even lead to apparent resistance) with his model, he acquires for his own personality both direction for further developmental movement and necessary self-limitation through a pronounced alien personality.

Not only do older poets influence younger ones, but the reverse
is also true: schematism has no place in literary activity. Šalda says
something interesting on this in *On the Most Recent Czech Poetry*:
"Poetism has even profoundly influenced poets alien to it, for
example Josef Hora. Take his last book *Struny ve větru* of an
incontestably new, in places sovereign, beauty. This feature of
spiritual purity, of an inner bright farsightedness, in places of a
special, genuinely new spiritual monumentality—all of this is

inconceivable without the goad of Poetism. Let this not be said to Hora's discredit. On the contrary: elaborating an influence is greater than avoiding it. . . . When the history of modern Czech poetry is written from a subtler and more spiritual standpoint than it is being written today, it will become clear, for example, that there was a moment in Neruda's development when he was under the influence of Vrchlický's poetry, a poet younger than he, but was elaborating this influence; in the same way there was a point in the life of the later Vrchlický when the influence of the so-called Decadents, hence younger people, manifested itself in the greater musicality of his verse."*

Among the problems regarding the relationship between the poet and the work is that of *the subject of the work,* namely, that "I" from whom the literary work as an utterance proceeds and who is perceived to be the most intrinsic carrier of all the feelings and thoughts contained in the work. The subject is the point from which the structure of a work can be surveyed in its entire complexity and unity. It is therefore a bridge from the poet to the reader, who can project his own "I" into the subject and thus identify his own situation regarding the work with that of the poet. The subject in a work either can remain hidden (though not absent), such as, for example, in the "objective" narrative, or it can attain a stronger or weaker realization (through the first person of verbs, the emotional coloration of the work, the identification of the poet with one of the characters in the work, etc.). The subject cannot therefore be identified a priori with the poet even when the work seems to express directly his feelings, his attitude toward the world and reality. Drda has described this very well in his study accompanying the new edition of Rubeš's *Humoresky*: "The songs, the second part of Rubeš's verse creation, are at first glance full of subjective signs and are seemingly closest to his human 'I.' But certainly we must see in them service to the common taste of young people rather than a confession springing from an inner necessity. All those abandonings, betrayals, painful amusements, moanings in vain, fading suns, black forks in the road, and whatever all those requisites of the sung love poetry of that time are called must be taken with reservations. After all, Rubeš himself gives us a recipe for this when he mentions several times in his prose works a favorite sentimental trick of the young men of his day who tried to move young beauties by reading them a fake letter from a dying friend. Rubeš perhaps never sang of his genuine pain and resignation, either amatory or existential." *

And there are even more complex cases. Subjectivity which during the poet's development has been a reflection of a literary convention can at another time manifest itself as a living reflection of the poet's existential situation. Halas says about Vrchlický: "It is surprising how relationships are constantly being discovered between Vrchlický's first book called *Z hlubin* [From the depths] and his last book *Meč Damoklův* [The sword of Damocles]. From the depths to the depths, from the artificial pessimism of the beginning to a recognition equally bitter, the pulp of which, however, is full of blood and not of literature." †

Worthy of further comment is the poet's *attitude toward the artistic value of the work* which he creates. This attitude is determined by whether the orientation is toward the scope or the permanence of the effect, and it can exert a considerable influence upon the artistic structure of the work in progress. Emphasis on the scope of the effect, for example, can incline the poet toward conventional artistic clichés; emphasis on permanence can incline him toward strict normativism. The poet's attitude toward artistic value also manifests itself negatively. If the poet rejects scope of effect, exclusive poetry (such as Symbolism) results. If he rejects permanence, an intentionally topical work (a political song, for example) results. Although the poet's attitude toward the value of the work influences the artistic structure of the creation, his intention need not be fulfilled by the actual fortunes of the completed work. A work produced with a regard for permanence may have only a short period of effectiveness (Polák's *Vznešenost přírody*); a work designated for a passing effect may become a permanent value (Havlíček's poetry). The same holds true for the poet's *attitude toward the function (the purpose) of the work.* This attitude also influences the work in progress, but it does not determine the actual conception of the work by the reading public. A work meant to be tendentious can, for example, be received as a purely artistic one (Bezruč's poetry) and vice versa.

Now we must take a look at *the relationship between the poet and the individual components, both linguistic and thematic, of a work. Language* is the poet's material, hence the object of artistic reorganization. The basis for the reorganization of linguistic means by the poet consists in the fact that he, just as every speaking individual, has certain individual linguistic habits which derive from inherited and acquired linguistic dispositions. Acquired dispositions include, for example, the "family" language, the influence of which upon the poet's linguistic expression becomes apparent if several members of the same family create poetically (consider the common linguistic features in the Čapek brothers and their sister Helena Čapková), the language of the native city and region, the language of the social milieu in which the poet has grown up or, in some cases, of those milieux with which he has been in temporary contact. The poet's conscious or unconscious artistic intentionality, partially governed by the previous tradition of poetic language, is superimposed upon the individual linguistic pattern described above. Through the mediation of literary creation the characteristic mode of expression of the poet as an individual is not infrequently transposed into the suprapersonal tradition of poetic discourse or even into general linguistic usage. From the standpoint of this usage the poet often appears as a mediator between the standard literary language and various non-literary linguistic patterns. Even the imperfect knowledge of the language in which a poet writes can have a positive effect upon the linguistic tradition of literature or upon the language in general. The Ukrainian Gogol became the founder of the linguistic tradition of Russian literary prose. "I don't know any good writer who isn't a linguistic creator," says Karel Čapek.* We must, of course, add that in the same way the national language has an influence upon the linguistic possibilities of a poet's creation. A cultivated language "writes poetry for a poet," an insufficiently cultivated one hinders it; on the other hand, of course, the excessive cultivation of a language can be a fetter for a poet and its insufficient maturity a stimulus.

The relationship between the poet and the thematic aspect of the work is founded on the polarity between the poet's existential experience and the thematic tradition of the given national literature. The poet's experience, rooted in his family, regional and social origin, and occupation, colors the traditional literary themes in a new way and, in some cases, introduces a new thematic sphere or new types of characters. On the other hand, of course, the thematic tradition of literature influences the poet's experiences which enter literature, coloring them by its semantic ambience or recasting them completely into traditional subjects and motifs.

Another relationship between the poet and the thematic aspect of the work is provided by the fact that some motifs or themes enter into an especially intimate bond with the poet's personality. These are the motifs and themes which recur many times in a certain poet. The motif of the pursuit of a fleeing criminal, for example, occurs several times in Karel Čapek ("Hora" in *Boží muka,* "Oplatkův konec" in *Povídky z jedné kapsy*) and in his brother Josef (*Stín kapradiny*)—hence is even a "family theme." We also find frequently recurring motifs in Mácha (the motival pair "stone – bone," the motif of flickering lights). There are several reasons for such *an affinity between a poet and a motif*: (1) artistic—namely, through its semantic ambience a motif agrees with the character of the artistic structure of a poet's work (the choice of words, the rhythm, etc.); (2) biographical—a motif has its source in an experience which has become deeply rooted in the poet's mental life; (3) psychological—a motif corresponds to a certain inclination of the poet's character or to the entire structure of his mental life. The biographical and psychological bases of a poet's themes can also manifest themselves in a work in a concealed form—in some cases, figuratively. It can happen that a poet explicitly declares some motif to be his own experience. But such a declaration can also be a mere artistic device. On the other hand, one of the poet's actual experiences is sometimes presented as a literary fiction—again for artistic reasons.

The relationship between a poet and a literary genre also involves the internal structure of the work. The common differentiation among prose writers, lyric poets, and dramatists as well as ballad writers, fable writers, satirists, novelists, and short story writers, in itself expresses the bond of poetic personalities with literary genres. The lyric poet is a poet who creates only or mostly in the lyric form, the ballad writer is a poet in whose creation ballads prevail, and so forth. In this way a genre becomes the characteristic feature of the poet. Even when the poet sometimes expresses himself in a different genre from the one which is basic for him, this expression bears traces of his dominant genre. Thus the poet sometimes reshapes a genre which is relatively alien to him by introducing into it the properties of the genre that prevails in his creation. The prose writer Karel Čapek, for example, renewed the style of Czech lyric poetry because in his translations of French poetry he transferred—drawing support in this from the

French originals—into lyric poetry the undeformed word order of prose, which was his proper artistic realm. His feat then became a powerful factor in the further development of the Czech lyric by lyric poets (Nezval et al). Conversely, Mácha and Zeyer transferred the deformed word order of verse into their prose creations. There are, of course, cases in which the poet is equally at home in several realms of literature. Neruda, for example, made both the lyric prosaic (especially through the "lowering" of vocabulary) and prose lyrical (Arne Novák on the *Malostranské povídky*: "Neruda who is always so painfully subjective and exclusively lyrical! Nowhere is he more subjective than in his short stories"*). The poet can also influence the development of a poetic genre by joining two genres together. The Byronic short story is thus rightly conceived by contemporary literary theorists (such as Boris Ejxenbaum) as the fusion of the epic with the lyric poem. Finally, at other times the poet becomes the founder of a genre or at least of a generic nuance: Arbes's *romaneto,* Karel Čapek's "moralizing" detective story.

Just as the poet fluctuates among individual genres, he can also do so *among several arts.* There are cases in which the artist is both a poet and, for example, a painter (Karel Hlaváček, Josef Čapek) or an actor (J. J. Kolár). At other times an artist who is primarily a poet intervenes in another art as a dilettante (Mácha, Karel Čapek in painting; Nezval in music), or, on the other hand, he resorts to literature as a secondary possibility for his creation, the center of gravity of which lies in a different art (the actresses Hana Kvapilová and Eva Vrchlická, who also wrote poetry). The type of the poet—an artist oriented toward the linguistic sign—can also be found in other arts, even in an artist who never produces literature. We then speak about a painter-poet or a musician-poet.

Other kinds of human creativity besides art can be linked to literature in the person of the poet. Especially common is the joining of the poet with the scholar (take, for example, Erben, a poet and a historian). Poetry and scholarship can also interpenetrate in the person of the poet (consider Jan Kollár, about whom Čelakovský said, "He writes poetry philologically and practices philology poetically"†). The joining of literature and other arts and other kinds of creativity is not only a matter of the personal gifts and inclinations of the individual concerned but also of the developmental orientation of the time. The union of a poet with a scholar in a single person, for example, frequently occurred in Czech literature during the period of the National Revival (Erben, Jungmann, Šafařík, Palacký, etc.).

Another set of questions concerns *the poet's position in the development of literature as well as the interrelation of the poetic individualities of the time.* The literature of a certain nation and a certain language is not only a set of works but primarily a continuous series developing uninterruptedly. The *single individual* seems to be a mere accidental vehicle of this suprapersonal flow. Upon close inspection, however, it will be evident that the developmental dynamics of literature has its source precisely in the individual unpredictability of each literary personality. The literary personality, especially the strong one, is the point of intersection at which forces collide and intermingle; these forces arise, on the one hand, from the impetus of the developing national literature itself and, on the other, from outside, from foreign literatures, the other arts, different realms of culture (religion, politics, economic life), and from the social organization and its development (the regrouping of the social stratification, the interpenetration of different social milieux, etc.). The resultant of this unique encounter of forces to which the poet's inherent dispositions also contribute their share is the poet's intervention in the suprapersonal developmental flow in literature. In this sense the poet is the force that determines development, being reciprocally determined by it. The selection of poetic individuals, their arrangement in a developmental scheme, the gradation of their significance, their interrelations and the tension among them—all of this is to a considerable extent predetermined by the pressure of the developmental tendency and its needs. If a certain literary personality asserts itself according to its natural gifts, the possibility of its assertion is nevertheless provided to a great extent by the fact that development at a given moment needs a personality gifted precisely in this way.

The individual personality is not therefore—despite its uniqueness—an accidental point in the set of the other literary personalities—the previous, the contemporary, and the following—but is determined by them and reciprocally determines them. In this sense Šalda has outlined Vrchlický's developmental position by means of the following scheme: Vrchlický - Neruda, Vrchlický - Zeyer, Vrchlický - Březina. It can also happen that the developmental relations between poets are "realized" in the form of interpersonal tensions, even hostility (the tension between Čelakovský and Mácha, between the Lumírians and the Ruchovians, between Vrchlický and the Symbolists). Of course, there are many variations in this tension: sometimes, though felt, it does not result in hostility (Neruda – Hálek); sometimes it is limited to the followers of the leading poets, whereas the poets themselves (e.g., Čech – Vrchlický) remain untouched by it.

The developmental relations among poets can also manifest themselves in the opposite way: in their *association* in generations, schools, groups around artistic journals, and so on. Association is seemingly the negation of individual uniqueness, but in reality it is an expression and a consequence of it. Personalities joined on the basis of some common features emphasize their difference from personalities outside the association which lack these features. Within the group itself the individual differences of the members are, as a rule, felt more intensely, for they are perceived against a background of similarities. Thus there is a differentiation of personalities within the association, and this can result in its dissolution: the gradual loosening of cohesiveness among aging literary groups is a common phenomenon. Association also contributes to the development of literary personalities in that one of the poets in the group sometimes prevails over the others. His individual features become the features of the entire association. The group then appears as a multiplication of a single leading personality. But even without the dominance of an individual it can happen that the literary group appears from outside as a single "collective" individual. This occurs if the association of poets requires from its participants an absolute unity of artistic views and methods (certain postwar groups, especially the Surrealists).

The interplay of relations among literary personalities, both positive and negative, is not, however, the result of the accidental encounters of individual sympathies and antipathies but a matter of the internal differentiation of the suprapersonal developmental flow. Personalities converge and diverge, associate with and oppose one another, because they are vehicles of forces deriving from the prior development of literature, the ultimate resultant of which determines once again the direction of further development. In this sense we can speak about "places" assigned to individual poets by a suprapersonal developmental tendency. There were two such

"places," for example, in the Czech lyric of the Máj school. There
was a need for a lyric poet spontaneously expressing emotion and
one for a lyric poet suppressing it (the difference between these
two lyrical types had existed in Czech poetry previously—between
Čelakovský and his sentimentalizing epigones, Vacek Kamenický
and Picek—but it gains the value of a developmental antinomy for
the first time among the Májovians). The first of the two "places"
was occupied by Hálek, the second by Neruda. In addition, however, this generation had yet a third pronounced lyric individuality, Adolf Heyduk, likewise a poet of spontaneous emotional
expression ("Every joy and sorrow have found an echo in his
songs," says Neruda). The "competition" between Hálek and
Heyduk was felt (Neruda: "Even though there wasn't a clash
between Hálek and me, there was one between 'Hálek's adherents'
and 'my adherents.' Heyduk, of course, belonged to mine, and I
frequently had to take an energetic stand for him"*). The stronger
Hálek assumed the position of Neruda's antipode. Heyduk then
moved into a peripheral position: he became a poetic regionalist,
the poet of Southern Bohemia and Slovakia.

The relationship between the poet and literature includes not
only the colorful variety of literary individualities but also *the
internal heterogeneity of literature itself,* the horizontal and
vertical articulations of literature: its stratification into high and
peripheral literature, both further differentiated internally, then
its differentiation into various parallel spheres, such as urban and
rural literature, or literature for adults and for youth. In each of
these literary strata and spheres the poet's task is conceived differently, his personality is viewed in a particular way. For example,
if the poet's name is emphasized in high literature, the product in
peripheral literature sometimes prevails over its creator to such an
extent that the choice of reading matter is made not with regard
to the author but with regard to the content and the nature of
the writing (the adventure novel, the detective story, the amatory
novel) or even to the extent that the author's name is unknown
(the hackneyed song).

Even in other respects, in the view of originality, for example,
we find a different conception of the poet's task and status in
different spheres of literature. The poet is usually more distinctly
limited to a single sphere of literature than the reader. All boundaries are not, of course, equally uncrossable. The dividing line

between adult literature and children's literature, for example, is for the poet much less sharp than the boundary between high and peripheral literature (though, of course, not even this one is always uncrossable: consider Kalina's *Kšaft*). The relative infrequency of one and the same writer's working in two different literary spheres is not, however, an obstacle to contact between different spheres; poets often mediate between them by transferring artistic devices and themes from one which they know only passively as perceivers to another in which they actively create (for example, Hálek's mediation between high literature and the street song, Nezval's between high poetry and "verses from readers").

The bond between the poet and a certain literary sphere in itself involves the question of the relationship between the poet and *society,* for many of the literary spheres correspond to particular social milieux whose views and taste they reflect. The poet is usually connected with a certain social milieu through his creation. Sometimes it is the milieu from which he himself comes, sometimes the one to which he addresses his works, coming himself from a different milieu (for example, the authors of literature "for the people," the authors of children's literature, or poets of plebian origin creating for the nobility and the courts: Corneille, Racine et al). The poet can also be an exponent of a certain milieu vis-à-vis others, its propagator and defender (the poets of the countryside, for example, the Ruralists, writing for city people; "proletarian" poets). He can also act through his work in raising the consciousness of the very milieu for which or in whose name he creates (the role of Sládek's poetry in the formation of Czech agrarianism; here, too, we can include the participation of the greater part of nineteenth-century Czech literature in the awakening and guidance of national consciousness).

Through his work and then through his person the poet can acquire the value of a representative, indeed of a symbol, of a certain milieu, for example, a nation (Björnson's position in Norwegian literature, Goethe's in German, Pushkin's in Russian, Čech's and Jirásek's in the appropriate periods of Czech literature, etc.). But there are also poets who resist any social incorporation, especially those who did so at the end of the nineteenth century and after. Thus originates a special milieu composed of poets and other artists who separate themselves from the social hierarchy. A negative attitude toward the contemporary social organization has manifested itself in the creation of some poets (the Decadents et al) in their claim of allegiance to a non-existent social formation, namely, a past one (for example, the feudal nobility) or even a completely fictitious one. Here, of course, we have a literary autostylization which, however, frequently expresses the poet's negative attitude toward the contemporary social reality.

Besides the poet's attitude toward a certain social milieu there is his attitude toward human society in general. It becomes apparent when the poet feels himself to be excluded from human society either by the impossibility of communication with others (Mácha) or by his awareness of his superiority over them (Romantic spleen) or finally by his aversion to man in general (Swift in book 4 of Gulliver's Travels). There are also periods when the poet feels himself and is felt to be superior to other people (the poet as prophet, saint, hero). In these cases as well it is a matter of the poet's stylization, in some cases autostylization, which figuratively expresses the real relationship between the poet and society.

Another aspect of the relationship between the poet and society appears if we look at the poet from the standpoint of his *social origin*. Whether the poet's attitude toward his native milieu is positive or negative, whether he addresses his creation to this or that milieu, his social origin is always evident. Sometimes a work bears direct traces of an intimate knowledge of the objective atmosphere, the social conventions, the ideology, the ethical and aesthetic feeling of the native milieu; sometimes this milieu manifests itself in a work figuratively (Hlaváček in *Mstivá kantiléna*); in some cases it turns into its direct opposite, but it is always present. For example, Šklovskij has shown that Leo Tolstoy is a typical Russian nobleman even in his work. The difference between Neruda and Hálek is usually explained in part by the difference between a poet of urban origin and a country man.

Occupation comprises another bond between the poet and society. There are times when poetic activity is an occupation in itself (among the court poets, for example); there are others when it lacks a professional character (the Czech poets of the nineteenth century); there are also, of course, numerous transitional possibilities. The fact that some occupations are connected with literary activity more often than others is also important. This is the case, for example, with journalism. In contemporary Czech literature, however, there is a relatively large number of doctors among the leading poets. Connections of this kind are, of course, different according to the time and the nation. Sometimes literary activity is even accompanied by an inclination toward frequent changes in occupation (J. K. Šlejhar).

Occupation can influence the themes of a poet's works (Šimáček's novels and novellas from the sugar factory milieu) as well as his manner of conceiving reality (for example, medicine, which presupposes training in the natural sciences, otherwise rare among literary people) and even the artistic structure of his works (see Karel Čapek's type of novel-feuilleton, such as *Továrna na absolutno, Válka s mloky,* or his "newspaper" short stories, *Povídky z jedné a z druhé kapsy, Apokryfy*).

The *reading public* is the mediator between the poet and society. Direct contact between the poet and society as a whole occurs only when his work becomes the object of public interest on account of one of its aspects—most often an extra-artistic one or when he is generally considered to be a representative of a certain society, such as a nation. In both these cases the poet becomes known even to those who do not know his works from personal reading; hence the poet prevails over the work. If *the work,* however, becomes common property, its author's name usually disappears from the general consciousness—hence the anonymity of quasi-folk songs, the unimportance of the author's name in folk reading.

Regular contact between the poet and society occurs *through the mediation of the reading public*: every poet has "his own" community of readers. The poet's reading public is usually characterized socially in a certain way: by belonging to a certain social milieu, by a common level of taste, by common views, sometimes even by age or sex. Through the manner in which he creates, the poet can tend to acquire as numerous a reading public as possible, in some cases a reading public as varied in its social composition as possible. Nor, however, is the opposite extremely rare, namely, that the poet seeks a maximal limitation of the number of his readers (for example, some Symbolists). There is a constant tension between the poet and the reading public, a tension which manifests itself not only through the poet's influence on the reading public but also through the reading public's influence on the poet. Even the mere image that the poet has of his reading public often influences his creation: ". . . the real aim of this or that choice, this or that effort on the part of a creator, often lies beyond the creation itself, and is the result of a more or less conscious concern for the effect that will be produced and its consequences for the producer" (Valéry).* The poet's image of the reading public need not, of course, coincide with reality. Indeed, there are even cases when the poet intentionally presupposes a non-existent reading public (a past, future, or imaginary one—an "ideal" reader; see Stendhal's statement that his works would be understood only around 1880). The relationship between the poet and the reader is so essential that even after the poet's death it sometimes appears almost personal: a *cult* of the poet.

The conception of the poet that we have outlined here does not treat the literary personality either as a resultant of external influences or as a self-regulating phenomenon but as a changeable point of intersection of forces pressing from all sides and entering into oppositions with one another. The initiative of the literary personality, then, consists in the fact that it organizes these numerous oppositions into a unique arrangement (which is often far from harmonious). The way in which the personality combats the forces which press upon the individual from all sides is determined by his psychophysical organization, which is not unique in itself but has the ability to become the axis of crystallization for a unique grouping and balancing of forces. Theoretical knowledge of the literary personality must not, therefore, be limited to a taxonomy of the influences which affect the poet, nor, on the contrary, must it proceed from an a priori conviction that the poet's mental life is an absolutely or almost autonomous world. Both of these views wrongly schematize the complexity of the poet's figure.

The picture of the poet which we have drawn here is only valid from the standpoint of artificial literature where the creating individual is distinctly differentiated from the perceiving individual (the reader). In *folk* literature the entire process of the origin of the literary work is completely different. Here, too, an individual is the primary originator of the work, but only after its origin does the folk work of verbal art begin a further life in tradition, where it is subject to the constant changes and restructurings through which "alone it becomes a genuine expression and, as a rule, creation of a folk collective."†

7

The Individual and Literary Development

The problem of personality is becoming more and more urgent in the humanities and in everyday life. We are witnessing a renewed interest in the individual. In everyday life the individual's responsibility is at issue, and this is evident especially when it directly influences the course of events. Scholarship cannot afford to bypass the individual if it wants to grasp the real complexity of developmental activity. The problems of the individual in everyday life are too complicated to be dealt with here. As far as theoretical study goes, it is apparent that the inclusion of the individual entails one danger: that the individual will become a convenient excuse for avoiding difficult problems and will bring into our studies an irrational element (unprovable claims, etc.), which is contrary to the very essence of scholarly thought.

The epistemology of personality must therefore be constructed from the outset. Each of the separate disciplines which this problem concerns must construct an epistemology on its own and with a sense of responsibility toward its material. It is likely that a different aspect of the problem will appear in each instance; however, without regard for a specific material it is impossible to attain useful general results. The relative independence of general conclusions from a material which is too individualized can be attained in theoretical thought only by applying results gained from one material to another and adjusting them.

The purpose of this study is an attempt to examine the epistemology of personality on the basis of material from the history of the arts, primarily that of literature. Here the problem of personality is very evident, for language, the material of literature, is individually differentiated even before it enters art. Moreover, it is the most common communicative sign (system of signs) which man has at his disposal. We want to examine personality as a factor in the historical development of literature. We want to

This essay was translated from "Individuum a literární vývoj," a lecture at the Prague Linguistic Circle, 1943-45; published in *Studie z estetiky* (Prague, 1966).

juxtapose a dynamic conception of personality as the force which constantly sets the development of literature into motion with the usual static conception of personality as a self-enclosed and self-determined whole.

The static aspects of the artist's personality cannot, of course, be overlooked. Here, as everywhere else, when we question an already existing notion designated by a traditional term, we must be careful not to confuse several concepts linked to one and the same matter and even designated by one and the same word. We shall therefore try to differentiate a few of the various aspects in which the artist's personality can manifest itself to us, especially so that the boundary between the static and dynamic aspects will be distinctly marked.

Let us proceed from the concrete impression which the work of art makes upon us. One of its most essential components is the impression of unity that is produced even when we experience contradictions which resist this unity. Indeed, it is precisely then that we experience unity the more intensely as an overcoming of the dissonances. Hence the old definition of an aesthetic impression as "unity in variety." The question of where this unity comes from cannot be answered as long as we have in mind only the "material" work of art. The unity of its individual properties-components will appear to us only if we consider the mental state which this work evokes in the observer. This psychic state, or rather the act by which we grasp the work of art, is the unity. This act is not essentially different from any kind of apperception, but because the work of art lacks the disturbing influence of a practical orientation, the apperceptive act stands out distinctly in its entirety. Since then the work of art which causes the apperceptive act is experienced as the stimulus of this act and its wholeness, and since the work is outside the observer, the appropriate psychic state is also projected beyond the observer's interior, and he who has created the work, the artist, is posited to be its vehicle.

The proof of this is the perception of a drama as a work of art. Insofar as we feel someone who causes the characters to act (insofar as we do not attribute the responsibility for their actions and words to the characters themselves) behind the dramatic work, we evaluate the event that we see before us as a drama. If there were a moment when we were seized by the feeling that each of the characters was acting on his own initiative and responsibility, we would begin to perceive the drama as a *real event,* not as a work of art. The creator's personality is therefore always felt to be behind the work even if we do not have the slightest information about the concrete creator and his actual mental life. It is a mere projection of the perceiver's mental act. The same thing can be expressed differently. The work of art is a sign mediating between two individuals as members of the same collective, and like every sign it needs two subjects for the fulfillment of its semiotic function: the one who provides the sign and the one who perceives it. But unlike other kinds of signs in which the relation between the sign and the object represented by it (the reference) is primarily manifested, the connection between the sign and the subject is what comes to the fore above all in the work of art, an autonomous sign with a weakened reference. And therefore behind each work of art the perceiving subject intensely feels the subject providing the sign (the artist) to be responsible for the mental state which the work has aroused in him. From here it is only a step to the involuntary hypostasis of the concrete creative subject, constructed only on the basis of the premises given by the work. It is clear that this hypostasized personality, which we shall call the author's personality, need not coincide with the artist's actual psychophysical personality.

But the question which concerns us here regarding the author's personality is whether this personality is dynamic or static, whether it is a historical or static fact. If we assume the attitude of a naive perceiver (a perceiver without a theoretical orientation), then there is no doubt that the author's personality is an ahistorical fact for the very reason that perfect unity must appear unchangeable in time. Just as the mental state evoked by the work appears to the perceiver as necessary and unchangeable (hence the theory of eternal value in art), the author's personality on which it is constructed must also appear as independent—in its unchangeability— of anything, but especially of time. This unchangeability is, however, a mere illusion. It is well enough known that the structure of a work changes with the flow of time (the incorporation of an old work into a new developmental context, if it is perceived long after its origin), and therefore the mental state which is its equivalent (correlate) in the perceiver's mind, and thereby the image of the author's personality must change, too. To sum up: the author's

personality is a mere shadow, a mere reflection of the structure of
the work on the perceiver's mind. It does not have any theoretical
interest in itself, for it does not contain anything which could not
be more precisely expressed by an objective description and an
analysis of the work itself. It becomes interesting only in confrontation with the artist's actual psychophysical personality.

Let us therefore turn to this other aspect. The artist's psychophysical personality is a bundle of dispositions, either inherent or
acquired (through education, environment, social status, etc.).
Since every disposition can be both inherent and changed by
external influences at the same time, it is difficult to distinguish
precisely the two levels. Nevertheless, a psychological analysis of
the artist's personality must be oriented toward inherent dispositions, must therefore be directed at a conception of the artist's
personality as a unity which finds its ultimate justification in itself,
in the act of its birth, hence as an ahistorical unity. Here, of
course, the material can hardly be limited to the work but must
include all the author's expressions, his written and spoken words,
as well as his acts.

If such an analysis is carried out precisely, it will frequently
appear that the artist's personality is broader than the author's
personality, that certain of the author's dispositions have remained outside the work or that at least they have manifested
themselves in the artist's life with a different force and in a different manner than in the work. A single example is sufficient:
Karel Hynek Mácha. Mácha's biographers have stated with some
surprise that this poet, who liked to use words predominantly as
sound values and, in doing so, was intentionally imprecise in joining them into semantically definite wholes, was actually a good
mathematician and an excellent lawyer. Thus he exhibited different dispositions in his life and in his work. As far as changes in
the same dispositions go, it is enough to recall the abysses between
the eroticism of *Máj* and that of his *Diary*. (For an analogous
example consider Verlaine's *Sagesse* and the records of his private
life.) Recently, in a private conversation, one of the leading Czech
writers ascertained in himself the difference between his practical
memory and the memory which furnishes him with materials for
his works, although both memories draw from the same source,
the artist's life and experiences.[1] The clash between the author's

1. Sometimes monographists consider it their duty to hide from the public that part
of the poet's personality which has remained outside the work for fear that they will

and the artist's personalities can even result in a contrast. Yet, on the other hand, an almost complete agreement can occur in certain cases.[2]

The relationship between the two personalities is therefore characteristic of the poet's works, but it is not as dependent on the artist's will as it might seem. The author's personality, as we have seen, is only a projection of the structure of the work into the psychic realm. And structure is not dependent on the artist's will alone but is primarily determined by its own development, comprising a continuous series evolving in time (for example, the structure of Czech poetry). Thus the relationship between the poet's dispositions and the author's personality is simultaneously determined from two sides: by the development of the structure in a given literature and by the dispositions of the poet who takes the structure from his predecessors' hands. It is therefore no surprise that we can trace in particular developmental periods the very typical relation between these two personalities which is characteristic in each instance of the given period, as Jakobson has shown in the aforementioned study (see footnote 2) by comparing a Romantic poet with a modern one (Mácha with Nezval) with respect to eroticism. Hence the poet's psychophysical personality, at first glance completely ahistorical, appears upon closer inspection to be incorporated into the development of poetry, though only through its relation to the author's personality. In other words, even if a psychological study of a poet's personality is undertaken, it cannot be done without regard for the development of literature. The two aspects of personality which we have just discussed—the personality as it asserts itself in a specific work and the actual personality—have in common the feature that both, at least at first glance, appear to be static. But we can and even have to approach the problem of personality from the perspective of development, hence from the very outset to conceive personality as a historical and dynamic fact.

Thus arises the question of the relationship between development and individuality (personality). If we consider a tendency toward uniqueness, indeterminacy, and unchangeability to be the basic features of personality, then personality necessarily appears

---

spoil an illusion of the poet. It would be superfluous to dwell on the scholarly impermissibility of this method.

2. See R. Jakobson, "Co je poesie?" [What is poetry?], *Volné směry* 30 (1933-34): 229-39.

to us as an antithesis of the immanent development of every cultural series in which it intervenes (we are concerned with literature). From the standpoint of a developing series, the intervention of a personality appears, on the one hand, as a disturbance of its continuity in time but, on the other hand—and at the same time, through the same act—as a force setting this series into motion. The more strongly the personality asserts itself through what is really unique in it (inherent dispositions and especially their hierarchy), the more visible will its intervention be for the observer. A rigid conception of personality as independent of development therefore leads first to Carlyle's famous thesis that the history of the world is the history of great personalities; ultimately it would lead to an absolute negation of development (personality outside of time). This conclusion is patently absurd, but not even Carlyle's thesis is correct. Regardless of the fact that development conceived in this way crumbles under the hands of the historian into an irregular sequence of explosions, two questions cause problems. Is an absolutely undetermined personality thinkable at all? In the opposite case, if we admit partial determinacy even in the strongest personalities, where are the boundaries: how can we prevent even the strongest personality from dissolving under the theoretician's hands into a bundle of determinacies?

We must look for such a relationship between the development, that is, the immanent development, of a given series, on the one hand, and a personality, on the other, which will allow us not to lose sight of the opposition of the two but will not threaten the basic precondition of development, namely, the continuity of the developing series. Development as a regular changing of a thing in time is the result of two opposing tendencies. On the one hand, the developing series remains itself, for without the preservation of its identity it could not be understood as a series continuous in time; on the other hand, it constantly disturbs its own identity, for otherwise there would be no changes. The disturbance of identity maintains developmental motion; its preservation adds regularity to this motion. The developing thing itself is the source of the tendency to preserve identity; therefore the sphere from which the impulses for disturbing identity arise must lie outside the developing thing. These external interventions are accidents from the standpoint of developmental regularity. The accidents which can interfere with a developing literature in this way are numerous. They can come from other cultural developmental series (other arts, science, religion, politics). All of them are the reflection of changes in the organism of society, but they intervene in literature immediately through the creator's personality.

These "accidents" are, of course, absolute accidents only from the standpoint of the series that is involved in the given case. From the standpoint of the series from which they come they appear as regular results of the immanent development of each of these series, and they can therefore be objectively described and defined. After all, even from the standpoint of the series whose development we follow continuously (literature, in the given case) the "accidentality" of these interventions is limited by the fact that their order, intensity, and developmental use depend largely on the needs of the developing series. Furthermore, it is important to note that all the mentioned external interventions do not operate on the same level. The relation of the social organization to all cultural phenomena is different from the relationships of cultural phenomena among themselves, because society is the bearer of culture, and its organization is the riverbed of its development. This has its consequences for the relative significance and disposition of the external influences. Every change in the structure of society manifests itself in some way in the entire structure of culture and in the interrelation of its individual series, such as the individual arts and sciences, whereas the influences of individual series of cultural phenomena upon one another have a much more limited range.

Now we must ask: What is the status of personality as an external factor of literary development? What is the degree of its accidentality with respect to this development, and what is its relation to the other external factors such as other arts, science, social organization? As regards the degree of accidentality, we must admit that personality, whose concealed but nevertheless very effective basis is comprised of inherent dispositions, is— precisely because of this basis—less predetermined by historical antecedents than cultural phenomena and social organizations. Therefore if it intervenes, for example, in the development of literature as an external influence, it can produce more of the unpredictable and can more strongly disturb the identity of the previous literary development. As we have said above, the accidentality and the indeterminacy of personality are strongly limited by the fact that the individual is a member of a social whole, the development of which he shares, and literature, just as any other cultural series, is for the individual only a part of a common cultural property, the development and effect of which exceeds by far the individual's sphere of influence and decision making.

In his relation to literature the individual is therefore bound by a great many ties and is by no means an absolute and independently self-asserting accident. Nevertheless, if we speak about his greater accidentality with respect to the development of literature, we have in mind only the relatively greater indeterminacy of the personality's intervention than is the case with other external interventions. The status of personality is also special with respect to its relation to the other external factors of literary development. If we had to place the social organization outside the other external factors of literary development because society is the source and the bearer of culture, we must also reserve a separate place for the interventions of personality, for personality comprises a focal point at which all the external influences that can affect literature meet, and at the same time it is the starting point from which they penetrate literary development. Everything that happens to literature happens through the mediation of personality. Personality is the only one of the external developmental factors which enters into immediate contact with literature; the others enter into this contact only indirectly through its mediation. All the other external factors can be included in the realm of personality (but we may not, of course, reduce their problems to the problem of personality).

Therefore the antinomy of literary development that we have abstractly characterized above as a contradiction between the affirmation and the negation of the identity of literature can, in fact, be concretely formulated as a contradiction between literature and personality. The individual stages of the immanent literary development constitute the theses in this antinomy; the personalities which intervene in literary development at a given stage function as the antitheses to them. They are antitheses because the negation of the identity of literature, the tendency toward changing it into something other than what it has previously been, derives from them. The antinomy literature – personality is therefore the most basic of all the possible antinomies of literary development, but it is also, of course, the most complex because it implies all the other antinomies.

As soon as we conceive the relation of personality to development in this way, it becomes even clearer that the question of personality as a developmental factor cannot be limited only to strong personalities whose influence in development is manifestly evident, in that it has as its result a radical reorganization of literary structure. Even when other impersonal influences clearly prevail over the apparent effect of personality, we must remember that *all* external influences enter the work through the mediation of personality and that even in the study of historical periods the problems of personality as a developmental factor do not lose their urgency.[3] Both the presence and the absence of strong personalities in a given developmental period must be ascertained and systematically explained. If a regard for the effect of personality upon the development of literature is to be fruitful for scholarship, personality must be conceived as a permanent force functioning uninterruptedly as a counterpressure to the immanent inertia of literary development.

Viewed as a permanent factor of development, personality no longer, of course, appears as a foreign body penetrating the tissue of developmental contexts in order to tear them apart, but as a dialectic negation of immanent development which, being its necessary accompaniment, in fact derives from it. As a dialectic negation, personality does not always automatically relate to development destructively. There are, of course, developmental stages in which it contradicts the direction of previous development or at least tends to do so, but there are also periods in which it appears as the culmination of the preceding development or as the factor synthesizing previously diverse tendencies into a single developmental current. Personality is therefore not outside of development but rather within it; it is its negative aspect. In order to elucidate and substantiate this assertion we shall attempt to enumerate the ties which incorporate personality into development as an evolutionary factor and bind it to it:

The most striking feature which seems to suggest the independence of personality from development is the intensity with

3. Personality as a developmental factor in folklore.

which so-called strong personalities assert themselves in literary evolution. The strong personality seems absolute with respect to development and its regularity. There are, nevertheless, facts which demonstrate that the conditions for the arrival of a strong personality are prepared not only in the social and cultural atmosphere of certain periods but even right in the immanent development of literature itself and that not even the intensity of the personality's expression is therefore independent of the immanent development. For example, Mácha's personality appears as a peak conspicuously rising above all others at the beginning of the development of modern Czech poetry. The strong ties which connect him to the preceding local development are obvious: in the area of metrics, for instance, the developmental need for creating the Czech iamb whose form, provided by Mácha, is closely connected to the other structural components of his *Máj,* such as its vocabulary and its syntactic and semantic structure. But all of this does not weaken the unexpectedness and surprise of Mácha's appearance and his sharp distinction from his contemporaries. Let us, however, note that Mácha appears at a developmental moment when everything has already been prepared for a turn. The theoretical struggles and practical strivings for reorganizing Czech verse had prepared for a definitive crystallization after a series of experiments. The effort at creating a work of monumental character, having resulted several times in mere voluminousness (Vojtěch Nejedlý, Hněvkovský, Polák, Kollár), finally had to reach the conclusion that monumentality does not consist in the scope of the work but in its mode of presentation.[4] Moreover, we must not forget that the conspicuousness of Mácha's figure is heightened by the situation that placed him at the beginning of the new development of Czech poetry after its weakening in the Baroque period (the limitation of poetry to a single genre: religious poetry) and after a period of indecisive fumbling in an effort to regain broad thematic scope and generic variety in the first decades of the nineteenth century.

If we wanted to take into account the general cultural and social situation as well as the immanent situation, we would most certainly see still other moments contributing to an objective explanation of the conspicuousness and visibility of Mácha's poetic

---

4. Cf. a similar process in Russian literature—namely, Ju. Tynjanov, *Arxaisty i novatory* [Archaists and innovators] (Leningrad, 1929).

figure. We do not intend, of course, to claim that after the exhaustion of all these moments the intensity of Mácha's poetic figure is completely explained as a fact of regular development. We are not forgetting that all these favorable moments converged at a given time around a single psychophysical individual with these and those dispositions and with such and such a quantum of energy for their realization. We only wanted to illustrate by this example the assertion that not even a thing so seemingly accidental from the standpoint of development as the force of personality is unrelated to the preceding development. We could also elaborate the generally known and common fact that strong personalities often appear in the development of a particular art in clusters and that again there are entire periods without them. Even at first glance this fact raises the question of whether or not there is any connection between a certain period of development in a given art and the number of strong personalities which assert themselves in this period. We shall not elaborate this allusion, but mention of the temporal parallelism of several strong personalities leads us to the next point.

The individual differences among contemporaries continuing the state of the preceding development in a given art also seem to be a direct expression of the indeterminacy of personalities and their independence from development. If we take a closer look at the differences separating parallel personalities, however, we discover that a certain correlation of personalities as developmental factors manifests itself precisely in these differences. They occur, for example, in many facets, resulting in a direct opposition, in the interrelation of the pair Mácha – Erben. This opposition is not, however, merely a matter of the personal dispositions of the two poets, but it can also be formulated objectively as the opposition of two developmental tendencies which complement one another precisely because of their antithetical character, so that the individuality of one poet cannot be properly understood without confronting it with the other. Jakobson offers an objective formulation of the opposition between Mácha and Erben as the antinomy of a revolutionary Romanticism and a Romanticism of resignation or—from another aspect—as the opposition between the ontogenetic and the philogenetic orientations of the experiences of terror.[5]

5. "Poznámky k dílu Erbenovu, I" [Notes on Erben's works, 1], *Slovo a slovesnost* 1 (1935): 152 f.

This can even be formulated as the opposition of two poetic structures: one, Mácha's, tending toward an extreme lack of motivation
of the components and parts, the other, Erben's, oriented toward
extreme motivation.

Mácha's personality can be subjected to still other comparisons,
especially with J. K. Tyl. Even here the essence of their relation to
one another—again an antithetical relation—would probably appear
only in a comparison of the developmental tendencies which they
represented in literature. This seems to be suggested by Tyl's
novella *Rozervanec* criticizing Mácha and emphasizing the literary
rivalry between the two friends, as well as by some words from
Hindl's letter to Svoboda to the effect that Tyl and Mácha "considered themselves rivals (here I mean only in literature) and *the
further they went, the more they would have to become rivals.*"[6]

The developmental predetermination of differences among personalities is even more distinct in the triad Neruda – Hálek –
Heyduk of the Máj generation than in the preceding two cases.
Grouped according to their human relations, Neruda and Heyduk
are closer to one another than Hálek is to either of them. Poetically, however, Heyduk obviously stands next to Hálek. Especially
in lyric poetry Heyduk and Hálek fulfill the developmental tendency of an emotionally unfettered lyric in opposition to Neruda's
lyric with strong emotional censorship. This distribution of
distinctive properties in the given case is therefore rooted in
literary development, although lack of emotional censorship,
emotional spontaneity, was also a significant biographical trait,
especially in Heyduk.[7] Hence the relationship among contemporaneous personalities is frequently and largely provided not by
the poets' personal characteristics but by their interrelations as
developmental factors and as representatives of different developmental tendencies.

Besides the intensity with which a personality asserts itself as a
link in the developmental series, besides the distinctiveness with
which it differs from its contemporaries, the image of the poet's

6. Italics mine; cited according to the afterword to Krčma's edition of *Rozervanec*
(Prague, 1932).

7. See, for example, Neruda's statement in the article "Rozmanitosti o Adolfu
Heydukovi" [Miscellanea about Adolf Heyduk] in *Kritické spisy J. Nerudy* (Prague,
1910), 6, pt. 1: "He befriended me alone with that ardency which characterizes his
entire vital, even passionate, emotional, rich nature" (p. 337). There are other numerous
statements and direct facts in this study.

psychophysical dispositions as they appear in his work also functions as an immediate expression of personality undetermined by development. Although we have shown above that the image of the personality in a work and the poet's real personality do not have to coincide in scope, that they can even substantially diverge, it nevertheless cannot be denied that there is a certain agreement even in cases of different scope and that there are, moreover, cases in which the poet's personality appears in a work fully and without inhibition. At least in this instance may we speak without reservation about the undetermined, historically independent intervention of personality in development? We have said above that cases in which a tendency toward an uninhibited assertion of a poet's entire personality occurs are developmentally determined. In addition, however, at every stage of development individuals who undertake literary creation find in their path certain preconditions provided by the preceding development, and these have the character of postulates with respect to their own work. It is true that the individual who is to influence future development strongly almost always demonstrates the force of his individuality precisely by disturbing this state as much as possible,[8] but to disturb the previous state of an artistic structure so that it is developmentally transformed into another state—hence not removed without a trace—implies a considerable amount of agreement with it, a considerable ability to assimilate it.

Therefore the dispositions of the individual, even of one who strongly reorganizes the prior state of a structure, are largely determined by the preceding state of literary structure. Only an individual who corresponds to the structure which he is to affect in his dispositions and their hierarchy will appear as a strong developmental factor. Dispositions which do not correspond to the prior state of the structure and which are therefore capable of reorganizing it (inadaptés) will also necessarily appear in a strong personality in addition to the agreements. But not even the direction and the appearance of these disagreements between the personality and the preceding literary structure are always and necessarily completely accidental from the standpoint of the immanent development of literature, because the direction of

8. See the chapter "L'Initiative des inadaptés" in F. Baldensperger, La Littérature: Création, succès, durée (Paris, 1913), pp. 109-28.

future development is already implicitly contained—at least in outline—in a particular developmental stage. If we view development as a genuinely continuous event, it is not, even for a moment in its shortest segment, a permanent state. A completed work which seems to stabilize a certain moment of development is the vehicle of a developmental current only at the moment of its origin. Immediately thereafter the development of the structure overflows into new works. Such a continuous motion, of course, has its direction.

Here the past and the future are always implied in the present, and therefore not even the disturbance caused by the partial disagreement between the creator's (the poet's) dispositions and the preceding state of the structure lacks predetermination. The choice of appropriate individuals for the realization of a certain developmental tendency must certainly be presupposed with respect to a negative relation to the preceding structure. Thus not even the very contents of a personality, the set (the quality and the hierarchy) of its dispositions, are unrelated to the immanent development of literature, are accidental with regard to this evolution.

We have attempted to ascertain the bond between personality and the development of literary structure, and it has become clear that personality is incorporated into development even by those of its aspects which at first glance seemed to be the least determined externally: the intensity of its effect, its differences from other contemporaneous personalities, and the set (the quality and the hierarchy) of its dispositions. We must, however, emphatically point out that this assertion does not in the least lead us into the danger of determinism. None of the aspects of personality, even when its contact with development is as strong as possible, can ever be disconnected from its vehicle, the structure of the personality, of which it is a part. If the literary structure constitutes a unity, from the standpoint of which a personality's interventions appear as accidents violating its immanent regularity, then the personality as well constitutes a self-centered unity. And from its standpoint that regularity of the development of literature which, in compelling the personality to assimilate it, violates its immanent order appears to be an accident. Every component of a literary work can be viewed in its relation to the structure of the work, that is, the degree of its regularity can be ascertained, as well as in its relation to the poet's personality, that is, the degree of its accidentality from the standpoint of the previous development of literature can be ascertained. On the other hand, every component of a poet's personality can be observed in its regular relation to the structure of the individuality of which it is a part as well as in relation to the work where it must submit to the external pressure of an alien regularity. The history of literature is a struggle between the inertia of literary structure and the forced interventions of personalities. The history of a literary personality, a poet's biography, depicts his struggle with the inertia of literary structure. Croce's theory of the poetic work as a direct expression of a personality requires restrictions.

The unpredictability of the literary personality, and thereby its importance as a developmental factor, cannot, however, be fully appreciated as long as we have in mind a single personality in each instance. We must realize that from the standpoint of the entire development of literature the accidentality and unpredictability of personality is provided, on the one hand, by the exchange of personalities in time and, on the other, by the alternation of contemporaneous personalities. The picture of the succession of personalities in the history of any art is by no means as simple as Vrchlický's line attempts to express it: "Druh druhu pochodně si podáváme" ("We pass the torches from one to another, from comrade to comrade"). Personalities following one another immediately can come from the most varied geographical and social spheres, can represent the most varied types of inherent dispositions, can be weak or strong; it is the same with contemporaneous personalities which struggle for dominance. A personality which has intervened once is already a more or less predictable factor, in some cases an absolute constant, in its further interventions. Personalities following one another or acting simultaneously are, however, heterogeneous and incomparable factors. It is mainly for this reason, therefore, that personality is a source of perpetual agitation and a focal point of reversals for development. And thus from a different perspective we again arrive at an assertion which we have made above: we can experience the whole significance of personality as a developmental factor only if we view it not as an isolated, unrepeatable point in time and space but as a constant force exerting upon development a constant pressure, the direction and intensity of which, of course, continually change.

Another circumstance that allows us to detect the indeterminacy of personality with respect to development is the following. We have said that if we view every developmental stage as the
present, it implies partly a past stage and partly a future stage, in
other words, that the direction of future development is always
given to a certain extent by the necessities which follow from the
preceding development. But this given pertains only to its overall
direction, not to its concrete realization. Let us assume that the
concrete movements a b c d, put into practice by personalities
A B C D, have appeared at a certain developmental stage both as a
reaction to the immediately preceding developmental state and as
its resultant. We could hardly conclude that these movements are
logically necessary to the extent that one of them could be missing
if the appropriate personality were not at hand or that movements
e f g, and so on, could not be added if there were more personalities at hand at the given moment. In any case it will be those
movements which have been realized and not those which we
might anticipate or rather merely surmise as unrealized that will
become the bases for further development. Here the decisive
developmental influence of personality—with all of its accidentality with respect to development—is therefore fully apparent. The
situation as we have depicted it is, of course, abstract. In reality—
at least in most cases—it is probable that the realization or non-
realization of a particular movement will be influenced not only
by the originator's personality but also by the regular developmental preconditions for which it will be more suitable than another that is likewise a priori possible. Here we have been concerned only with proving how personality through its accidentality
determines the path of immanent development which has seemingly been fully determined by suprapersonal forces.

Not even the fact that a personality appears in development as a
representative of a certain milieu or social stratum need imply
only a passive role for personality. On the contrary, it is obvious,
though difficult to prove concretely, that the relative force of the
representatives of different milieux (or immanent tendencies) can
determine the hierarchy.

If we examined all the components and aspects of a literary
work in this way, it would be clear that each of them can be
defined in direct connection with the poet's personality. But to
deduce from this the absolute dependence of a literary work upon

the poet's personality would be as incorrect as the other extreme, to deny the dependence of a work upon the poet's personality. Every component of a literary work and its structure in general can a priori be determined just as much by the poet's personality as by the development of the structure. Scholarship must reckon with this duality, must proceed from it as from a working hypothesis and innovative principle. This means that with respect to every component of a literary work and the whole we must ask to what extent it arises from individual motivation and to what extent from developmental motivation. In this sense the sphere of individual motivation includes, of course, all the influences of other developmental cultural series and the influence of the development of social organization, for the individual is, as we have said above, the bearer—and by no means a passive one—of all of this. As soon as such an influence is exerted upon the development of literary structure, it will immediately appear incorporated into this structure with respect to the past and the future: it will be apparent how development needed and exploited it. A developmental necessity is not, however, identical with a logical necessity. We can always presuppose that the developmental function which the influence borne by a certain personality fulfilled could have been fulfilled by another influence if another personality coming from a different milieu had intervened. The further development deriving from this other influence would probably appear different from what actually occurred. No matter how rigorous the organic unity of an immanent developmental line might seem to be, it always gives complete freedom to accident—to the individual—not in the sense that the individual can break the developmental tendency (such an intervention is not only beyond the reach of the individual's will but also outside of the realm of his intention, for the individual intends to change the previous state, but this also means to preserve the identity of the changed thing), but in the sense that the developmental tendency is much broader than its concrete realization. Every realization of a developmental tendency is only one of many or, at least, several possible ones.

Only the inclusion of the individual as a developmental factor in the theoretical study of literature means in fact the definitive liquidation of the causal conception of development. As long as we see only the immanent development and the other series intervening in this development at just the moment when and in just the manner that it needs their intervention, there is always the danger that the word *regularity,* even if the scholar himself understands it teleologically, will contain some latent mechanical causality, will incline toward the scheme of causes and results necessarily and unequivocally following from them. But as soon as we have in mind that accident, represented by the individual (the individual as genus), constantly and continuously operates behind this regularity as its latent aspect, the notion of regularity is divested of the last traces of causality. Accident and law cease to exclude one another and conjoin into a genuine, always dynamic and energizing dialectic opposition.

The indeterminacy of personality will, however, appear even more distinct if instead of looking at it from the inside of development we choose to examine it from the outside, if we view personality as a source of impulses and the point of intersection of the external influences which intervene in literature. Personality will then appear to us (as we have mentioned above) as a bundle of dispositions, either inherent or acquired (through education, through the influence of the natural and social milieux, through occupation, etc.). We have also said that it is difficult to distinguish between inherent and acquired dispositions, for very often one and the same disposition can be both inherent and additionally modified by external influences. Even what is inherent in personality and what has been brought into it by the fortunes of life have a considerable amount of accidentality in themselves. But even more unpredictable are the resultants into which these individual components are bound, and then even more so is personality as a structure binding both parallel and antithetical forces into a fixed whole. The uniqueness of personality as a whole is apparent, and therefore the assumption of Taineism and movements deriving from it that personality can be wholly determined through its analysis into individual components of biological (heredity) and social (milieu, race) origin is fundamentally fallacious. The well-known axiom that a whole is more and something different from the sum of the parts of which it is composed is in itself enough, in fact, to reveal this fallacy.

This does not, of course, mean that scholarship must give up the analysis and objective classification of personality. We have mentioned above that it is possible and necessary to attempt a psychological description and typological classification of the creative personality, that it is furthermore necessary to solve as well the general problems of the psychology of creativity, for example, the question of poetic invention and imagination, the question of the relationship between sexual life and artistic creation—all of this, of course, under the condition that the scholar always keep in mind the possibility of the historical changeability of the seemingly extratemporal laws which follow from the material. But the specific question of the poet's personality must also be raised; in other words, the epistemology of biography must be systematically considered. The biographer's duty is to answer the question of which external influences have formed the poet and how they have done so. All the poet's actions must be explained from the structure of his personality. If the poet's personality is to be grasped in its uniqueness, it must be conceived as an activity, not as a permanent, petrified configuration. It is therefore incorrect if the biographer limits himself to an unhistorical affirmation or rejection of the poet's behavior, to a positive or negative idealizing of the poet's personality (the poet as a hero of good or evil).[9]

But if we want to view the poet's personality as an activity, it is not enough to break it down mechanically into the parts which have gradually formed it. The very succession in which these parts—individual influences—have entered the personality has become a fact of its structure. It is not indifferent whether influence x has affected the structure of the personality before influence y or only after it has been reshaped as a whole by this influence. Moreover, the biographer must always keep in mind that the contact between the personality as a structure and a certain influence is not mechanically necessary or unequivocal. The fact that a poet comes from a certain social stratum, for example, can be—and most probably will be—a factor of his mental structure, but even the extreme case in which this fact remains—especially if it is paralyzed by another stronger influence—without any effect is conceivable. If social origin has become a factor, its influence is not necessarily direct; the poet can be an exponent of another stratum than the one from which he has come or of several strata in succession. Indeed, he can even become an adversary of the stratum from which he has come.

9. Furthermore, idealizing is an equally unscholarly approach whether it is provocative—the poet as a rebel against the conventional ideal of man—or philistine—the poet as a perfect realization of the ideal of the orderly citizen. The poet's biography thus turns into a moralizing treatise in which only the facts introduced—provided that they are new—can have any scholarly value.

8

Detail as the Basic Semantic Unit in Folk Art

The conception of folkloric creation has undergone a basic change in recent decades. There has been a fundamental change in the view of the relationship between subjectivity and objectivity in folk creation, of the relative participation of the individual and the collective in it, of the relationship between folkloric creation and "high" art, of the incorporation of folklore into the life of society. Questions of artistic form in folklore have also taken on a new appearance. Moreover, new problems, in fact new sets of problems, are looming on the horizon. There are in particular the questions of functions as well as those of the sign and semioticity. It would be too extensive an undertaking and would lead to a repetition of things already known from elsewhere were we to attempt to elucidate the new conception of folklore in its entire breadth and magnitude. The following study will deal with the questions of the sign and semioticity in folkloric art, not in their entire scope but only with the problem of the semiotic nature of detail in the folkloric work of art.

We must nevertheless say at least a few words about semioticity in folkloric art in general.[1] A folkloric creation of whatever kind has the very pronounced character of a sign. It even happens that semioticity connects a folkloric work, for example, a song, so firmly to certain kinds of situations in life that the semiotic function suffices to veil the content of the text of the song. Martha Bringemeier quotes the song "Wir sitzen hier so fröhlich beisammen," the first line of which speaks about the pleasure of sitting

This essay was translated from "Detail jako základní sémantická jednotka v lidovém umění" (1942), *Studie z estetiky* (Prague, 1966).

1. If we say "folkloric art," we have in mind those folk creations which correspond to the individual categories of "high" art, for example, folk songs, folk paintings, folk theater, and so on. We must be aware, however, that folkloric creation as a whole by no means occupies only the sphere of art and that the relation of the "artistic" folkloric work to the life of the collective is completely different from that of "high" art. It is more concrete and more immediate. For this reason there is also no boundary in folkloric creation between works with a prevailing aesthetic function and works in which the aesthetic function, though present, does not prevail over the others.

with a friend but the text of which is a patriotic song from the period of the Napoleonic wars. The meaning of this text is, however, absorbed by the meaning of the first line to such a degree that "sometimes when sung, the entire first stanza disappears and, nevertheless, the song retains the meaning which the first line gives it."[2]

The folkloric work of art as a whole, therefore, generally relates to specific kinds of real situations which it signifies. The individual and the collective can strive to affect reality (magic rituals and objects) through the mediation of the folkloric work as a sign. A significant property of folklore is that each folkloric work is a set of rather loosely connected signs, and thus they are capable of migrating freely from one whole to another. It has been known for a long time that folk tale motifs, for example, are capable of migrating from tale to tale separately and in sets and of regrouping freely even within individual tales. This also applies, however, to other kinds of folkloric art. Karel Šourek mentions how a certain detail in folk painting and sculpture is sometimes exaggerated for emphasis regardless of its actual proportion to other elements: "Let us look, for example, at the proportions of the individual characters in the scene 'The Flight into Egypt' on the underlayer of the glass: the landscape, the ass, St. Joseph—all of these diminish next to the dominant silhouette of Mary hiding the Holy Son while fleeing. The exaggerated head of the statue of St. John of Nepomuk (the proportion of head to body is 1 : 3) pressing his silent lips together with poignant zeal is evidence of the same principle of sculpture. Here again the semantically important details of the saint's face are exaggerated . . . because for the folk artist they are the vehicle of the expression and hence the total meaning of the statue."[3] This is, of course, a completely different conception of the unity of the work of art from that to which we are accustomed from works of contemporary "high" art. As proof of this let us juxtapose a passage from Šalda with the preceding citation from Šourek: "A poetic work is not the individual speeches or deliberations of certain characters but an *inseparable, integral whole* of characters, actions, fates, *the entire poetically*

---

2. *Gemeinschaft und Volkslied* (Münster, 1931), p. 107.
3. *Lidové umění v Čechách a na Moravě* [Folk art in Bohemia and Moravia] (Prague, 1942), p. 118.

vital tissue, as it unfolds before the reader from the first letter to the last sentence."[4]

Does the folkloric work of art therefore never achieve the closed form which we require of the works of high art? An observation made by Jungbauer[5] provides an instructive answer to this question. The author succeeded in recording both the original form of a broadside ballad about a murder, composed in 1845, and the rendition of this song as it existed in folk tradition in 1905, sixty years after its origin. The original song had twenty-one stanzas, the version of 1905 only seven. In comparison with the verbose original, the text which had passed through tradition is a closed balladic form. This form did not, however, result from a creator's intention but came about through creative forgetting, in brief through a collective collaboration on its transformation, a collaboration which cannot be denied intentionality and at the end of which a folk (in fact, in the case of the broadside ballad, semi-folk) work corresponds to the creative principle of artificial poetry. The independence of individual details, the "additive" character of the entire composition of the song, however, remain in effect even in the collective collaboration on the transformation of the existing work. As soon as an artificial song becomes folklorized, it not only loses some of its motifs but also acquires others.

The appending of details in folk art does not always correspond to the laws of logic and experience. We shall speak about this later. A detail maintains its semantic independence, and a work comes about through the appending of details which are usually part of tradition and have therefore originated a long time before the author of a particular work used them. Thus the theory of the spontaneous origin of a work from the author's experience is shown to be invalid for folkloric art. Karel Jaromír Erben, who held to this theory, explains in the introduction to his anthology the origin of the song "Červená růžičko, proč se nerozvíjíš?" in a way that was for a long time considered a generally valid explanation of the genesis of folk songs: "A girl hears a tune, for example No. 93 of this collection, being played in a pub. These heartrending sounds—which in my opinion can best be produced on a violin,

4. "Doslov autorův," *Loutky i dělníci boží,* 4th ed. (Prague, 1935), p. 418.
5. G. Jungbauer, "Zur Volksliedfrage," *Germanisch-romanische Monatsschrift* 5 (1913): 68 f.

and even their form indicates a more perfect instrument—stick in the girl's memory; her entire soul is filled with them and takes on their color; day and night this tune is on her mind; wherever she goes, she hums it, seeking only the words which would allow her to pour out through her mouth what abounds in her heart and soul. Suddenly her gaze accidentally falls on an open red bud of a rose bush in the garden in front of her window. This is the spark for her soul; in this bud she sees a real image of that emotion which the music has caused in her soul. Immediately seizing this opportunity, she makes the half-opened rose the beginning of her song; the tune establishes the word order, the form of the lines and also governs the rhyme, when the girl begins:

> "Červená růžičko, proč se nerozvíjíš?
> Proč k nám, můj holečku, proč k nám už nechodíš?"
> "Kdybych k vám chodíval, ty by si plakala,
> červeným šátečkem oči utírala."[6]

> "Little red rose, why don't you open?
> Why don't you come to visit us any more, my darling,
>   to visit us?"
> "If I came to visit you, you would cry,
>   you would wipe your eyes with a little red
>   handkerchief."

According to Erben, the actual impulse for the origin of the *text* of the song (the melody is provided in advance) is an accidental sensory perception and the emotional experience attending it. But this is contradicted by the fact that the first line of the song has a traditional character and even stands at the point of intersection of several traditional formulae for a beginning. (1) Its beginning has the form of a question, like, for example, the first line of the song "Čí je to koníček?" [Whose little horse is this?]. (2) It has the character of an apostrophe, like, for example, the beginning of the song "Ach cesto, cestičko ušlapaná" [Oh path, little path trampled down]. (3) It is introduced by the adverb "why," and fifteen songs in Erben's collection begin with this word, in addition to others which have "why"—just as our song—within the first line. (4) It begins with an adjective signifying a color, as do, for

6. *Prostonárodní české písně a říkadla* [Czech folk songs and sayings], 4th ed. (Prague, 1937), pp. 8-9.

example, the songs "Černé oči, jděte spat" [Black eyes, go to sleep] and "Červený, bílý, to se mně líbí" [Red, white, that's what I like]. (5) Its first line contains the name of a plant, as do, for example, the songs "Červená, modrá fiala" [Red, blue violet], "Trávo, trávo, trávo zelená" [Grass, grass, green grass] and indeed even "Růžička červená, krví pokropená" [Little red rose, sprinkled with blood].

The genesis of a folkloric work of art thus begins with an accumulation of traditional motifs and formulae even though we must presuppose an individual creator at its origin. And the origin of a work of folk art is only the beginning of a process of constant changes occurring through the regrouping, the addition, and the loss of details. These details are the basic semantic units of the contexture of the folkloric work of art. They can be of different scope. Thus the very coupling of words can be a basic traditional semantic unit in folk poetry, but so can a line or even an entire stanza ("wandering" stanzas).

In the linking of details into a contexture, of course, there often occur semantic "junctures" which in folk art are neither an accidental phenomenon nor the "defect" about which scholars of the older generation, such as Gebauer and Bartoš, used to speak. Although the "junctures" are perceived, the semantic connection between them is only apparent. It is the listener's task to establish it. This semantic process of connecting the unconnected manifests itself most distinctly in folk poetry (although it also occurs, for example, in folk visual art). Thus the introductory lines of folk songs often have to be connected with what follows afterwards. It sometimes happens, of course, that the connection is direct even though the beginning of a song has a formulaic character:

Pod tú černú horú	Under that black mountain
husičky se perú.	geese are fighting.
Pod'me, moja milá,	Let's go, my darling,
zabijem některú.[7]	we'll kill one of them.

More often, however, the connection must be sought afterwards—in our relating the beginning of the song metaphorically to what follows:

7. F. Sušil, *Moravské národní písně* [*Moravian folk songs*], 3rd ed. (Prague, 1941), p. 271.

Co je po studýnce,	Why should one care about a well,
dyž v ní vody néní?	when there's no water in it?
jako po panence,	as about a maiden,
dyž v ní lásky néní.	when there's no love in her?

[Sušil, p. 287]

There are also cases in which the connection between the beginning and the very context of the song is simultaneously direct and figurative:

Rostó, rostó konopě	The hemp is growing, growing
za cestó,	beyond the road,
už só pěkný zelený.	it's already nicely green.
A za nima roste	And beyond it grows
černovoký děvče,	a dark-eyed girl,
až vyroste, bude mý.	when she grows up, she'll be mine.

[Sušil, p. 287]

But we also find examples in which there is a lack of any apparent or hidden semantic connection between the beginning of a song and what follows it:

Na nasilskym poli	On Nasily field
stromeček stoji	a little tree stands
a na něm žulty květ;	and on it there's a yellow flower;
o! dočkaj ty, dočkaj,	oh! wait you, wait,
moja najmilejša	my most beloved,
hodzinu sedym let.	seven years for the moment.

[Sušil, p. 299]

Here the semantic juncture between the beginning of the song and the continuation of the text is almost displayed. The semantic "leap" which subsequently occurs is striking precisely for its absolute incomprehensibility.

A comparison of the variants of the same song, each of which has a different beginning, can be interesting. In Sušil's collection we find on p. 271 the song:

Sokolove oči,	Falcon's eyes,
jastřabove peři;	hawk's feathers;
každa panna blazen,	every maiden is crazy,
co pacholkům věři.	who trusts young men.

The variant closest to this version has the beginning:

Šuhajova hlava,	A swain's head,
za klobóčkem péří,	feathers in his hat,

každá panna blázen,	every maiden is crazy,
kerá chlapcům věří.	who trusts boys.

The entire meaning of this stanza (and of the rest of the text) is: swains are handsome but deceitful. The first variant feigns a semantic break between the first and second distychs. It actually only feigns it, because it does not name the proper subject of the statement, the swain, but only suggests it by the predicates: eyes, hawk's feathers (in the hat). In the second variant the subject concerned is explicitly named. The semantic leap is still present to a certain extent, because the adversative "but" (handsome but deceitful) remains unexpressed. The third variant completely suppresses the semantic leap:

Kolik je klásečků	As many ears as there are
v ječmenném snopečku,	in a barley sheaf,
tolik falešnosti	so much deceitfulness
při každém synečku.	is there in every young man.

Here an entire pattern book of the possible semantic connections (and disconnections) between the beginning and the text of a song is gathered within the negligible span of a single little song.

Scholars noticed the peculiarities of the semantic relationship between the beginning and the text proper of folk songs long ago, but their evaluation was different from ours. Let us cite as an example Gebauer's study "On the Beginnings Favored by Folk Songs, Especially Slavic Ones" (1875). There we read: "Besides beginnings with fully realized images we frequently encounter in folk songs *disfigured, stunted and corrupted* beginnings and images. In order for an image to be *fully* realized, the object should be placed next to it and the *tertium* pointed out. And whenever one of these things is missing, the image lacks something for its completeness. Sometimes, of course, the meaning of the image is not greatly obscured and understanding is not hindered, although something has been omitted. . . . But more frequent are cases in which the image is obscured by disfiguration and its meaning and purpose become unclear. The detriment to the art of poetry and the debasement of poetic technique are palpable when dark and often nonsensical disfigurations occur instead of clear images and when there is a preference for *stereotypical* image beginnings which are sometimes suitable but more often not."[8]

8. J. Gebauer, "O začátcích v jakých si libují národní písně, zvláště slovanské," *Stati literárnědějepisné*, ed. A. Novák (Prague, 1941), 1: 80-81.

Today it is already clear that—in contrast to Gebauer's view—not even the semantic leaps between the beginning and the text are a manifestation of a "corruption" but only an exaggeration of the general tendency of folkloric art toward composing a work from details which are semantically more or less independent. Today we already know very well that the starting point from which a folkloric work of art is constructed by addition is not an image (even one only gradually realizing itself in the work) of a semantic whole but that it is details created and fixed by tradition which are subsequently put together to form a whole in a mosaic-like fashion. This is valid for the work as a whole, not only for one of its parts, for example, the relationship between the beginning and the text of a folk song. Let us cite some examples of this artistic method, typical of artistic folklore, again verbal folklore.

First let us call to mind the rather frequent cases in which the coupling of a fixed epithet (*epitheton constans*) clashes with the occasional context precisely because of its traditional nature; for example, "louka zelená sněhem se bělá" ("the green meadow is whitening with snow"),[9] where the semantic leap between the lexicalized coupling of an adjective with a substantive and the remaining contexture of the sentence is readily apparent. The way in which subjects are handled in folk songs provides another illustration of the mosaiclike composition of a contexture in them. The folk song, unlike artificial poetry, exhibits an excessive preference for emphasizing the subject from whom the utterance proceeds or to whom it is addressed. Linguistically this tendency manifests itself in the frequent use of the personal and possessive pronouns of the first and second person (I - you; my - your) as well as the first and second persons of verbs. At the same time the speaking and addressed subjects alternate with one another frequently and vividly in the course of the same song. This also results in a certain kind of semantic leap. In a folk song the repertoire of possible speaking subjects is often increased because not only people but animals (for example, a horse to his rider) and inanimate objects, even immaterial states of mind, speak here:

Plyň, lásko falešná,	Flow, false love
až do Prahy,	right to Prague,
jednoho mládence,	[false love] of one youth,
jedné panny!—	[false love] of one maiden!—

9. Erben, *Prostonárodní české písně*, p. 385.

Já láska falešná	I, false love,
pluju v řece;	flow in the river;
byla jsem puštěna	I was launched
po potoce.	on a brook.

[Erben, p. 176]

The deceased, too, are often addressed and speak in the folk song, even when evoking an impression of something miraculous is not intended. In epic songs, for instance, the depiction of death is presented through the mouth of the dead person himself:

Na kohos, Mariško,	Whom, Mariško,
na kohos vouaua,	whom were you calling,
dyž ti ta vodička	when that water
ústa zalévaua?	was flooding your mouth?
Byua bych vouaua	I would have called
na svoju mamičku,	my dear mother,
ale sem nemohua	but I couldn't
pro prudkú vodičku.	for the rushing water.
Byua bych vouaua	I would have called
na svého tatíčka,	my dear father,
ale sa mi vliua	but the water
voda do srdečka.	was pouring into my heart.
Byua bych vouaua	I would have called
na svého miuého,	my beloved,
ale sem nemohua	but I couldn't
pro boha živého.	for God's sake.

[Sušil, p. 120]

The folk song can also use an indefinite subject ("someone") for the purpose of making the listener feel the semantic leap, in this instance provided by the semantic span between the extremely concrete first person of the verb and the diffuseness of the semantic contour of the subject "someone":

Když jsem já k vám chodívával	When I used to walk to your place
přes ten hájíček,	through that little grove,
na cestu mně svítívával	my way was usually lit
jasnej měsíček;	by the bright little moon;
měsíček mně svítívával	the moon used to light my way,
já jsem sobě zpívávával,	I used to sing to myself,
popošel jsem kousek cesty,	I'd gone a bit of my way,
někdo zavolal.[10]	*someone* called me.

10. Italics mine, J. M.

Zavolal jest smutným hlasem:	He called in a sad voice:
"Stůj a zastav se,	"Halt and stop,
jde za tebou potěšení,	your darling is following you,
něco ti nese:	is bringing you something:
nese ti smutné psaní	is bringing you a sad letter
černě zapečetěny;	sealed in black;
málo inkoustem je psáno,	with little ink it is written,
více slzami."	more with tears."

[Erben, p. 163]

From artificial poetry we are accustomed to perceiving the fact that someone addresses or is addressed as a part of the theme. In folk poetry, however, the fact that someone addresses or is addressed is often motivated very freely. Precisely for this reason folk poetry can exploit the changes in speaker for the mere achievement of semantic leaps. A comparison of two variants of the same song appearing in Erben's collection (p. 162) provides us with a good illustration. The song contains a girl's complaint about her lover's infidelity. In one variant the girl is the sole speaking subject right to the end; in the last stanza of the second variant the lover suddenly starts speaking and ironically answers the girl. The two versions are as follows:

First Variant

Zafoukej, větříčku,	Blow, little wind,
v pravou stranu;	to the right;
že mého Jeníčka pozdravuju;	that I greet my Johnny;
že ho pozdravuju,	that I greet him,
za lásku děkuju,	thank [him] for [his] love,
za jeho falešné	for his false
milování!	loving!

Second Variant

Zafoukej z Dunaje,	Blow from the Danube,
můj větříčku,	my little wind,
pozdravuj ode mne	greet from me
mou Ančičku:	my Annie:
že ji pozdravuju atd.	that I greet her, etc.

Since the alternation of subjects in the folk song is therefore largely freed from thematic motivation, folk poetry can transfer the spectator to the perspective of one subject, then of a second, and sometimes even of a third. Within the contexture of a song there occurs, therefore, a sequence of semantic shifts which results from the semantic independence of the detail, an independence that is a property of folk poetry:

Teče voda, velká voda	Water, a flood is flowing
kolem dokola jabora.	all around the maple tree.
Všecky lavičky pobrala,	It has carried away all the
	footbridges,
jenom jednu tam nechala.	it has left only one there.
Po kerej Honzíček chodí,	Over which Johnny walks,
Marjánku za ruku vodí.	leads Mary by the hand.
Byl jest tam jeden	There was one
stromeček,	little tree there,
na něm bylo moc	on it were a lot
jabliček.	of apples.
Utrh Honzíček, utrh dvě,	Johnny picked, picked two,
jedno je pustil po vodě.	one he launched on the water.
Kam, jablíčko, kampak	Where, little apple, where
kráčíš,	are you going,
že se ani nevotáčíš?	that you don't even turn around?
Kráčím já, kráčím	I'm going, I'm going
po dolu,	down,
až k mej Marynce	right to my Mary's
do domu.	house.
Když připlynulo k okýnku,	When it had reached the little
	window,
zaklepalo na Marynku.	it knocked for Mary.
Vyjdi, Marynko, vyjdi	Come out, Mary, come
ven,	outside,
Honzíček stojí před	Johnny is standing in front of
domem.	the house.
Pročpak bych já ven	Why would I go
chodila?	outside?
Dyt' já nejsem jeho	You know, I'm not his
milá.	beloved.
Pročpak bys milá nebyla,	Why wouldn't you be [my] beloved,
dyt's mi dávno slibovala!	since you promised me long ago!
Slibovalas mně o duši,	You promised me on [your] soul,
že se ta láska nezruší.	that this love wouldn't be broken.
	[Sušil, p. 312]

There are six changes of the speaking subject in this twelve
stanza song (if we disregard the neutral stanzas): the lover, the
singer, the apple, the apple, the girl, the lover. However, not only
the speaker can change in a song, but so can the one to whom the
utterance is addressed. If the change occurs without preparation
and transition, there is a semantic leap here as well. In the following song a girl speaks all the time but at first to her lover, then
suddenly to her mother:

Jen jednou za tejden,	Only once a week,
potěšení moje,	my delight,
můžeš přijít;	can you come;
až se pomilujem,	when we've made love,
můj zlatej holečku,	my golden lad,
můžeš si jít:	you can leave:
v sobotu podvečer,	on Saturday evening,
to sejdem se,	we'll meet,
když hodinka příde,	when the time comes,
rozejdem se.	we'll part.
Krájejte, má milá,	Cut, my dear,
mamičko rozmilá,	beloved mother,
drobnej salát;	the salad fine;
já nejsem uvyklá,	I'm not used,
má mamičko milá,	my dear mother,
dlouho spávat:	to sleeping long:
já vstávám raníčko	I get up early
za svítání,	at dawn,
když češe můj milý,	when my dear,
holeček rozmilý,	beloved lad,
koně vrany.	grooms [his] black horses.

[Erben, p. 170]

Here the change in listener occurs only once. The change is,
however, very striking not only because it happens unexpectedly
but also because the two utterances are semantically independent
of one another to a great extent. The semantic leap at their boundary is therefore striking.

Under the conditions which we have just depicted, it is not surprising that the folk song is mainly oriented toward dialogue. The
composers of the echoes,[11] especially Čelakovský and Sládek,

11. *Editors' note.* The "echo" (Czech: *ohlas*) is a particular type of Czech poetry
which imitated the folk verbal art of the Slavs both in theme and in form. Cf., e.g., F. L.

were clearly aware of this property of the folk song. This is true
not only of Czech folk songs. Gesemann cites three common
compositional schemes of Serbian folk poetry: the fairy's calling,
the raven's message, the dream and the interpretation of the
dream.[12] All three imply the dialogization of epic material. By
calling, the fairy warns the hero of danger, and the hero replies;
the ravens come forward, they are asked questions, and they
answer; the dream is narrated by the person who had it, and it is
then interpreted by another person in reply. The reason for which
dialogue is so prevalent in folk poetry does not stem from its
themes alone, nor is it merely a matter of an external technique;
rather it follows from the very principle of the semantic structure
of the folkloric work of art, from the tendency to build its semantic contexture from partial units which are relatively independent
of one another.

In addition, let us mention so-called balladic terseness as another property characteristic of this genre. Heussler even declares
it the main feature distinguishing the epic song from the epic.[13]
From the example cited by Jungbauer and quoted above it is
obvious that abbreviation is the result of the economy of memory.
But terseness is likewise *facilitated* by the very structure of the
contexture composed of units relatively independent of one another. If we view the ballad from the standpoint of artificial
poetry and hence from the perspective of a unified semantic
intention, its terseness may appear to us as a dramatic quality in
the sense of the definition favored by Jaroslav Vlček (a ballad is a
drama narrated in the form of a song), but for the poetics of folk
poetry it is only one of the consequences of the basic semantic
law of this manner of creation.

Another consequence of the validity of this law is a phenomenon common in the folk lyric whereby all of a sudden and without transition a laudatory song can become deprecatory, a
sympathetic one antipathetic, a seriously intended one ironic, by
the mere addition of a stanza which is in sharp opposition to the
preceding stanzas. In the foreword to his *Anthology of Czecho-*

Čelakovský's *Ohlas písní ruských* [The echo of Russian songs] (1829) or *Ohlas písní
českých* [The echo of Czech songs] (1839).

12. G. Gesemann, "Kompositionsschema und heroisch-epische Stilisierung," *Studien
zur südslawischen Volksepik* (Reichenberg, 1926), pp. 65 f.

13. A. Heussler, *Lied und Epos* (Dortmund, 1905), p. 22.

slovakian Folk Songs (1874) František Bartoš mentions a number
of examples of this, of course, only to show how he himself "has
purged the text of all kinds of inappropriate additions." It was not
his fault but rather the spirit of the age that caused him to overlook the fact that such striking semantic turns in the text are only
extreme manifestations of a property omnipresent in the folk
song, namely, the constant oscillation of semantic contexture. The
contexture of a folk song is always ready to surprise the listener,
to take another path than that which its previous course has indicated. But if we imagine the conditions under which a folk song
used to be sung—for example, at a folk dance before a circle of
listeners who evaluated every initiative on the part of the singer—
we understand that the deviations from an already known text,
which brought a traditional text closer to the immediate situation,
were not considered by the audience to be a "detriment" to the
effect but rather an enhancement of it. Thus Erben cites (p. 114,
No. 117) a song in which a lover complains how he came to visit
his beloved at her parents' house, how the dog Kuráž started bark-
ing at him and summoned his master, whose arrival chased the boy
from the yard. The text ends with an apostrophe to the dog
Kuráž:

Kuráž, Kuráž!	Kuráž, Kuráž!
ty lásky neznáš;	you don't know what love is;
sic bys byl neštěkal,	otherwise you wouldn't have barked,
když jsem byl u vás.	when I was at your place.

The song is thematically closed, but Erben has recorded one more
stanza. Of course, he introduces it with the note: "The following
stanza is probably a later addition and is only detrimental to the
preceding ones." The stanza reads:

Vždyť' já jsem neštěkal,	Well, I didn't bark,
já jsem jen vrčel,	I only growled,
kdybych to byl věděl,	if I had known this,
byl bych radš mlčel.	I would rather have kept quiet.
Špetni jen, Kuráž!	Just whisper, Kuráž!
kůrčičku tu máš;	here's a crust for you;
já ani nemuknu,	I won't even open my mouth,
když budeš u nás.	when you're at our place.

If Erben says that the stanza is "detrimental," he is speaking
from the standpoint of the compositional unity to which he himself strictly adhered in his own epic poems and fairy tales. The

requirement of compositional closure was not, however, valid for the folk singer and his listeners. Instead, the song was more charming for them if Kuráž, who had hitherto only been addressed, unexpectedly joined in the end of the song with a good-natured afterword in order to proclaim his previous behavior a mistake. This corresponds exactly to the principle of additive composition in which the listener could expect a surprise from an unforeseen semantic break after every line, not to say every stanza.

By remaining alive and being transformed from reproduction to reproduction, the folk song and other forms of folk poetry do not, therefore, have the unity of semantic intention which makes a work of artificial poetry an integral creation characterized by a particular set and sequence of parts. In the perception of a work of artificial poetry, the tendency toward semantic unification operates from the very beginning, when the total meaning of the creation is still unknown. Every part, every detail which enters the perceiver's consciousness during perception is immediately evaluated and understood in its relation to this total meaning, and only its incorporation into this meaning determines the specific semantic quality and import of every detail of the work. If some detail slips out of the sequence of the others, if it resists incorporation into the total meaning, the perceiver expects that another detail will appear by means of which the seemingly errant detail will be connected with the total meaning. Even when all the parts (details, motifs) of a work are not incorporated into the total meaning or when this total meaning remains hidden from the perceiver, the orientation toward the semantic unity of the work is not invalidated. There will merely be a feeling of artistically intentional semantic "deformation." It is, however, otherwise in folk poetry. The semantic sequence created by successive individual motifs remains open. The total meaning which is, of course, gradually created in the perceiver's consciousness from a sequence of units can change in the course of the work. Even in folk poetry, though, there are cases in which the meaning of the work is unified, indeed very tightly unified, but in such cases semantic unity is not a precondition, a norm; it is simply one of the possible results. The inconsistency of successive motifs in folk poetry is neither a "mistake," as the old school believed, nor an intentional deformation (as more recent theoreticians have said), but a simple fact.

Let us demonstrate what we mean by an example. It is a song recorded in Sušil's collection (p. 98) which narrates how a daughter, married far away from her mother, arrives for a visit a year later but does not find anyone in the house except a little boy sitting at the table. She starts to talk to him:

Ptam se ja tě, pachole,	I ask you, little boy,
hdě moja maměnka je?	where my mother is?
Mamička nam umřela,	Our dear mother has been dead
to včera od večera.	since yesterday evening.
Leža tamto v komůrce	*She's lying there in that little room*
v malovanej truhelce.	*in a painted coffin.*
Dcerka, jak to učula,	The daughter, as soon as she heard this,
hned k mamičce běžela.	immediately ran to her dear mother.
Ach mamičko, stavajtě,	Ach dear mother, get up,
požehnani mně dajtě.	give me your blessing.
Dy stě nám ho nědaly,	After all, you didn't give it to us,
když stě nam umiraly.	when you were dying on us.
Ach mamičko, stavajtě,	Ach dear mother, get up,
slovečko ke mně mluvtě	speak a word to me.
Ma dceruško, něvolaj,	My little daughter, don't call,
těžkosti mně nedělaj.	don't give me a hard time.
Ja bych rada mluvila,	I'd like to speak,
dyby ja živa byla.	if I were alive.
Ležim blizko kostela	*I'm lying close to the church*
a neslyšim zvoněňa.	*and I don't hear [the bells] ringing.*
Ani ptačka zpivati,	Or the birdie singing,
tej zezulky kukati.	the cuckoo calling.
Těš tě už tu Pan Bůh	May the Lord himself comfort
sam,	you here,
matka Boži, svaty Jan.	the mother of God, Saint John.

The inconsistency which violates the unified meaning of the song is apparent here. It is said that the deceased lies in a little room, but several lines later the deceased claims that she is close to the church. This contradiction can very easily be explained genetically. In both cases it is a matter of fixed folkloric motifs which we find in other songs in very similar, even identical wording:

I. Tvůj Heřmánek v komoře je,   Your Herman is in a little room,
   leží v malovanej truhle.   he is lying in a painted coffin.
                                                      [Sušil, p. 83]

II. Nežadaj to, ženo ma,   Don't ask, my wife,
    by ses ku mně dostala.   to join me.
    Ležim blizko kostela   I'm lying close to the church
    a něslyšim zvoněňa,   and I don't hear [the bells] ringing
    ani ptáčka zpivaňa.   or the birdie's singing.
                                                      [Sušil, p. 152]

What is important is the fact that the first of the motifs is
presented both in our song and in the other one as a *report* about
a dead person, the second likewise in both occurrences as a part
of an *utterance of the deceased himself.* Therefore there is an
"incongruity" in our song where these two motifs are presented
simultaneously in such a way that the deceased is both narrated
about and then allowed to speak herself. Each of these two modes
of presentation is accompanied by an appropriate motif. The fact
that the two motifs contradict one another does not matter in folk
poetry where the emphasis rests much more on a gradual *creation*
of the total meaning than on the unity of meaning intended from
the beginning and revealed at the end of the work.

Those who claim that such contradictions are "mistakes" might,
of course, object that here we have a mere oversight, a distortion
of the original "correct" reading from repeated reproductions. Let
us therefore present another example which will show us that an
"accidental" successive arrangement of motifs is also creative
energy. We are referring to a song recorded in Sušil's collection on
p. 122. It is a ballad about a "young man" who comes to visit a
girl at night, against her father's will. The father gets up and chops
his head off. The girl then laments her lover's death and runs to
the Danube, into which her father has thrown the severed head.
After this passage comes a very strange but tragically effective
depiction:

Synečkova hlava   The young man's head
po Dunaju plyve   is drifting on the Danube
a za tú hlavičkú   and behind that dear head
štyry krápě krve.   four drops of blood.

Za tymi krapjami   Behind those drops
klobúček s pentlami   a hat with ribbons
a za tým klobúčkem   and behind that hat
botky s ostrohami.   some boots with spurs.

Za tymi botkami	Behind these boots
truhelka s pokrovem	a coffin with a lid
a při tej truhličce	and with that coffin
štyřé mládencové.	four young men.
A nad hrobem stála,	And she stood above the grave,
žalostně plakala,	plaintively weeping,
chudobným žebráčkom	to poor beggars
almužnu dávala atd.	she was giving alms, etc.

The head drifts along the surface of the river and several different objects drift along behind it: blood, a hat with ribbons, boots with spurs. All of this can be put into the frame of a single picture, into a single, empirically possible scene. But does "a coffin with a lid and with that coffin four young men" also drift along the Danube? Here we obviously confront another scene: we see a funeral before our eyes. Here the folk song has achieved a semantic effect by means of a "dissolve," known today from the film which has attained it through a complex technical development. But how did the song achieve it? Through the simple juxtaposition of motifs without regard for a close connection between them. In the semantic composition of the folk song, motifs appear as units precisely delimited from one another, not continuously connected so that there can be gaps, semantic leaps, contradictions, and so on in their succession. And thus the device of the "dissolve" of two different scenes which is used in the song follows quite regularly from the very principle of the semantic structure of folk verbal art. We also find proof of this in the preceding verses in which we see drifting one after the other the head, four drops of blood, a hat, boots. The detail of the "four drops of blood" on the surface of the river which do not dissolve in the water, if conveived optically, has a ghastly and phantasmal effect. Lyrically expressed, it is blood which cries for revenge. But again this powerful impression is achieved by a mere successive arrangement of motifs sharply delimited from one another. What is presented here is not a verbal equivalent of a visual impression but an enumeration of motifs which the perceiver projects into a visual image only afterwards.

From this example we can conclude that a certain incongruity or even a contradiction among successive motifs, which always potentially accompanies the progression of the semantic structure in folk verbal art, follows from the very essence of this kind of creation. It is a principle that cannot be evaluated either positively or negatively but must be considered as existing and operating. At the same time, however, it is apparent how mistaken anyone is who approaches folk verbal art with the presupposition of "deformation." Folk poetry attains a considerable span between empirical reality and its representation simply on the basis of the fact that its aim is a combination of signs, not a reproduction of the empirical relations among things. Awareness of the correspondence between the sign and reality persists in this; the folk artist (not only the poet) is always convinced that what he writes or paints is reality. We find a very nice observation about the direct relationship between the work and reality in the folk artist's consciousness in Papoušková: "[A folk glass-painter] answers the question 'According to what did you paint Janošík and the brigands?' surely and without hesitation: According to reality (p. 40).—[The same painter] called himself a naturalist because he painted according to nature, but the legend about Geneviève was just as real for him as his neighbor's cat which he painted in his spare time" (p. 61).[14] Here, of course, the explanation is the same as in poetry. A folk visual artist puts his work together from signs, and for him the impression of the "reality" of his creation is based on the fact that each of the partial signs of which he composes his work has its own relation to reality.

Therefore the mode of creation in folk art is different from that of high art to the extent that it is absolutely unjustified to approach a work of folk art with the habits which we bring with us from high art, even if they seem to us completely self-evident and necessary. In this respect, the semantic structure of folk poetry is a very good means for explaining the semantic structure of folk art in general. Let us thus take a closer look at the notion of *motivation*. This notion is, of course, very special; it is limited not just to literature but specifically to narrative and dramatic literature. As we shall see, nevertheless, taking this concept into account can also result in a general explanation.

Motivation is a basic requirement of plot construction in artificial narrative and dramatic literature. Every motif entering the work should be related to another or several others, and it should

---

14. N. Melniková-Papoušková, *Československé lidové malířství na skle* [Czechoslovakian folk glass-painting] (Prague, 1938).

be related in such a way that the motifs bound together by it determine one another semantically and are thereby incorporated into the total meaning of the contexture. On account of reciprocity, motivation has at the same time a progressive and a regressive character. When the initial member of a motivational bond appears, it evokes an expectation in the perceiver; the next then directs the perceiver's attention backwards to what has already been perceived. At one time the necessity of motivation was formulated epigrammatically as follows: if at the beginning of the narration it is said that a nail has been driven into the wall, it is necessary that the hero hang himself on this nail at the end of the work. Even in artificial literature the "requirement" of motivation is not, of course, an inviolable norm, the observance of which determines the value of the work. It is not an imperative, but rather it is the semantic background against which the course of the action in artificial literature is perceived. The effectiveness of motivation increases with the distance between the motifs which are bound by it into the contextural sequence. The longer the connection of a certain motif with the others remains hidden from the reader, the more the reader's expectation contributes to the "tension," and the more strongly the action is bound into semantic unity by means of motivation. The linking of motifs over a distance could perhaps be represented schematically as follows:

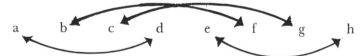

Here the letters represent motifs, their alphabetic order indicates their succession, the curves symbolize the semantic relations between individual motifs, and the arrows at the two ends of the curves are to indicate the reciprocity of the motivational relations. It is clear that the more densely the contexture is permeated with motival interrelations, the more the cohesiveness of its semantic structure is enhanced.

Frequently the "explanatory" motifs, that is, those which semantically determine and incorporate other preceding motifs, are accumulated at the end of the narration; in some cases the "key" motif, which has either a direct or indirect motivational connection with many of the preceding ones, is placed here. This results in the perceiver's being kept as long as possible in the dark about the semantic range of the entire contexture—an impression well known from detective novels. If we take into account the fact that in the case of an extremely unified motivation the solution is usually provided at the very end of the sequence, we could alter the motivational scheme as follows:

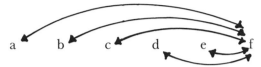

By concentrating the curves on the letter *f*, we wish to indicate the "key" motif, elucidating at once the meaning of everything preceding. We should add, of course, that neither of these schemes nor the two together grasp the real variety of the alterations of which motivation is capable in different situations. Their purpose is only illustrative.

Let us now deal with the question of motivation in the folk epic. We must, of course, be aware of the great variety of phenomena which are included under this term. Here we have the entire range between the heroic epic and the fairy tale. Indeed, even if we limit ourselves only to the fairy tale, we shall find a considerable variety of genres, and this variety certainly has an influence on the formation of semantic structure. Polívka says: "In a formal analysis, tales should certainly be more precisely differentiated from fairy tales and other novelistic and humorous short stories. But so far the question of whether various folk stories differ in this respect has not even been raised."[15] Nevertheless, the question of whether we can detect—despite this great variety—at least indications of a general attitude toward motivation that characterizes folk creation as a whole is not unjustified. From what we have already said above about semantic structure in folk art in general and folk poetry in particular, it seems to follow that such an attitude exists. The composition of semantic structure from partial semantic units relatively independent of one another necessarily has consequences in this respect as well. As we have seen, motivation *unifies* a literary work semantically, but folk poetry—according to its constructive principle—tends, on the other hand, to disturb the static semantic unity of the work. We should not, of

15. J. Polívka, "Doslov" [Afterword] in J. Kubín, *Lidové povídky z českého Podkrkonoší: Úkrají východní* [Folk tales from the Bohemian Krkonoše region: the eastern part] (Prague, 1926), p. 445.

course, think that there is no motivation in the folk epic. In the fairy tale we encounter at each step motifs whose ultimate incorporation into the plot occurs only in its further course. Let us take, for example, the fairy tale about Zlatovláska as we find it narrated in Erben.[16] Here the hero starts to understand the speech of animals because he has eaten snake flesh in violation of an interdiction. This violation causes him to be sent out to win Princess Zlatovláska for his master. Knowledge of animal speech turns out to be useful when he communicates with the animals that he helps, and this aid rendered to animals is again to the hero's advantage in accomplishing the tasks assigned to him when he strives to win Zlatovláska. This is a continuous and even complex motivational chain (the complexity lies in the fact that one and the same deed in relation to what follows is incorporated into two motivational series: the eating of snake flesh both brings the hero the task of winning Zlatovláska and helps him in fulfilling it). Each motif has its precise place in the sequence of the others; any displacement of the individual motifs would upset this motivation. There is nothing here that differentiates the motivation of a fairy tale narrated in this way from motivation in artificial literature.

But let us look at the variants of this fairy tale recorded in Tille's *Index of Czech Fairy Tales.*[17] Among them we find a variant which proves that the attitude of the folk epic toward motivation is indeed different from that of artificial literature. It is the version recorded by Kubín[18] to which Tille adds the note "Confused." The "confusion" is not, however, such that it has upset the continuity of the fairy tale; rather we might speak about a rearrangement of the plot. In Kubín's version, Zlatovláska is the daughter of the king whom the hero serves, and thus the competition for the bride between the king and the hero which was one of the mainsprings of the plot dynamics in Erben's version is lost. The king assigns the hero the job only as a punishment for eating snake flesh against his interdiction (in Kubín only he who has eaten the flesh first understands animals—the king was therefore cheated out of the effect of the snake flesh). In the organization of motifs,

16. *České pohádky* [Czech fairy tales] in *Dílo K. J. Erbena* (Prague, 1939), 3:45.
17. V. Tille, *Soupis českých pohádek* (Prague, 1934), 2, pt. 1, pp. 374-79.
18. *Lidové povídky z českého Podkrkonoší: Pohoří západní* [Folk tales from the Bohemian Krkonoše region: the western range], pt. 1 (Prague, 1922), pp. 269-74.

however, the hero's journey in quest of Zlatovláska is also lost, and thus the encounter with the animals, which was presented in Erben as an adventure experienced by the hero during his journey, has lost its motivation. The necessity of placing the encounter with the animals somewhere else arose because of this rearrangement, and Kubín's narrator does not hesitate to place this encounter at the very beginning of the narration. During the encounter the hero speaks with the animals that he helps, and thus a particular inconsistency occurs in Kubín. The hero speaks to the animals first, and the narration about snake flesh comes only afterwards. In Kubín's version, therefore, the hero actually speaks with the animals before he has the ability to understand them. From the standpoint of artificial literature Tille was correct to call this version "confused," for in artificial literature such a transposition of motifs disturbing the motivation is possible only as an intentional breach of it (for example, for comic effect). It simply does not matter to the folk narrator and his listener (who are otherwise accustomed to hearing about speaking animals without any previous motivation in songs and fairy tales). For them motivation is not the basic principle of the successive arrangement of motifs to the extent that its breach is felt as a deformation. They do not avoid motivation; they use it, but they can also do without it.

And thus the fairy tale, just as other forms of folk verbal art and folk art in general, experiences and evaluates each motif as an independent semantic unit. The folk narrator does not, therefore, care too much whether he has prepared the listener for a newly introduced motif or not. In Kubín, for example, the miraculous horse says to his master Honza: "But now, dear boy, you've got a hard nut to crack. You must destroy that Brandiburk so that your entire fate as well as mine is fulfilled."[19] But the listener is hearing about this "Brandiburk" for the first time and learns only from the further narration that Brandiburk is the commander of a great army, but even here he is mentioned only in passing: "Well, Brandiburk has suddenly moved, and he has declared war on that king."[20] In the folk fairy tale the only matter occupying the narrator's and the listener's attention is a direct sequence of motifs.

19. "Kokeš," *Lidové povídky . . . Úkrají východní,* p. 154.
20. Ibid., p. 155.

Whenever there is a transition from one motif to another, it is
always felt more strongly than in high literature, where attention
is focused more on the reciprocal bonds of non-contiguous motifs.
The basic principle of semantic structure in the folk narrative
could therefore be represented by the scheme:

a   b   c   d   e   f   g   h

And in the folk story this principle is the only scheme on the
basis of which the motivation can be realized. For this reason
motivation in the folk narrative tolerates a breach much more
easily than that in high literature.

Another manifestation of the tendency toward successive arrangement is so-called staircase construction (a model being the
fairy tale about the rooster and the hen) represented by the
scheme:

$$a \to b \to c \to d \to e \to d^1 \to c^1 \to b^1 \to a^1$$

Even where there is a genuine motivation in a folk narrative, it is
influenced by the tendency toward successive arrangement: the
tasks (one and the same hero gradually does various tasks, or
several heroes do one and the same task and only the last suc-
ceeds). But the principle of successive arrangement is realized not
only in the folk epic but also in other genres of folk poetry,
especially in the lyric. In lyric poetry the transition from motif to
motif is realized especially sharply as a surprise factor, as a place
where semantic reversals occur.

In folk art, therefore, detail is much more than a subordinate
structural element. It is not static but is the basic vehicle of initiative in the semantic structure of the folkloric work of art. Folk
art does not proceed from an image of the whole but from an
ordering of details provided by tradition, and unexpected wholes
arise from the always new ordering of these details. It is, of course,
clear that an image of closure, perfection—an image not very often
realized and not basically important for folk art—hovers as the
final goal at the end of the development of the folkloric work of
art as well. It could be said aphoristically: Was Hanka aesthetically

correct when he ordered the motifs in his "Kytice" [The bouquet][21] in such a way that a girl who "fell, ah, fell into the cold water" still has the time and the opportunity afterward to consider who "planted the bouquet in the loose soil," or was it Goethe who by merely rearranging the motifs had "Das Sträusschen"[22] end on a balladic note: "Da fällt, ach! da fällt sie/Ins kühlige Wasser" ("She fell, ah, she fell into the cold water")? From the standpoint of high poetry Goethe was indisputably right, and his intervention reveals an artist of genius precisely because of its seeming insignificance accompanied by a powerful poetic effect. From the standpoint of folkloric poetics, however, Hanka was right because he perceived the folkloric law of ordering motifs.

The thesis which we have attempted to formulate in this study has been documented (rather than explicitly stated) many times in the great number of folklore studies of recent years. But this in no way means that the study of folklore has already drawn all the necessary conclusions from it. Modern folklore studies have not exhausted all their possibilities but rather have just begun to realize them. The continuation of the semantic analysis of folkloric art can push not only folklore studies but also the theory of art miles ahead.

21. *Rukopis Královédvorský* [The Královédvorský manuscript], 1835 edition, pp. 44–45.

22. "Das Sträusschen: Altbömisch," *Goethes Werke*, part 1, vol. 3 (Weimar, 1890), p. 210.

9

Between Literature and Visual Arts

I

Comparative literature owes its origins to the Romantic interest in the historical and geographical heterogeneity of cultural activities. In the course of its development it has created a number of methods, each of which has entailed not only a different modus operandi but also a different approach to material, a different conception of it. Sometimes the path of a certain theme or thematic element (motif) is traced through different literatures; sometimes the literary activity in a broad cultural sphere differentiated into a number of national literatures is examined with a unifying vision. The questions arise as to what is the center of this activity, what the impulses originating from it, and how do literatures bound into a unity of a higher order influence each other. Furthermore, the question of the general regularity of literary activity and its historical variations arises. In the last few decades the foundations for a comparative study of literary forms have been laid.[1] In connection with the comparative study of the literary form we should mention Jakobson's fruitful idea of investigating those literary forms which are closely tied to language, for example, meters in literatures related by language (such as Slavic). The influence of language for the differentiation of literary development is thus revealed. It appears that even slight differences between kindred languages determine the completely different natures and developments of the same meter in two linguistically related literatures. Even in more complicated literary phenomena, for example, in international literary movements (such as Symbolism), we can often deduce to a considerable degree the heteromorphism of such a movement in different nations from differences in their linguistic systems.

This essay was translated from "Mezi poesií a výtvarnictvím," *Slovo a slovesnost* 7 (1941).

1. See, for example, F. Wollman's *K methodologii srovnávací slovesnosti slovanské* [On the methodology of Slavic comparative literature] (Brno, 1936), p. 86.

The above methods of study are not, of course, the ultimate ones which comparative literature is capable of deriving from its basic orientation. Neither has structuralism, penetrating the methodology of literary theory, threatened comparativism with its presupposition of the immanent development of every individual literature; rather it has enriched its possibilities. Structuralism proceeds from the presupposition that every compared literature comprises an individual structure. The contribution of structuralism is that it does not compare individual facts as independent values but as representatives of the literary structures into which these facts are incorporated. Comparison thus eliminates the risk of fortuity and the arbitrary interpretation of the compared facts. In each case, even the most detailed ones, its object is, in fact, entire developmental series and their polarity. The concern for polarity, for the tension between comparative series (literatures), however, causes structuralism, unlike older comparative scholarship, to take into account not only similarities between the matters compared but also, and above all, their differences (an example of this being the comparative studies of metrical schemes that we mentioned above).

Polarity manifests itself not only among different literatures but primarily within each literature itself. The essence of literary structure lies in the polar tension among individual components, the tension that maintains the structure in constant developmental movement. From the standpoint of structuralism, therefore, there is not a substantial difference between the comparative study of several literatures and the study of a single literature; even within a single literature the scholar is always compelled to make comparisons. It is impossible, for example, to understand the developmental dynamics of a given literature without taking into account the influence that the tension between verse and prose exerts upon this development. Prose continuously adopts its artistic devices from verse, altering their function and appearance in terms of its intrinsic preconditions (the difference between rhythmic and non-rhythmic speech) and its current developmental situation,[2] and poetry borrows from prose in the same way.

2. See our article "Próza Karla Čapka jako lyrická melodie a dialog," *Slovo a slovesnost* 5 (1939): 1 ff. *Editors' note.* For an abridged English translation see "K. Čapek's Prose as Lyrical Melody and as Dialogue" in *A Prague School Reader on Esthetics, Literary Structure and Style*, ed. Paul L. Garvin (Washington, D.C., 1964), pp. 133-49.

If, however, the scholar decides to take into account this and similar tensions, he will approach his material in exactly the same way that a comparativist deals with the literatures compared. In the case mentioned, prose and verse appear as two independent developmental series interpenetrating and repelling one another. The assignment of individual poets within the development of a given literature also requires the comparative method: the poet in question appears to be determined by his polar relation to predecessors, contemporaries, and younger poets (consider Šalda's famous scheme: Vrchlický – Neruda, Vrchlický – Zeyer, Vrchlický – Březina). If comparative study thus penetrates more deeply the very kernel of literature than seems to be its primary design, we may obviously presuppose that it can expand in the opposite direction as well, namely, into the sphere where artistic literature touches upon other arts.

Neither do the relations among individual arts, including literature, differ from those among individual national literatures. Similarly, as individual literatures usually differ from one another most conspicuously through language, the individual arts differ from one another according to material. Czech literature, for example, differs from German, French, and Russian literature primairly (if we disregard, of course, other differences) in the fact that its material is the Czech linguistic system with such and such individual features that both make possible and limit artistic creation in this language. Likewise, literature as one of the arts differs from painting and music in its material, the boundaries of which it cannot overstep and from which it draws its typical developmental possibilities. As early as 1776 Lessing discovered (in his *Laocoön*) the delimitation of the arts according to the nature of their material. In the spirit of his time he interpreted this limitation as a directive for artists, whereas the real development of art shows that every art sometimes strives to overstep its boundaries by assimilating itself to another art. Boundaries are, however, uncrossable, not *de iure* but *de facto,* for material can never give up its nature. Other questions of contact among the arts also find their analogues within literature. For example, the transposition of a theme from one art to another (painting, drama, film with a theme adopted from literature or vice versa) has some aspects in common with the transfer of a theme from one literary structure into another or even from one literary genre into another. Thus the transition from the comparative study of literature to the comparative theory of the arts is likewise continuous with the connection between the comparative study of literature and the study of a single literature. There is an uninterrupted scale of correlations and tensions from the polarity among individual components of a literary work to the polarity between literature and the other arts, and only a total survey of this multiply stratified scheme of forces would yield a complete picture of the "internal" development of literature as an art. In the following section we shall attempt a more detailed characterization of the relations which link the individual arts to one another as well as a closer examination of the situation of literature within this interplay of forces.

II

What links the individual arts to one another is the community of their goal. In general the arts are activities with a prevailing aesthetic consideration; what separates them from one another is the difference in material. Both these circumstances manifest themselves simultaneously and, of course, dialectically, creating a basic antinomy in the relation among the arts. Community of goal leads to the fact that every art—as we have already said—sometimes strives to attain through its own means the same effect that another art attains. Sometimes literature seeks to portray like painting, sometimes it strives to achieve the semantic polyvalence of music (to which the perceiver can attribute a large number of meanings and can at the same time oscillate among manifold meanings). At such a moment, however, the character of the material intervenes. A word remains a word, and by copying painting, literature attains only the discovery of a new possibility (in some cases, a new configuration of possibilities) of the artistic exploitation of the word. For example, if the verbal imitation of painting emphasizes shades of color and light, this tendency necessarily manifests itself in linguistic material as an excessive need for terms (most often adjectives and substantives derived from them) expressing colors and lights. To achieve necessary variety foreign words can be adopted, and the exploitation of foreign borrowings as a literary device can thus be increased. The differentiation of expressions signifying colors and lights can also

be achieved through unusual derivations, and derivation is therefore elevated to a means of poetic effect.

Let us cite another example. One of the important factors in
the "imitation" of music by poetry can be the euphonic organization of speech sound elements in combinations which repeat; the
phonological composition of a text which, of course, does not
resemble a series of tones except for its temporal succession is thus
deautomatized. Of course, it also happens that an art striving to
achieve an effect characteristic of another art has at its disposal an
element common to this art and utilizes it for "imitation." If
Hlaváček entitled one of the poems in the collection *Pozdě k ránu*
with the line "Svou violu jsem naladil co možná nejhlouběji" ("I
tuned my viola as low as possible"), he expressed not only the
figuratively musical orientation of the collection but also (perhaps
involuntarily) the real tonal level of the voice that his poems compel during an oral reading. Here the tonal level of the voice has
been exploited (by means of the syntactic, phonological, and semantic composition of the text), or, more precisely, the differences among the three tonal levels which every individual has
at his disposal. Hlaváček's poems force the reader to remain on
the lowest of these levels. Despite the fact that tone is a factor
common to the human voice and to music, it is exploited in a
poem in a completely different way than in music. Musical melody
is based on variations in tone; the "musicality" of the poem, however, has made it necessary to remain as much as possible on the
same tonal level, has required vocal monotony.

An art inclining toward another art can never, therefore,
transcend its own essence. There are even cases in which this impossibility itself becomes an object of poetic effect. Thus Nezval
has created the impression of the fantastic in a poem of his
Absolutní hrobař (the cycle "Bizarní městečko" No. 6) by trans-
posing the perspective of a picture into the poem.[3]

The imitation of one art by another is not unambiguous. If,
after a certain time in the course of development, the same two
arts encounter each other several times, the imitating art can focus
attention each time on a different aspect of the other art. For

3. See our study "Sémantický rozbor básnického díla" [The semantic analysis of a
poetic work], *Slovo a slovesnost* 4 (1938): 1 ff.

example, during the period of descriptive poetry, poetry sought, in its contact with painting, support for the predominance of static (descriptive) over dynamic (plot) motifs. On the other hand, in the period of Parnassianism and especially in the period of literary Impressionism immediately following it, it was a matter of the imitation of color which, as we have already suggested, especially influenced the selection of words. There is neither a totally passive nor totally active party in the contact of the arts with one another. The same art which inclined toward another in one period itself becomes an object of imitation in another period. For example, theater and film have alternated between activity and passivity in very rapid succession several times during the last few decades. In its beginnings film sought support in theater (the photographed theatrical scene, theatrical acting in film), it then influenced theater itself (lighting, the dynamicity of scenic space), but finally, in the period of the soundtrack, film has again attempted to become, in part, theater (theatrical dialogue). As for literature, sometimes it has been the object of imitation in relation to music (program music), sometimes it has sought support in music itself (Symbolism). Neither is painting always simply a model with respect to literature, for in certain periods it itself seeks a poetic effect, sometimes by attempting narrative, sometimes by pursuing lyrical emotiveness, and sometimes by striving for the painterly equivalent of poetic metaphor, metonymy, and synecdoche.

There are not only temporary encounters but also permanent contacts among the arts. It is precisely here that the tension among the arts is most conspicuous. For literature, illustration and vocal music, in particular, constitute such an area of interconnection. In both these cases, the problem of the transposition of literary devices into music and painting is raised again and again with the same urgency. Frequently, however, the opposite problem also occurs: the transposition of musical and painterly devices into literature. A picture is not always an illustration of a literary work, for sometimes a literary work is an illustration of a painting; the poetic word is not always the foundation of music, for sometimes music is the basis of the poetic word.[4] The materials of the participating arts and their expressive possibilities collide with

4. See J. Ort, "Zrození české dikce operní" [The origin of Czech opera diction], *Kritický měsíčník* 2 (1939): 197 ff.

one another in illustration and vocal music especially. The histories of these two fields show how differently their materials can be interrelated and how diversely they can project themselves into one another.

Quite often arts meet in the person of the artist himself. Thus a literary talent is often combined with a talent for the visual arts, especially painting (Wyśpiański, Josef Čapek), or for music (Nezval). Even more frequent are cases in which the second art remains a dilettantish activity (Mácha, Pushkin). These cases are not less interesting than the former for the study of the interrelations between literary structure and the structures of other arts.[5] There are also cases in which the poet is the illustrator of his own writings (Karel Čapek in his travel books); here the question of the interpenetration of word and picture is of the utmost urgency.[6]

Finally, we should mention that the encounters of the arts need not always have the character of an influence of one upon the other, for they can appear as a quite extraneous competition and struggle for popularity. For example, during the last few decades we have witnessed a competition between film and theater in which film had the upper hand for a while, whereas theater now enjoys this advantage. Painting and sculpture have frequently been in a similar competitive tension. Sometimes competition has to do with different branches of a single art; in literature, for example, a predilection for poetry alternates with a predilection for prose. If we continued this consideration of competition among the arts, it would of course lead us into the sociology of art. Nevertheless, some of the factors which are decisive in this competition can have their source in the development and state of artistic structure (for example, verse will probably be more popular when it stresses the emotiveness of poetic expression than when it renounces emotive effectiveness); others can have their source in the epistemological range of the artistic work which is closely connected with its structure (the art that at a given moment is based upon an epistemological stance accessible to the broadest strata will be more popular than the others).

5. See, for example, A. Èfros, *Risunki poèta* [A poet's sketches] (Moscow, 1932) and V. Volavka, "Mácha a výtvarné umění" [Mácha and the visual arts] in the anthology *Věčný Mácha* [The eternal Mácha], ed. V. Hartl et al (Prague, 1940).

6. See our article "Významová výstavba a komposiční osnova epiky K. Čapka" [The semantic structure and compositional scheme of K. Čapel's narrative], *Slovo a slovesnost* 5 (1939): 113 ff.

Meeting and struggling in the course of their development, the arts enter into very complex relations which influence the character of the entire set. Thus during the period when Symbolism began to incline toward music, painting (or at least some of its movements) also sought support for its tendency toward the harmonization of colors in music. Consider, for example, one of Karel Hlaváček's reviews: "Thinking and feeling artists are returning to the reduction of natural color tones, to the basic unshaded levels of pure, rich, singing colors. They are returning to where Japanese art is clearly preeminent. Depth, airy perspective, motion, and rest—all these can be expressed by simple, pure and broad primary and secondary tones resolved by the crystal corundumlike prism of the artist's soul. From the entire symphony of colors, viewed and heard, the modern watercolorist chooses only broad, harmonious tones in a minor key in order to express the present state of his soul. And if you give the same color symphony to several modern watercolorists, each of them will sing a different aria from it. . . ."[7]

At the turn of the century, however, architecture also approximated literature and music. As late as 1929 Ozenfant treats the last relics of this aesthetic trend ironically: "The architect's client, when he dreams of his future house, has a whole poem in his bosom. He rocks himself with dreams of the perfect symphony he will dwell in. He unburdens himself with some architect. And the ordinary architect is all fire to be a second Michael Angelo. Under pressure, he puts up an ode in concrete and plaster that generally turns out very different from what the client brooded over: whence arise conflicts: for poems, particularly those engendered by others, are uninhabitable."[8]

After all, all the arts are always interrelated in particular ways so that they are bound into a structure of a higher order. Even if two arts do not confront one another head on at a given moment, they feel their common existence and react to one another. For instance, it is quite possible that when poetry "imitates" music, it simultaneously exhibits detectable traces of a kinship with the visual arts. We have in mind the state of poetry in the Symbolist period when poetry demonstrated a certain affinity to the move-

7. "Výstava českých akvarelistů roku 1896" [The 1896 exhibit of Czech watercolorists], *Dílo Karla Hlaváčka* (Prague, 1930), 3: 65.

8. *Foundations of Modern Art* (London, 1931), p. 139.

ment in the visual arts called Art Nouveau at the same time as it was approximating music (we shall deal with Art Nouveau in poetry in more detail in the following section). The structural makeup of all the arts is thus as complex and dynamic as that of any individual art. It is also hierarchically organized and even has its dominant component if one of the arts in a certain period is felt to be the art κατ' ἐξοχήν, the most essential one, the representative of artistic creation in general. During the Renaissance, for example, the visual arts held such a position; during Romanticism, literature enjoyed this status. If the entire structure of the arts undergoes a change, the relations among its individual components, indeed the components themselves, also undergo a change. Thus the interrelation of literature and theater changed when film became a member of the set of the arts (I gather that the influence of film can be seen, for example, in the fact that the relation of theater to narrative literature has become more intense: the frequent staging of novels); indeed, even the intrinsic structure of these arts has changed as a result of the influence of film. Despite this perpetual changeability in the hierarchy of the arts, certain constants underlie the relations of individual arts. For instance, under any developmental situation literature is closer to music (with which it is connected through the sound aspect) and painting (with which it has in common the capacity of expressing the phenomena of external reality through signs connected in a continuous contexture) than to sculpture and architecture.

The concept of the interrelation of the arts as we have depicted it in the previous paragraphs is based upon the contradiction between the commonality of aim and the difference in material of the individual arts. In this it differs from the former concept, the typical expression of which, at least as far as literature is concerned, may be found in the appropriate chapters of Oskar Walzel's *Gehalt und Gestalt im Kunstwerk des Dichters* (1923) and in his earlier study *Wechselseitige Erhellung der Künste* (1917). Walzel's concept reduces the unity of the arts to the undynamic parallelism of artistic configurations, in the given case, of the literary configuration with the painted and musical ones. Its difference from the contemporary concept lies in the fact that Walzel tries his utmost to remove from sight the specific distinctiveness of the individual arts. He thus devotes much space to the weakening of the division between the temporal arts (literature, music) and the spatial arts (visual arts). He does this in such a way that, with a polemical thrust against Lessing, he discovers the element of successiveness in the perception of the visual arts as well.

There is no doubt that Walzel's achievement was developmentally necessary and progressive in its time. In Walzel the dogma of the nontransgressiveness of the boundaries between the arts yields to the unprejudiced study of the correlation between individual arts. From the modern standpoint, however, it is equally clear that Walzel's method goes too far in its direction away from Lessing. In rejecting the *dogmatic* separation of the arts, Walzel loses sight of their *factual* delimitation by the nature of their material. He applies to literature the principles created by Wölfflin for the analysis of works of visual art, finding it quite possible to seek the differences between linearity and the "picturesque" in the verbal aspect of literature. Such an application of terms adopted from the theory of the visual arts to literary devices can be, of course, only figurative and therefore ambiguous. Proof of this is the fact that Walzel himself admits a dual possibility in applying the aforementioned opposition. The difference between linearity and the picturesque can, according to him, correspond either to the difference between a literary technique emphasizing the contours, in some cases the plasticity, of objects and one emphasizing colors, or to the difference between a literary style which articulates distinctly and one which weakens the articulation by obliterating the transitions between syntactic units, sentences, and so on. It is obvious that it is a matter of a mere analogy, in the discovery of which quite a lot of leeway is left to the scholar's fantasy. Walzel himself, of course, frequently arrives at very valuable results, but this is often for reasons of clairvoyant perception rather than methodological precision.

The adoption of the periodization of the visual arts, especially architecture, by other arts stems from an attitude similar to Walzel's, though not completely identical with it. This method is based upon the presupposition of a common epistemological and psychic tendency from which all the arts of a certain period arise. In all of the artistic creation of a given period there is the same will toward form (*Formwille*—Worringer's term) which renders its works similar to one another. Periodization following that of the visual arts has enjoyed considerable success in the history of literature (and elsewhere): such terms as Gothic literature or

Baroque literature have the value of technical terms today. The advantage is obviously that the styles of the visual arts in their rather distinct periodization lend support to the division of the much more continuous development of the other arts. In recent years, however, attempts have been made to work out this method in detail. Not only the great epochs but also the secondary temporal segments of literary development are designated by terms adopted from the history of the visual arts: the literature of the Empire, the Biedermeier, and so forth. Nor is this detailed confrontation of literature with the visual arts without value. It is like projecting a sharp light from the side so that the aspects of literature which have previously escaped our attention are now revealed.

There are, however, certain dangers, among which the principal one is that regard for the specificity of literary material and for the autonomous development of literature will be neglected in this confrontation. The developmental boundaries need not be the same in every detail in all the arts, and the character of individual periods is also usually different in different arts. Let us take as an example Impressionism in painting. In its beginning Impressionism was parallel to Naturalism in verbal art (an effort to grasp reality without the veil of conventions); however, in its later phases it is related to further stages of literary development. Its effort at suggestiveness (the landscape as "the state of the soul") brings it closer to poetic Symbolism; the laying bare of devices (for example, individual styles of painters, color-patches) renders it similar even to more recent literary movements. Nevertheless, Impressionism does not give up the basic unity of its approach throughout the entire period of its development. The consistent application of the developmental divisions of the visual arts to literature would necessarily lead to the separation of phenomena related from the standpoint of literature, the application of phenomena alien to one another, and so forth.

Must we therefore abandon the confrontation of literary development with the development of the visual arts? We think not (and it would also be wrong to give up the advantages which result from this confrontation). It is only necessary that the scholar look for dissimilarities as well as similarities between these two developments. Only if he takes into account these similarities and dissimilarities at the same time, will he avoid the danger of deforming

the material under study. In the following section we shall attempt
to present an example of a developmental study oriented in this
way.

III

The subject of the comparison that we are attempting here is
the way in which the movement in the visual arts called "Secession"[9] projected itself into the development of literature at the
turn of the century. First we must make a few brief remarks about
the nature of this movement.

Art Nouveau is rooted in the craft industry, and its origin
derives from the revolt against the imitation of historical styles.
Tendencies of this kind first appeared in France and especially in
England where the revival of the artistic craft was proclaimed by
Ruskin and put into practice by Morris. For central Europe this
movement is usually marked by the years 1895–1905.[10] From the
craft industry Art Nouveau penetrated the visual arts, and we may
thus speak about Art Nouveau painting, sculpture, and architecture. Here, however, the boundaries are not definite. Recently
there has been an effort to broaden the notion of Art Nouveau;
for example, van Gogh, Gauguin, Munch, and the Czech artist
Preisler are included among Art Nouveau painters today.[11]

We could enumerate many of the features of Art Nouveau,
especially if we took into account heterogeneous peripheries of
this vaguely defined movement, but we shall limit ourselves to the
most essential of them. Above all, Art Nouveau is characterized
by a tendency toward ornamentation. For the Art Nouveau artist
the ornament is not something additional and optional but the
very essence. We can already find emphasis on the importance of
the ornament in Morris's theoretical discussions. He supports his
thesis with interesting arguments. Figure painting is without any
doubt the highest form of the art of painting, but pictures repre-
senting man and his activities frequently arouse human passions
and instincts; indeed, sometimes they even cause suffering and
dread. This tires the body and the soul, and like an animal man

9. *Editors' note.* The term Secession is used in Czechoslovakia and other parts of the
former Austro-Hungarian Empire. Its English equivalent is *Art Nouveau.*

10. See the entry "Jugendstil" in J. Jahn's *Wörterbuch der Kunst* (Stuttgart, 1940).

11. Cf. J. Pečírka's introduction to *Vincent van Gogh a Paul Gauguin*, ed. E. Filla
et al (Prague, 1935), pp. 5-8.

longs for rest, while at the same time he resists fatigue. He is therefore reluctant to experience tragic feelings day after day and hour
after hour. On ordinary days he must accordingly surround himself with an art which, though perhaps not worse than high art, is
less exciting. This is why he covers the walls of his home with
ornaments reminding him of the face of the earth and the innocent
love of animals and people who spend their days between work
and repose. This is how Morris expresses himself about ornamentation in a lecture on decorative painting, and his essay reveals the
very foundation of the Art Nouveau attitude. Though we do not
claim that every Art Nouveau artist would agree with this opinion
word for word, we can, nevertheless, deduce from it that the dis-
like for strong emotional fluctuations and for the strong force of
will which such fluctuations necessarily cause is inherent in the
very essence of Art Nouveau. For Art Nouveau, emotion seems to
be a monotonous mood, sometimes a bit asthenic, qualitatively
characterized as dreaming, weariness, resignation. The supple
ornamentation of Art Nouveau is the expression of this mood and
the means of its evocation. A predilection for line and plane is
closely associated with the ornamentality of Art Nouveau.

The *line* of Art Nouveau is a continuous curve without sharp
breaks and without geometrical regularity, a curve that evokes in
the viewer an impression of undulatory, pacific movement through
a sympathetic motor reaction. This curve is found not only in
ornaments and paintings but also in the construction of furniture,
and even in architecture (the contours of walls, gables, etc.). Some
favorite motifs of Art Nouveau painting—hair, streams of smoke,
hands outstretched sideways and upwards, dangling twigs—are
linked to its linearity. A predilection for the *plane* finds its application especially in Art Nouveau painting but elsewhere as well,
for example in architecture (the flat facades of Art Nouveau
buildings). Color compensates for the monotony of the plane.
The color-patch gains coherence after the trembling quiver of
Impressionism: firm contour is furnished by the line. Art Nouveau
color is a value in itself rather than a mere characteristic of an
object. Even the craft industry of this period frequently chooses
colors that conflict with the usual coloration (indeed, sometimes
the designation) of an object (for example, pink or blue furniture
in Art Nouveau kitchens). The essential requirement of Art
Nouveau color is the interrelation of the colors of a painting, of

an ornament, or even of an entire interior. The harmonization of colors or their contrast is the means of achieving this interrelation; harmonization is sometimes produced by the decomposition of light. Decomposition and harmonization lead to the selection of unusual, even previously non-existent, shades of color. The emphasis on the shading of color is one of the most characteristic features of Art Nouveau.

A predilection for a combination of heterogeneous materials is connected with this passion for color—for example, colored tiles, colored glass, colorful mosaics, polished stones, and metals combined in surprising compositions on the facades and in the interiors of Art Nouveau buildings. A predilection for materials themselves thus arises. Unlike the later conception, however, this predilection concerns primarily the optic impression that a material creates.

Finally, we must mention the Art Nouveau concept of stylization. Seeking to detach itself from historical ornamental formulae, Art Nouveau favors natural shapes (leaves, flowers, the human or animal body) which, however, it arranges according to the principles of proportionality, symmetry, and eurhythmy. Thus arise shapes subtly oscillating between the imitation of reality and ornamentation. The contradiction between reality and artifact is therefore felt more sharply in Art Nouveau than in other periods. There are even theoretical writings about this phenomenon.[12] Stylization becomes the central feature of Art Nouveau perception, and not only in the visual arts; gestures, forms of social contact, and clothing are stylized. Through stylization Art Nouveau penetrated the whole of life, all of its expressions and activities, and it is thus not surprising that we can find its reflection in artistic activity other than the visual arts.

Having briefly characterized Art Nouveau, let us now turn our attention to the Czech literature contemporary with it, the literature of the years 1895-1905. What was happening in Czech poetry at this moment? It was about 1895 that the generation of the Symbolists and Decadents gained ascendancy. Sova's collection *Soucit i vzdor,* with which "the anteroom of his poetry ends" (Šalda), was published in 1894. The year 1895 brings Březina's *Tajemné dálky.* In 1896 Hlaváček publishes the book *Pozdě k ránu,*

---

12. See, for one, L. Volkmann, *Naturprodukt und Kunstwerk,* 3rd ed. (Dresden, 1911).

and Karásek ze Lvovic publishes *Zazděná okna*. The situation is
not, of course, so simple. Besides the generation of the Lumírians,
whose profile was already unalterably complete (but whose younger members—the trio O. Auředníček, J. Borecký, and J. Kvapil—
had prepared the way for Symbolism), we find the unique figure
of Machar here. The contradiction between Machar and Symbolism
provides the basic scheme of the developmental plan for a long
period: poets such as Neumann, Dyk, and Bezruč are, each in his
own way, syntheses of this antinomy.

From this point up to the [First] World War, the development
of Czech literature continues without any further distinct genera-
tional division, but it is richly differentiated by strong personalities. Previously accustomed to the system of leading individuals
(Hálek and Neruda in the Máj school, Vrchlický and Čech in the
generation of Ruchovians and Lumírians), Czech poetry at this
time acquires a new, unusual organization. There are a number of
equally important poets interconnected and separated by complex
relations. This individualizing differentiation of poets as a whole
was accompanied by a strong upsurge in criticism. Šalda's *Boje o
zítřek* [Battles for tomorrow] (1905) shows graphically that the
purpose of this critical effort was not only the struggle for a new
conception of poetry and its task but also the need to impose
some order upon the individualizing process of literature. Šalda
never stops repeating that individuality and the individual cannot
do without internal regularity, that they are not natural phenomena but values which must be created by a great ethical and
artistic effort. This volcanically restless activity and its mediation
gave birth to the particularity of the Czech cultural awareness,
basing it for the moment on the personal responsibility of individuals to themselves.

At first glance nothing is more alien to this maximally active
contemporary attitude than the playful and relatively passive
nature of Art Nouveau. We would be unjust to every one of the
poets of this period (at least every outstanding one) if we declared
Art Nouveau as the basic feature of his profile. As long as the
historian does not distort actual conditions, there is no chance for
a section called "The Literature of Art Nouveau" to appear in the
history of Czech literature. And yet . . . In 1896 *Almanach secese*
[Almanac of Art Nouveau] appears under the editorship of
Stanislav K. Neumann. In his introduction the editor declares:

"I invited all of the modern camp [to contribute], independently of any faction, whether they stood in either of its wings or alongside of it, as long as they did not stand against it." Thus we find the names of Březina, Hlaváček, Karásek, the pseudonym of Dyk, and even the name of Zeyer among the contributors. It would therefore appear that Art Nouveau made the claim of being synonymous with modernism. Even more conclusive for the influence of Art Nouveau on poetry is the way in which Šalda formulates his ideal of the self-determining poetic figure: "But the kingly artist and the chaste donor of a blossom and a second, who gave only overflowing froth, gave infinitely more: he gave his *height,* the highest height which he ever reached and thereby his entire *depth,* for froth is the blossom of the depth and its measure. . . . There are no greater artists than the artists of the froth of life." [13] The inner order of artistic individuality required by Šalda takes on the form of contemporary stylization, a purely Art Nouveau stylization, as the motifs of the *blossom* and the *froth,* both borrowed from the typical stock of ornaments of Art Nouveau painting, indicate.

If we need even more distinct proof, we can cite Šalda's words from his article "The Ethics of the Modern Rebirth of Applied Art": "All the arts are slowly liberating themselves from the solitude of their material isolation and feel more and more intensely that their foundation and roots are *ornamental and symbolic* and that their purpose is to work on the adornment of life, to work on totality and to serve totality: *style* as the highest cultural value, the unity of art and life, becomes the object of our hope."[14] Here we are quite explicitly within the Art Nouveau conception of art, but at the same time it is also clear that the pathos on which Šalda's words are borne does not belong to the nature of Art Nouveau but has its roots elsewhere. In Šalda Art Nouveau is only the stylization of the ideal, not the ideal itself. Nevertheless, it is not without significance, for Šalda himself or for the poetry of the turn of the century, that recently he wrote a penetrating study of literary autostylization (a phenomenon not rare in other periods either, but intensified in the Art Nouveau period by the general

13. "Osobnost a dílo" [Personality and the work], *Boje o zítřek* (Prague, 1905), p. 25.

14. "Ethika dnešní obrody aplikovaného umění," ibid., pp. 123-24.

stylizing tendency derived from the visual arts) in which he says: "As we can see, we have found that in all the leading representatives of the so-called generation of the nineties autostylization is an essentially important structural component and sometimes even a lyrical motif of their poetry. It goes hand in hand with the budding and outpouring of their lyrical talent, and almost all of them ostentatiously underline it and place it in the most significant vantage points of their works, either as the introductory prelude or as the concluding and synthesizing chord."[15]

The greatest critic of the turn of the century, who programmatically formulated the tendencies of his generation, thus bears witness—though not explicitly—for us of the intervention of Art Nouveau in the conception of the poet and poetry at that time. Just as conclusive as Šalda's statements is the voice of the poet Jiří Karásek ze Lvovic writing about poets. If Šalda speaks about the stylization of the poet's personality, Karásek goes on to speak directly about the poet's stylization of nature. In his study on Karel Hlaváček we read: "Though the book is full of natural details, it is not a book with a 'natural scent.' You can go through all of it and you will not find there a single trace of where Hlaváček captures nature or a natural mood just as they are; Hlaváček is not a man of 'nature.' He studies it—hence his landscape and natural details—but not to grasp it, instead, on the basis of what he finds in nature, to stylize and to create what we do not see there. He works with nature against nature like Japanese artists."[16]

We should point out that the "Japanese artists" mentioned are painters, whereas Hlaváček, though both a poet and a painter, is discussed here as a poet. Here the confrontation of literature with the visual arts is as explicit as in Hlaváček himself who says: "Female Japanese painters used their special colors, a small number of special brush strokes, each of which could still express all the subtlety of their miniature dreams . . . —and he differed from them only in the fact that he wanted to use, instead of colors and contours, words melted in the hermetic furnace of his refined style."[17]

---

15. "O básnické autostylizaci, zvláště u Bezruče" [On poetic autostylization, especially in Bezruč"], *Slovo a slovesnost* 1 (1935): 24.

16. *Impresionisté a ironikové* [Impressionists and ironists] (Prague, 1926), p. 67.

17. "Pseudojaponerie," *Pozdě k ránu* in *Dílo Karla Hlaváčka* (Prague, 1930), 2: 26-27.

Let us now consider literature itself. Here we cannot present a detailed comparison of literature with Art Nouveau in the visual arts, and this is certainly not the aim of this essentially theoretical essay. We shall therefore attempt to illustrate our assertion by means of only a few characteristic passages selected at random from the poems of the period around 1895–1905. The reader who wishes to get a more complete picture should consult the anthology *Modern Czech Poetry*,[18] in which the material is lucidly arranged. From today's standpoint this anthology could quite easily bear the subtitle "Art Nouveau in Czech Poetry."

We have spoken about the linearity of Art Nouveau. In looking for a reflection of this visual artistic feature in literature, we do not wish to interpret it figuratively as Walzel did. In Czech poets of the turn of the century there are plentiful examples of landscapes *actually* perceived linearly, hence examples of the verbal transposition of painted works:

> Klid bílých linií se tiše krajem snoval
> v šat slabě vzdmutých ploch a lesů mrtvých ladem;
> let ptáků v azuru čar sítě nerýsoval.

> The calm of white lines was moving quietly through
>   the landscape
> into the garment of the slightly raised planes and
>   the forests dead in fallow;
> the flight of birds was not sketching nets of lines
>   in the azure.
>   [Březina, "Siesty," *Tajemné dálky*]

> Kraj vymřel dokola. Je mrtvo. Nikde ruchu.
> Vše tichu podléhá. V snů jemně modrý klam
> Klid spících linií se kreslí v měkkém vzduchu.

> The countryside has died out all around. It is
>   deathlike. Not a sound anywhere.
> Everything is subject to silence. Into the fine
>   blue mirage of dreams
> The calm of slumbering lines is sketched in
>   the soft air.
>   [Karásek ze Lvovic, "Hudba siesty," *Zazděná okna*]

18. *Nová česká poesie*, ed. V. Dyk and A. Novák (Kruh českých spisovatelů: Prague, 1907).

Je večer sladký, lípy dech
petřínských voní na valech,
a polo bdí a na půl dříma
v oparu světel obrys čar
barvami do mlh vhozenýma,
pohádka, smutek, polotvar.

The evening is sweet, the linden's breath
wafts sweetly on the Petřín ramparts,
and half-awake and half-asleep is
the contour of lines in the midst of lights
like colors thrown into fog,
a fairy tale, sadness, a half-form.

[Sova, "Praha, věčná stráž," *Zápasy a osudy*]

We could not explain the similarities among these three landscape depictions if we did not take into account a common source,
the linear perspective of the Art Nouveau visual arts. Moreover,
there is the fact that Sova evidently conceives the landscape as a
plane ("a contour of lines"); thus even in this respect he follows
the model of Art Nouveau painting.

In the enumeration of Art Nouveau features in the visual arts
we have also spoken about the passion of Art Nouveau for color
and coloration. The verbal transposition of natural colors and
colors found in painting is not a rare phenomenon in literature;
nevertheless, if we find a predilection for grasping individual
shades of color among the poets of the turn of the century, we
can safely assume the kinship of poetry with Art Nouveau color
technique:

Sen modří šedivých ve stínech sněhu ožil,
však záře usnula ve zrůžovělých žlutích.

A dream of gray blues has revived in the
    shades of snow,
but the glare has fallen asleep in pinkened
    yellows.

[Březina, "Siesty," *Tajemné dálky*]

Březina's lines apostrophizing autumnal days demonstrate the
tendency toward the shading of color even more distinctly:

Svůj rozestřete lesk a plajte v chladný říjen
svou září karmínův a minií a sien.

Spread your luster and blaze into cold October
with your glare of carmines and miniums and siennas.

["Říjen," *Tajemné dálky*]

The designations "carmine" and "minium" refer to two shades
of the same color, red. This fact as well as the explicit naming of
color shades (not just the colors: red, brown) attests to the Art
Nouveau conception of coloration. And if we read (at a distance
of thirteen years from *Tajemné dálky*) in Růžena Svobodová's
Černí myslivci the sentence "It was after the great rains, the warm
earth breathed white vapors, the vapors created blue mists, lightly
ultramarine, which cajoled amorously about the crowns of trees,
filled up the valley, shaded the bluish forests, piled up unevenly,
cloudlike in the foreground of the picture, and created a subtle
harmony of bluish-green"—if we read this sentence which varies
the same color (blue) four times, we feel that we are still within
the range of Art Nouveau.

The internal cumulation of colors into colored chords which
we frequently encounter among poets of the turn of the century
reminds us of the harmonizing effort of the color technique of
Art Nouveau painting and ornamentation:

A v jeden akvarel skvrn rozteklých ted' splývá
Krev s černí spálenou a karmín s línou šedí
A slunce vyrudlé jak plátek staré mědi
se kalné, znavené v kraj jednotvárný dívá.

And into a single watercolor of run-together patches
Blood now merges with burnt black and carmine
    with lazy gray
And the sun faded like a piece of old copper,
    dull, tired, looks into the monotonous landscape.

[Karásek ze Lvovic, "Kalný západ," *Zazděná okna*]

In this stanza no fewer than five colors (blood, black, carmine,
gray, copper) mingle in the depiction of a sunset. At the same
time three of them (blood, carmine, copper) are shades of the
same basic color. And we should not forget the attendant
circumstance that watercolor painting (about which these lines

speak) is one of the techniques favored by Art Nouveau painters.
Another example reads:

> Za horkých červnových dnů, kdy všechno plápolá zlatem,
> a bílí holubi s radostným chvatem
> třesavě nad strání krouží,
> tu mladé dívky se šťastným smíchem do trávy se hrouží
> a shora dolů se to kotálí,
> jak plamínky v trávě když zapálí
> červené, žluté a bílé.

> During the hot July days, when everything flares up
>   in gold,
> and white doves with a joyful haste
> shakily circle above the hillside,
> then young girls immerse themselves in the grass with
>   happy laughter
> and roll down the hill,
> as if little flames were lit in the grass
> red, yellow and white.
>
> [Neumann, "Stráň chudých lásek,"
> *Kniha mládi a vzdoru*]

In the overall coloration of the picture, the triad of red, yellow,
and white creates an intentional color chord. We find an analogous
color harmony, bordering, however, almost on contrast, in the
following poem by Machar:

> Na hoře město. Zdí tré pásů chrání
> bezpečnost jeho. Prvá natřena jest
> svítivou barvou, jak ji má krev lidská,
> ta druhá mrtvou černí tmavé noci
> a třetí modrá, jako bývá nebe,
> když slunce slábnouc mdle jen usmívá se.

> On the hill a town. Three belts of walls protect
> its safety. The first is painted
> a shiny color, like that of human blood,
> the second the dead black of dark night
> and the third is blue, as the sky usually is,
> when the sun growing weak only weakly smiles.
>
> ["Krajina asijská," *V záři hellenského slunce*]

These rich colors that are simply juxtaposed bring us close to the poster, which was elevated to the status of art precisely by Art Nouveau.

Much could still be said about the expressions of Art Nouveau color sensibility in Czech poetry. For example, there is the question of the symbolic meaning of color freed from its characterizing function. There is the problem of the hidden coloration of poems which sometimes do not contain a single color designation. Further, there is the question of color monotony. We shall, however, turn to another point of contact between poetry and the Art Nouveau visual arts, ornamentation. We do not wish to look for it in poetic style or composition even though such ornamentation is not alien to the poetry of the turn of the century. We are concerned not only with the mere similarity between literature and the visual arts but with cases of a distinct transposition of visual artistic devices into poetry. In this respect, an instructive example is the gesture of ornamental nature, namely, that which yields very easily to visual artistic stylization. One of the most characteristic gestures of this kind is the outstretching of the arms to the sides or above the head, a gesture common in Art Nouveau figure painting. It is striking how often this gesture occurs, for instance, in Neumann's first books, later gathered into the collection *Kniha mládí a vzdoru* (1920). Thus in "Vypučel jsem nad bahna" the twice repeated motif of arms outstretched above the head is the basic motif of the poem. In its second occurrence this motif concludes and climaxes the poem:

> Sám
> pyšný
> uprostřed pláně stojím a vysoko zdvihám
> svá hubená ramena za nejdražší vlastí svých snů.

> Alone
> proud
> I stand in the middle of the plane and raise high
> my thin arms for the most cherished country of my dreams.

In the poem "Ad te clamamus exules filii Evae" we find the line "and the hands sticking into the air reproachfully"; in the poem "Ty, jenž jsi bledý Adonis" it is said "One should outstretch one's arms and strip bare one's breast"; furthermore, there is a poem entitled "Here I lie with outstretched arms" (this is also its first line).

In "Sen o zástupu zoufajících" the ornamental motif of the gesture of hands has this appearance:

> A tu se černá postava ze žhoucí té výhně vzepjala
> s rukama zoufale vztýčenýma
> a za ní druhá a jiné a jiné do set a do tisíců

> And suddenly a black figure rose up from that
>   glowing furnace
> with hands desperately upstretched
> and after it another and others and others to
>   hundreds and thousands.

Finally, in "Jarní apostrofa slunce" we find the lines:

> Kolikrát jsem tobě vstříc rozepial svou náruč,
> nahý a odevzdaný!

> How many times have I outstretched my arms
>   toward you,
> naked and resigned!

Sometimes we also find a similar ornamental stylization of gesture in Karásek ze Lvovic:

> Ale jitro! Jaká mdloba! S lože visí líně
> paže k ránu.

> But dawn! What a swoon! From the bed lazily hang
> hands toward morning.
>   ["V lyru ze slonové kosti," *Sexus necans*]

But in the poetry of the turn of the century we find even more direct transpositions of the Art Nouveau ornament. It is hidden where we would least expect it: in the central and title motif of Březina's last collection, *Ruce* [Hands]. Let us recall the lines from the poem of the same name:

> Hle, v této chvíli ruce milionů potkávají se,
>   magický řetěz,
> jenž obmyká všechny pevniny, pralesy, horstva
> a přes mlčenlivé říše všech moří vzpíná se k bratřím.

Look, at this moment the hands of millions are
   meeting, a magic chain,
which embraces all lands, virgin forests, mountains
and over the silent realms of all seas rises up
   toward the brethren.

The image of the mystical unity of being, which is the brace in the vault of Březina's poetry, is rooted deeply in his world view, and its semantic structure corresponds to his technique of imagery. But at the same time this image is also a verbal artistic transposition of the Art Nouveau ornamental belt—Art Nouveau because it is based upon the unmediated stylization of a real object. Moreover, hands, as we have already seen in Neumann, are a favorite Art Nouveau motif.

Let us mention as a further example of the transposition of Art Nouveau visual arts into literature the way in which Art Nouveau's predilection for palpable materials is reflected in poetry. Palpable material seems to be exclusively a matter of the visual arts, non-transposable into literature, which builds upon the immaterial word. Nevertheless, we frequently find a reflection of the substances which are the materials of artistic crafts in the poetry of the turn of the century. The poetic images of the Symbolists in particular draw from this semantic realm in expressing the color of objects by means of the names of precious or beautiful materials:

To bývá chvíle soumraku, kdy slunce,
mdlá lampa z ametystu, dohasíná.

This is usually the moment of twilight, when the sun,
a faint lamp made of amethyst, fades out.
             [Karásek, "Mrtvá touha," *Sodoma*]

srp měsíce jak stříbrný je plech

the moon's sickle is like a sheet of silver
           [Hlaváček, "Pršelo v noci," *Pozdě k ránu*]

a slunce vyrudlé jak plátek staré mědi

and the sun faded like a piece of old copper
         [Karásek, "Kalný západ," *Zazděná okna*]

Po černém koberci, jejž k mému loži stínem
v šat vonný z kašmíru Noc tkala kyprou vlnou,
tys přišla, Milá má.

Over the black carpet, which to my bed like a shadow
Night has woven into a fragrant cashmere garment
   out of fluffy wool,
you've come, my Dear.
              [Březina, "Tichá bolest," *Tajemné dálky*]

trav šumné království a s atlasovou řízou
sbor teskn7ch lilií

trav šumné království a s atlasovou řízou
sbor teskných lilií

the rustling kingdom of grasses and with a satin robe
the choir of melancholy lilies
              [Březina, "Březen," *Tajemné dálky*]

Some themes and motifs of the poetry of the turn of the century also bear obvious traces of the inclination of literature toward Art Nouveau in the visual arts. This is true, for example, of the theme of the dance, which is very common in the literature of this period. The connection with the visual arts is provided here by the suppleness of dancing movements, which is related to the suppleness of the Art Nouveau line, by the stylization of dancing posture, and finally by the emphasized colorfulness of the costume and the surroundings. The Art Nouveau conception of dance is distinctly apparent, for instance, in Neumann's "Salomé." In this respect the following lines are especially characteristic:

              Tanči!
Dej vyrůst nad koberců barvami zašlými
bílému zázraku těla,
jak bizarní květině s tvary vzácnými,
jež stále je nová a skvělá
s tisícem vděků, s tisícem tvarů,
s tisícem milostných vášnivých darů
vždy jiná.

              Dance!
Let the white miracle of your body
grow over the faded colors of the carpets,
like a bizarre flower with precious shapes,
which is always new and splendid
with a thousand graces, with a thousand shapes,
with a thousand amorous passionate gifts—
always different.
              [*Sen o zástupu zoufajících*]

It is apparent that color especially is connected very closely with the dance for the Art Nouveau vision, as Karel Červinka's "A ještě taneček" shows:

> Vzal jsem ji zlehýnka, bělounkou, křehkou,
> v Sardagni k tanečku vzal jsem ji, vzal,
> při hudbě vesnické jako pták lehkou,
> šatečky bílé jí roztancoval,
>
> I gently clasped her, pale, tender,
> in Sardagne I clasped her for a dance,
> to the country music, clasped her light as a bird,
> her little skirts I set dancing,
>
> [*Slunce v mlhách*]

where only the color white, however, is emphasized as the dominant component of the image. We find a similar case in Kvapil's "Valčík":

> Jako květ jsi vonný, bílý,
> na vlnách jenž kolébá se.
> Na břehu, slyš, flétna kvílí,
> umlká a volá zase,
> pláče ted' a jásá chvílí,
> povídá snad o tvé kráse,
> čarovný ty květe bílý,
> na vlnách jenž kolébá se.
>
> You are fragrant, white like a blossom
> which rocks on the waves.
> Listen, on the shore, a flute wails,
> falls silent and calls again,
> now it cries and then rejoices,
> perhaps it tells about your beauty,
> you magic white blossom,
> which rocks on the waves.
>
> [*Padající hvězdy*]

The motifs of water lilies and swans are another thematic element common to poetry and visual arts of the turn of the century. We find the two connected in Jan z Wojkowicz's poem "Labutě tesknily," the first four lines of which read:

Lekníny bílé voní, to voní na šero,
labutě teskní, teskní, že prší v jezero . . .
Labutě hlavy kloní tak smutně z večera,
bílá jejich křídla šumí hladinou jezera . . .

The white water lilies waft sweetly, waft
    sweetly for dusk,
the swans languish, languish, because it is
    raining into the lake . . .
The swans bow their heads so sadly by evening,
their white wings rustle over the surface
    of the lake . . .

[Poesie]

The above motifs had already occurred, of course, in poetry before the period of Art Nouveau, and the motif of swans in particular is a traditional thematic poeticism. Its semantic ambience has, however, changed in the course of time: the conception that we find in Wojkowicz is obviously inspired by the Art Nouveau ornamental stylization of the figure of the swan. Proof of this is already evident in the confrontation of the swan with the water lily, which is reminiscent of a theme of Art Nouveau painting. Thus Wojkowicz's swans have very little in common with the legend of the swan song which we find, for example, in the Old Czech *The Song of Záviš* ("The swan is a strange bird, it sings while dying") or with the medieval epic theme of the knight and the swan. The motif of the water lily is then patently substantiated here by the predilection of the Art Nouveau visual arts for this flower which nature herself has stylized into a harmonious linear contour of blossom and leaf.

Finally, we should mention the frequent use of the motif of the blossom, examples of which are abundant in the poetry of the turn of the century. No doubt, other literary periods also know the blossom as a favorite lyrical motif; here, however, we must again point out that what is important is the semantic ambience which accompanies the motif in a given period. What, therefore, is the blossom for the poetry of the Art Nouveau period? Toman's "Píseň" serves as a vivid example:

Divoký mák si natrhám
na poli zprahlém nejvíce,

pomněnky modré k němu dám,
jež u struh květou teskníce.

Na její lože nastelu
mák divoký, mák divoký.
Můj bože, já tam nastelu
mák divoký, mák divoký!

At' rdí se cudná světice,
at' stud a vztek jí v tvář krev hnal!
Mák rudý rád mám nejvíce.
Vždyt' krev jsem vždycky, vždycky dal!

Krvavě kvetla láska má,
jak krví plá má nenávist.
Umřela v krvi láska má,
Co slzami zrosila míst!

Ó ctnostná panno, světice,
můžete s pomněnkou si hrát.
Mák rudý rád mám nejvíce
a umím, umím pohrdat!

I'll pick wild poppies
in the driest field,
I'll add blue forget-me-nots to them,
which blossom languishing near ditches.

On her bed I'll heap
wild poppies, wild poppies.
My God, there I'll heap
wild poppies, wild poppies!

May the chaste saint blush,
may shame and fury drive the blood into her face!
I like red poppies the best.
For I've always, always given my blood!

My love has bloomed bloodily,
my hatred glows like blood.
My love has died in blood,
In how many places she has shed her tears!

O virtuous maiden, saint,
you can play with a forget-me-not.
I like red poppies the best
and I know, I know how to despise!

[*Pohádky krve*]

The poem which we have quoted in its entirety is obviously based on the contrast of two colors, but this contrast is conceived in a typically Art Nouveau manner. It is not a confrontation of two basic colors for the expression of which the words *red* and *blue* would suffice but two concrete color shades: the blue of forget-me-nots and the red of the wild poppy. The function of the motif of the flower in the poetry of the turn of the century thus lies (analogously to the canon of Art Nouveau painting and ornamentation) in the transposition of individual color shades into a linguistic expression.

We thus conclude our brief comparison of Art Nouveau in the visual arts with Czech literature of the years 1895–1905. If we have not quoted all of the outstanding poets of this period, this does not mean that we could not find traces of Art Nouveau in their works as well. There is abundant material, but the purpose of our study has not been the investigation of concrete artistic phenomena; rather we have been concerned simply with illustrating the theoretical assertions developed in the first two sections. A more consistent study would prove without a doubt the thesis that although Art Nouveau in the visual arts projected itself into literature very effectively, it neither created a special movement nor limited its influence to only one of the purely literary movements but scattered its colorful light over the entire range of the literature of its time. Art Nouveau intervened at the moment when the development of literature, if it tended at all toward a different art, had music, not the visual arts, as its goal. Moreover, the aggressive vividness of Czech poetry and cultural life of this period did not coincide with the languor of Art Nouveau. Despite all of this, or rather in conjunction with it, Art Nouveau intervened effectively in the fate of literature, complicating an already complex development. At a moment of extreme individualization its leveling influence affected almost all poets without exception. For the theoretician of literature the moral of the story is the following: If we study the relation between literature and another art, the influence of this other art must not be evaluated as a mechanical transposition of an alien periodization into literature but as a complex transference of an external impulse into the immanent development of literature, as a reflection which can strike literature at the most varied angles of incidence and with the most diverse results.

Appendix: Notes to "The Poet"

*Page 144: A. Novák, " 'Skalák' Karoliny Světlé, studie analytická" [Karolina Světlá's "Skalák": An analytical study], *Podobizny žen* (Prague, 1918), p. 133.

*Page 146: "Dva představitelé poetismu" [Two representatives of poetism], *O nejmladší poesii české* [On the most recent Czech poetry] (Prague, 1928), p. 95.

†*Page 146: "Předmluva" [Introduction] in A. Stašek, *Z blouznivců našich hor* (Prague, 1939), p. 14.

*Page 149: "O poetismu" [On poetism], *O nejmladší poesii české*, pp. 104-05.

*Page 150: J. Drda, "František Jaromír Rubeš," postscript to F. J. Rubeš, *Humoresky* (Prague, 1941), pp. 201-02.

†*Page 150: F. Halas, "Lyrik" [A lyric poet], introduction to J. Vrchlický, *Strom života. Meč Damoklův* (Prague, 1941), pp. 29-30.

*Page 151: "Chvála řeči české" [A eulogy for the Czech language], *Marsyas čili Na okraj literatury* [Marsyas, or On the periphery of literature] (Prague, 1931), p. 259.

*Page 153: "Večerní dialog o Janu Nerudovi" [An evening dialogue on Jan Neruda], *Mužové a osudy* (Prague, 1914), p. 17.

†*Page 153: F. L. Čelakovský in his letter of September 12, 1832, to J. V. Kamarýt, *Korespondence a zápisky Františka Ladislava Čelakovského* [František Ladislav Čelakovský's correspondence and notebooks] (Prague, 1910), p. 269.

*Page 156: "Rozmanitosti o Adolfu Heydukovi" [Miscellanea about Adolf Heyduk], *Kritické spisy J. Nerudy* 6, pt. 1 (Prague, 1910), p. 342 and p. 337.

*Page 160: "The Opening Lecture of the Course in *Poetics*," *The Collected Works of Paul Valéry*, vol. 13: *Aesthetics*, tr. R. Manheim and ed. J. Mathews (New York, 1964), p. 95.

†*Page 160: B. Václavek, "Jak krystalizuje lidová píseň" [How a folk song crystallizes], *Program D*[40] (October 24, 1939): 7-8.

Index